Sahaptins Studies

Columbia River Plateau
Cora Du Bois
Homer Garner Barnett
Gerald Raymond Desmond

Jay Miller, ed.

© 2018

Preface

This volume brings together classic studies of Sahaptins, especially Yakamas ~ Yakimas, of the past century:

3   The Feather Cult of the Middle Columbia by Cora Du Bois 1938

63   The Yakima Indians In 1942 by Homer Barnett, printed 1969

161   Gambling among the Yakima 1946 PhD by Abbot Gerald Desmond,
           published in 1952

202-205   Index

Slight editing has been done to these classics, whose opinions and observations do not always agree with current standards, ethics, and policies.
Providing them, therefore, also provides a measure of our progress and pitfalls in Plateau research.

To encourage research, original page numbers are within [square brackets], with the second column of each page marked as [b]. Other additons ~ commentaries are within {curved brackets}. The tilde ~ marks equivalences.

The Feather Cult of the Middle Columbia

Cora Du Bois

General Series in Anthropology: 7 1938

The Feather Cult of the Middle Columbia
Cora Du Bois

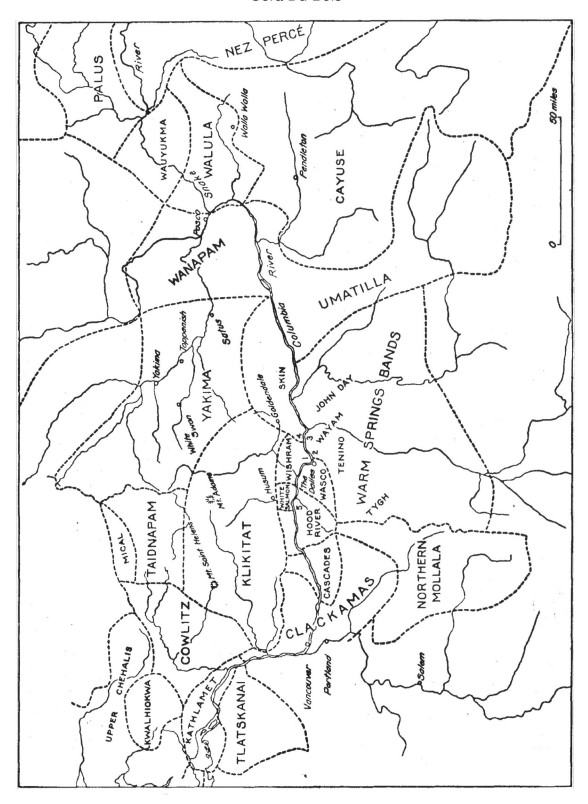

CONTENTS

	Page
INTRODUCTION	5
WASHANI RELIGION	8
Pre-Smohalla Data	8
Pseudo-historical Accounts of the Origin of the Washani	8
Historical Accounts of the Origin of the Washani	9
Smohalla and His Contemporaries	11
Smohalla (Wanapam)	12
Wiletsi (Umatilla)	12
Luls (Umatilla)	12
Hununwe and Nukshai	13
Shramaia (Skin)	14
A Wishram Prophet	15
Kutaiaxen	15
Klikitat Prophets	16
Lishwailait	16
Ashnithlai	18
Ashnithlai	18
ORIGIN OF THE FEATHER CULT: JAKE HUNT	20
Biography	20
Conversion	22
Clairvoyance and Miracles	24
Shamanism	25
DIFFUSION OF THE FEATHER CULT	26
Columbia River	26
Yakima Reservation	26
Warm Springs Reservation	27
Umatilla Reservation	27
Paviotso Converts	28
CEREMONIALISM	30
Initiation	30
Personal Experiences at Initiation	31
Ordinary Meetings	32
Curing Procedure	33
Accounts of Cures	34
First Food Feasts	35
Funerals	36
Morality and After Life	37
REGALIA AND ITS SYMBOLISM	38
Clothing	38
Feathers	38
Mirror	39
Colors	40
Tambourine and Bell	40
Meeting Places	40
Poles and Flags	41
Grace and Songs	42
SUMMARY	43
1. Tribes of the middle Columbia	
2. Sketch of Shramaia's drum	14
3. Jake Hunt's flag	19
4. Jake Hunt's Sunday ceremony at Spearfish	33
5. Women's dresses	38
6. Ceremonial mirror in buckskin pouch	39
7. Pole in front of Jake Hunt's lodge at Husum	41

Introduction

During the summer of 1934 a grant-in-aid from the Social Science Research Council permitted the collection of data on the Feather cult of the middle Columbia River. The material in this paper deals with the Columbia drainage from approximately Hood River in the west to Umatilla in the east, from Yakima reservation in the north to Warm Springs reservation in the south. In the western portion of this area the Upper Chinookan speaking people border the Saphaptins, but for the most part the region is the center of the Sahaptin stock with The Dalles as its approximate western boundary on the Columbia River.

Throughout the region three religions are current today; the Washani, the Feather, and the Shaker. Every community of any size has representatives of all three groups. The Washani and Feather religions are more closely related to each other, than either is to the Shaker. Field work was devoted primarily to the Feather cult, but because of its close affiliations with the other two religions, some orientation in their history was essential. At the time that the material was collected Spier's clarification[1] of the cult histories had not yet appeared. There will be a few preliminary sections presenting additional substantiations of Spier's Christianized Prophet cult dating from the early nineteenth century. There is also a short summary of some of the many prophets who preached contemporaneously with Smohalla on the middle Columbia. Particular emphasis is placed on the Klikitat prophets who preceded the founder of the Feather cult. These are presented as a necessary background for an understanding of the religious movement to which the bulk of this paper is devoted.

Certain clarifications in terminology should be made immediately. *Washani* or *washat* is generally translated as worship. It is a Sahaptin term which is known and used by Upper Chinookan speaking Indians. Actually *washat* means dance and *washani* means dancers. In Umatilla the equivalent terms are *walashat* and *walashine*. As the term is used by informants, it includes both the early Christianized Prophet dance of Spier and what has come to be known as the Smohalla cult. Actually Smohalla was just one prophet in a whole series of Washani dreamers. Smohalla is itself a Sahaptin term meaning [b] dreamer, which is usually used by both Chinookan and Sahaptin speaking individuals who apply it generically. In this paper Smohalla is used only in connection with the revival of the Washani during the last half of the nineteenth century. It should be recognized only as a subdivision of the Washani religion. The particular man called Smohalla was simply a powerful figure among many comparable leaders. He brought the cult to the attention of the whites but his activities were in no sense unique. The Chinook Jargon equivalent of Washani is *bum-bum* which refers to the tambourine associated with the cult. In the eastern part of the middle Columbia *pom-pom* is usually substituted for *bum-bum*. The term Washani has been adopted in this paper although there are drawbacks to its use. Chief among these is that it is a Sahaptin word while the religion is not limited to this linguistic group. On the other hand *pom-pom* or *bum-bum* is misleading since the use of the tambourine,

---

[1] Leslie Spier, The Prophet Dance of the Northwest and its Derivatives: the Source of the Ghost Dance, General Series in Anthropology # 1, 1935.

which gave rise to the term, may have been a post-1870 addition. Again, Spier's Christianized Prophet dance has the drawback of being some what cumbersome, of excluding the post-1870 manifestations and of assuming an earlier Prophet dance which is still inferential.

The Feather cult is known in Sahaptin as either the *waskliki* (spin) or *waptashi* (feather). In English, Feather cultists are generally referred to as the *bum-bum* or *pom pom* Shakers. The name is an acknowledgement of the twofold source of the Feather cult. Although the Feather cult has many features in common with the Washani, it should be differentiated from it as this paper will demonstrate.

One other subject should be mentioned. The greatest reticence was met among informants who still profess the Feather cult. This was particularly marked among those relatives of the founder who are still living and among the cultists on Yakima reservation who are in close touch with these relatives. In Warm Springs reservation, on the other hand, far more cooperative informants were secured. At present the founder's eldest sister is the most influential person among the cultists north of the Columbia River. While field work was in progress, she was travelling back and forth between the White Salmon River and Yakima reservation where [7] she seems to have discouraged local cult leaders from serving as informants. Despite this drawback there were many persons avail able as informants who had once been Feather cultists but who since have turned to the Shaker church. These were willing to speak freely and frequently they were without antagonism toward their earlier faith. Of the [b] twelve living relatives of the founder indicated in Table 1, only four could be persuaded to discuss the Feather cult. Although the others were friendly and courteous, the emotional blocks were practically insurmountable during the brief period for field work at my disposal. [8]

Washani Religion

Pre-Smohalla Data

There were two types of statement secured from informants concerning religious practices of a non-shamanistic variety prior to the 1870s when the Smohalla cult leaders came to the attention of the whites. One type was the pseudo-historical account of the origin of the Washani religion. It was often combined with prophetic tales concerning the coming of white settlers. This kind of prophecy continued after the settling of the middle Columbia by the whites, but the content was altered to prognostications of social and material changes. The second type of statement was rarer. It was an attempt to give a true historical account of the Washani religion in terms of Euro-American ideas of historicity. The fragmentary statements of these two types will be presented verbatim in the order named.

Pseudo-historical Accounts of the Origin of the Washani

Mary Lane (Klikitat) — "In the old days before the whites came, the Indians had many trances. That is how the Washani religion got started. Long before even my grandmother's time [i.e., before ca. 1830's] a woman on the Columbia River had things revealed to her. She died and came back to life and told all she had seen. She said a people with white hair and skin and eyes were coming. She said they had different materials to work with, different clothing, different food that they would give the Indians. They all got excited like Seven Day Adventists. They sang and danced all day and all night. They went crazy. They burned or threw in the river all their things. They destroyed every thing because the whites were coming to give them everything. They didn't store up any food that summer. Only a few of the wise ones saved everything they got. They had a bad winter that year. Many began to starve and the whites didn't come. The wise ones tried to keep the others fed. In the spring they found many who had crawled off trying to get food and had died of weakness."

Tom Bill (Klikitat) — "In the first generation a woman died and her soul went up to heaven. She was from a tribe near the mouth of the Columbia about five miles [b] from a cape, across from Astoria at Scavehill [?] but she was not a Chinook. Her tribe was the next one upstream from the Chinook.[1] When this woman got to the gate [of heaven?] she was told she had come with flesh on her and so she could not enter. She had to go back to this world to teach the Washani religion. When she woke up from the dead, she told her people what had been said to her. She had been told that the world was just a little speck and that the rest was under water. The Lord had pointed his finger at it and all the water drew back giving dry land. Just the streams and rivers were left. The Lord told this woman about the herbs and the foods on earth so that the Indians could prepare them and live on them. She was the one who started all this.

---

[1] The region across from Astoria and five miles from Cape Disappointment is certainly Chinookan territory. The next tribe upstream is either Mooney's Wakiakum or the Cathlamet, both of which were also Chinookan speaking groups.

She was the one who started counting seven days to a week. She began the custom of dancing on their knees. Drums were used in this old Washani, but bells have come in only since the whites. This religion was carried on for four generations after her and then Lishwailait arose."

The informant did not know the name of the woman who is supposed to have begun this cult. The same story was known to his Cowlitz wife who had heard the tale on Chehalis reservation where she was brought up. The Lishwailait mentioned in the last sentence was a Klikitat dreamer whose activities will be discussed later. He was a contemporary of Smohalla. Four generations preceding Smohalla and Lishwailait, who were active in the 1870's, would place this semi-historical beginning of the Washini in about 1800.

Sally Ann Joyce (Cascade-Klikitat) — "Katxot was a man who lived a long time ago, long before Lishwailait's time [i.e. before 1850's to 1870's]. He was not a Klikitat, but I don't know to what tribe he belonged. He used to travel up and down the Columbia River. He used to dream and foretell about the coming of the whites. Long before the whites came they danced and told during their worship that the day was coming when they would lose their homes. They were so afraid that they worshipped all the harder. These things were revealed to Katxot. He said they should dance on their knees. You kneel and jog up and down in time. Maybe you hop forward a step or two. Dancing on the knees [9] was revealed at the same time that it was revealed that another race was coming to this country. Dancing on the knees was carried on until Lishwailait's time." (See Lishwailait data for confirmation.)

This informant did not associate the seven day week with prophecies concerning the whites and knee dancing. For the seven day week she gave a Christianized creator explanation.

Charlie Selatkrine (Yakima) — "The Washani religion went way back to the ancient people. A long time ago they used to have the religion much harder. They used to dance on their knees. At that time people lived in their own old style houses and had none of the things the white people brought with them."

Oscar Ike (Warm Springs) — "A man died. They kept his body three days and then he came to. He told the people what he saw in heaven and what was right to do. He went to sleep and the creator told him to have this Indian religion every seven days and to sing. They counted seven days and every seventh day danced. This was the first religion. This was a long time back when people were dying like flies [during an epidemic?]. That was how the Washani religion began."

Elizabeth Lindsay (Umatilla-Tenino) — "There was a chief in Umatilla village when I was a girl who was already an old man. His great-great-grandfather had a dream and dance. He had said to dance for all they were worth because they wouldn't be able to dance much longer in the old way. There was to be a new order of things for the coming generations. This was before the Indians had horses or guns and while they were still living in earth houses."

It would appear from this account that some premonition of the arrival of the whites was current at the beginning of the 19th century and that it gave rise to dancing in the eastern extremity of the area under consideration.

From these accounts it may be assumed with some certainty that the settling of the country by the whites was anticipated on the middle Columbia early in the nineteenth century, that it gave rise to a religious furor with which knee dancing was associated. The Klikitat seem to have received these prognostications from the lower Columbia area. Both dreaming and death-like comas appear to have been legitimate forms of inspiration. [b]

Historical Accounts of the Origin of the Washani

John Watchino (Clackamas) — "The Smohalla [meaning Prophet cult or Washani] was the first church made by the Indians.[2][3] There was an old preacher called Father Woods. He was part Clackamas and part Cascade. He must have learned these words from the Hudson Bay Company. He said they came to him from God. He surprised the old people. They didn't know where he got these things. He was the one who made churches from the Clackamas to The Dalles. They used to have a Smohalla church at La Center near Lewis River. Father Woods was a fine speaker. He preached on Sundays and holy days like Christmas. That surprised the old settlers. They wanted to know how the Indians learned about Christmas. The Indians got it straight from God. They were almost like the Catholics. This religion existed long before I was born [1846?] and it existed in my father's time. After their preachers died, the people joined the Catholic church.

"The first Catholic bishop who came here [lower Willamette in Oregon] was Father Blanch. He travelled all over baptizing children. He baptized me in 1846. Father Blanch said Father Wood's church was just about like the Catholics. He gave the Smohalla church a large flag pole to put up outside the church. He also gave two small flags that the acolytes used. He gave them small bells too that they rang before praying. These had not been used by Father Woods before, but he and his two acolytes already used garments in the service. After Father Blanch's visit a cross was used over the church door." At Clackamas the church used by Father Woods was about sixteen feet wide by twenty-five long. There were no seats in it. There was no altar opposite the door, but during the informant's youth, the farther end of the building was decorated with candles and holy pictures. Father Woods stood in front of these. On either side of him stood an acolyte with a bell. When ever the bell was rung, everyone kneeled to pray facing Father Woods. They sang songs whose origin was unknown to the informant. They kept time to the songs by waving right arm up and down and by moving feet. All entered church, sat at far end. When Father Woods entered, all stood up and sang. Continued until he reached opposite end of building. Acolyte rang bell; all knelt and prayed. Then rose. Preaching and singing. All must be quiet. No musical accompaniment; no drum. Father Woods wore long black robe with white one over it. Acolytes wore white robes. Sign of cross used in services. Exhortations to be good, honest, kind. Good ones "given [10] credit" by God. Bad ones went to hell. Services held in midmorning. Father Woods chose a young man called Andrew as his understudy, but Andrew never preached. He died shortly after

---

[2][3] The informant had never heard of an individual named Smohalla. To him the word was simply a synonym for the Jargon term "*bum-bum*".

Father Woods. Woods preached in Clackamas. When he visited Grand Ronde reservation in Oregon he did not hold services, attended Catholic church instead. Many Catholic converts at Grand Ronde — "because it was just like the Smohalla."

Despite marked Catholic features of Father Woods' cult, the seven Catholic sacraments were not used, not even marriage; no holy water; no private confession and absolution. "You confessed right in front of everybody. You told what you did that was bad. You promised to do better. Anyone could confess whenever he wanted to."

This account is somewhat puzzling. The gist of the information indicates that more markedly Catholic forms were practiced among the Clackamas than elsewhere prior to consistent Catholic proselytizing. These similarities were so marked that the first missionary in the area considered it a religious form which might be sanctioned by him.

The Bishop Blanch of this account appears to be the Very Reverend F.N. Blanchet who arrived in the Willamette and lower Columbia area in 1838, two years before De Smet began his work in Montana.[3,4] This fairly definitely dates Christianized Indian cults among the Clackamas in the 1830's at the latest. Blanchet, however, makes no mention of Father Woods, although he does describe the conversion of the Clackamas in 1840.[4] At that time they had been under Methodist influences for at least two years. Blanchet states that he gave the Clackamas a cross, a red flag bearing a cross, and a "Catholic Ladder." The "Catholic Ladder" was a device widely distributed on the lower Columbia and on Puget Sound. It was a wooden oblong six feet long by fifteen inches wide on which Christian history was represented by a series of "marks and points." It served as a mnemonic device for Indians who were visited by the priests and who had received some instruction.[5] The converts of the particular Father Woods remembered by the informant felt the transition to Catholicism was easily made. The similarities between this cult and the true Washani are not very marked. No trace of Father Woods was found farther up the Columbia River although he is supposed to have travelled along the middle Columbia. It may be significant that the Clackamas informant just quoted agrees with the following Wishram [b] informant in attributing new religious changes to influences of the Hudson Bay Company at Ft. Vancouver.

Martin Spidish (Wishram) — "The Indians didn't know about Sunday and keeping track of the week. Some whites came here and made a camp near Big Eddy about one mile downstream from Wishram. They came in canoes. It was after Lewis and Clark [1804 - 1806]. They were the second white people to come through here. Some bad Indian stole a powder horn from them that was mounted with silver and gold. It belonged to a white doctor. He got mad and turned some kind of medicine loose to make disease. The Indians all got sick with a fever. They didn't know it was a fever so when they got hot they jumped in the river and died right away. This was smallpox. It

---

[3] L.B. Palladino, Indian and White in the Northwest; or, a History of Catholicity in Montana. (Lancaster Pa., 1922), p. 34.

[4] J.N. Blanchet, Historical Sketches of the Catholic Church in Oregon During the Past Forty Years (Portland, Oregon, 1878), pp. 119-20. (Portland, Oregon, 1878), pp. 119-20.

[5] Ibid., pp. 84-85 passim.

all happened one spring, perhaps in April. The people gathered together to consult. The big chiefs decided to go to Ft. Vancouver. The Hudson Bay people were living there. The white people questioned the Indians about the horn which had been stolen. The Indians said they would ask about it when they got back. Some white religious men were at Ft. Vancouver. They gave the Indians a piece of cardboard like the page on a calendar. It had holes punched in it. They taught the Indians the days of the weeks. On Friday they were told to get all dressed up and confess. One of the leaders was to ask what you had done and then you had to confess before all the people at the meeting. In this way they got the man who had taken the powder horn to confess. It had been traded back east as far as Montana but the thief got it back and returned it to the doctor at Ft. Vancouver. "These trips were the beginning of understanding about Sunday. After they came back from the second trip [when they returned the powder horn] the chiefs put up a flag and flag pole at Wasco. They had been given the flag at Ft. Vancouver. They also had a song which they said had been taught them down there. The sick people came around and were cured just through believing in God. The chiefs were told that the Indians must drink nothing but spring water for seven years; not drink water from the Columbia River. "This religion spread up the Columbia River way back east. This religion was a belief in God to help sick people. After that came, sick people stopped dying. In this faith you must not smile during the ceremony. If a man smiled at a girl during a meeting, she would have to be hand cuffed with big number two spring traps. [11] After that religion came, everything strict; you couldn't do anything but follow the religion. They had no (musical instruments) at their meetings; just sing.

"All this was about thirty or forty years after Lewis and Clark. It was much older than Smohalla's religion. Before this time there had been only Indian doctor beliefs. The four chiefs who got the religion from the Hudson Bay Company were Watilthkai, Tariutcus, Kumsuks, and Mut.

The informant's sister, Lucy Spidish gave separately a similar account. The common source of this version of the Washani was their grandfather who had lived to be very old man. A Wasco on Warm Springs reservation gave substantially the same information but with fewer details. In his version four Wasco chiefs went to Ft. Vancouver for assistance.

The informant's data imply that the Washani religion was a by-product of Christian influences secured at the Hudson Bay station at Ft. Vancouver. In 1836 Samuel Parker mentioned a delegation of Indians from The Dalles area who said that they had long been in possession of a flag and a seven day week with Sunday observances.[6]7 This implies that Martin Spidish's account antedates 1836 and that it refers to the earlier delegation mentioned by Parker. As early as 1782-83 the West was swept by an epidemic from the Missouri to the Pacific. In 1823 according to Hale, and 1829 according to others, a fever swept the Columbia from The Dalles westward.[7] It is probably to the epidemic of 1823 (or 1829) that Spidish' account refers. It is possible, however, that the Wasco from Warm Springs was referring to the later delegation of

---

[6] Quoted from Spier, op. cit., p. 20.

[7] James Mooney, Aboriginal Population of America North of Mexico (Smithsonian Miscellaneous Collections Vol. 80, No. 7, 1928), pp. 13-14.

1836.

There is one other hint which may assist in dating Martin Spidish's account of the stolen powder horn. Robert Stuart reports an attack on July 20th, 1812 at The Dalles "for a shining metal box which, containing dispatches for Astor, was strapped to the shoulders of John Reed."[8] It is, of course, just possible that the dispatch box in Stuart is to be equated with the powder horn in Martin Spidish' account and that the beginning of the Washani can be referred to 1812 or 1813.

One other statement by an informant gives a further hint for dating the Washani cult.

Jo Hunt — "Years ago this land turned dark for two days. There was no light. It [b] smelled awfully bad. It was as though Mt. Adams {*patu*} were sending forth ashes. From then on the Washani came out more seriously than before because people were so afraid that this land might be condemned."

A survey of volcanic activity in the region[9][10] reveals that Mt. St. Helens was active for twelve hours in 1831, 1841, 1842 when smoke and light ashes were ejected for two months, and again in 1843. Mt. St. Helens lies immediately to the west of Mt. Adams and the activity of the two might easily be confused in the memory of informants. Whether the earlier activities of 1831 or the later ones of 1841 to 1843 are referred to here cannot be determined, but on the basis of the preceding paragraphs it appears probable that the Washani antedated even the earlier volcanic disturbance.

Spier has suggested after an exhaustive combing of historical sources that there were three phases of cult development in the Columbia drainage. First there was the aboriginal Prophet dance, then a Christianized Prophet dance, and finally the Smohalla revival. He suggests that one source of the Christianized Prophet dance was the Iroquois influences emanating from Flathead country in about the 1820's.

The bearing of the fragmentary field data just presented upon Spier's thesis is the following. I believe that the cult which the middle Columbia Sahaptins term Washani is equivalent to Spier's Christianized Prophet dance. It can be dated in the first two decades of the nineteenth century as Spier suggested. Although Spier recognizes the possibility of Christianizing influences from Ft. Vancouver, he is inclined to believe that the Christianized Prophet cult was the result of Iroquois settlers in Flathead country in approximately 1820. It is quite possible that Christian influences closed in on the middle Columbia tribes from both the east and west during the decade from 1820 to 1830. The material presented here neither adds nor detracts from Spier's inferences concerning a Prophet dance which antedated Christian influences and existed as early as 1790.

Smohalla and His Contemporaries

From the middle of the nineteenth century onward, one begins to secure data on

---

[8] Philip Ashtan Rollins (ed.), The Discovery of the Oregon Trail. Robert Stuart's Narratives of his Overland Trip Eastward In 1812-13 ... (New York, 1935), pp. lxxix.
[9] Edward S. Holden, A Catalogue of Earthquakes on the Pacific Coast, 1769 to 1897 (Smithsonian Miscellaneous Collections, Vol. 37, No. 1087, 1898), pp. 26-27.

a whole series of dreamers along the Columbia. Among these was Smohalla, whose influence was widespread but not unique. In this section I shall treat him simply as one among many others. Most of my emphasis will be [12] laid in a subsequent section on his Klikitat contemporary, Lishwallait, who was the most influential dreamer in shaping the Feather cult to which this paper is primarily devoted. Personal names used as headings represent the prophets about whom most information was forthcoming. Under each heading, statements are preceded by the name of the informant from whom the material was secured.

Smohalla (Wanapam)

Martin Spidish (Wishram) — "Smohalla used to preach around here at The Dalles. I remember seeing him when I was a half grown boy. He preached at Wishram and Wasco. He talked Nez Percé and Klikitat. He didn't use jargon. When he preached he talked his own language and used an interpreter. He used three to seven drums."

Allen Padawa (Umatilla) — "Smohalla belonged somewhere up the Columbia River and gathered together many people. He told them the same things as Luls [q.v.]. Smohalla was told in a dream what he should do. There were many dreamers before Luls and Smohalla but I don't know about them. Some would tell what they saw just before they died. Smohalla held meetings at White Bluffs and a big one at Walula. All the river tribes went to the Walula meeting. There were Umatilla, Walla Walla, Nez Perce, Cayuse, Yakima and Warm Springs people there — all the people from the Snake and Columbia Rivers. They had a very long tipi. It was fixed up nice inside. They talked about religion and about the white man's right to settle in their country. This meeting was after Luls died [in 1880's]. There were two other Umatilla dreamers, Wiyetrinawit and Pinapuyuset, who went there."

Elizabeth Lindsay (Tenino-Umatilla) — Sunday meetings with drums existed long before Smohalla."

Jerry Bruno (Wasco) — "The Nespelem, Okanagan, Umatilla, Waiem, Yakima, and all who speak that language [Sahaptin] took over Smohalla's preachings. But the Wascos never had anything to do with it. A Wasco would never join in a meeting that used drums. [Confirmed by other Wasco informants.] This real old time Wasco religion has disappeared today [i.e. knee dancing?]. The (Sahaptins) used the drum in their Washani meetings even before Smohalla's time.

Wiletsi (Umatilla)

Ruth Jacobs (Umatilla) — "He was my grandfather. He was the oldest of four brothers. He lived near the mouth of Mackay Creek [on Umatilla reservation] where the dam is now. He appointed his son [informant's father] to protect roots and fruits in season. No one might eat them without giving thanks. He was leader about eighty years ago [1850's?], before Luls began. [b] They had no dances; just prayed and sang. At a signal with a bell, everyone had to be quiet and let him talk. This kind of meeting was held in a communal dwelling holding four or five families. He held Sunday sacred and supervised the first food feasts. Women were not allowed to dig roots on Sunday.

If anyone went digging he had them tied hand and foot and he would beat them [confirmed by another informant]. No other dreamer ever did that. He was stricter than anyone else. They had to kneel when they prayed. Later in Luls' time they weren't so strict. In Luls' time they danced and used drums but they didn't in Wiletsi's time. Both of them used the same root feast."

Luls (Umatilla)

Allen Padawa (Umatilla) — "The *pom-pom* comes from dreams. A man called Luls lived at Mackay Creek on Umatilla reservation. In his dreams he saw he should have six drums. He died before 1870. In his dreams he saw a lot of people coming down in the clouds as though they were standing on them. They were all fixed up nice with clean feathers in their hair. Their faces and hands were painted red. When he woke up from his sleep dreaming he saw his dream before him all the time. People talked to him and he didn't want to answer. He just wanted to think about what he saw in his dream. He was that way for maybe two or three weeks. He began singing what he had heard these people singing with their drums. His own family helped him. He told them for the first time what he had seen in his dream. He felt sad. He said, 'I saw the holy people in my dream. They almost came down to this ground where we live. They are singing this song with drums and they told me to do these things on the holy day. Clean yourselves well on the Sabbath day and be ready to do these things.' So they sang the song keeping time with their right arm [flexed upward at elbow]. He told the people, 'You must not think anything bad against your friends. You must not think of things in this world. Think about what I saw, of the beautiful people who almost came down to this world. They said they came from the holy country where our father, our children and our friends go when they die. If we do this, keep ourselves clean in our hearts, and be kind to each other, we shall go to the same place as our dead relatives.'

"Then the people worshipped in this way for many years. Luls became a mighty man. He could tell when a person did not believe or thought other things. Then he would point his finger at him and say, 'You must not think like that.' When he talked he raised his right arm. If he talked awfully strong and waved his arm, some people would fall over unconscious because his power was too strong for them. He could do that to whites, too." [13]

Meeting House — Long tipi, door on long side; no orientation of door or tipi. Made of tipi poles covered with reed mats. Canvas used now. Mats spread around sides for audience. Three fires down center. Floor kept clean and swept.

Meetings — Luls walked around and pointed finger at people telling them to join. At each meeting three or four new converts made. New member stood up in center, said, "I renounce my old bad ways and will try to do right so as to meet the dead in the holy country." Meetings held every Sunday from 10 A.M. to 3 P.M. Luls had four or five songs of his own. There were many other songs. Had meetings for Root feast.

Berry and Root Feast — Luls said, "Our Creator gave us this beautiful world and the streams and the nice trees with fruit, and roots of many kinds, and fish in the waters. We must remember our Creator in these things. We must not kill these fish, gather roots or berries, or kill deer on the Sabbath. We must honor our Creator. Whenever the first berries ripen we must pick them on week days and then eat them in our long tent. We must do the same with the first roots. Give thanks to our Creator who gave us this to live on in this world."

"This religion lasted until about the Paiute war [1878]. At that time the government asked people on the reservation to take allotments, have houses, schools, and churches. A little while after this Luls died. The Umatilla decided to accept these things from the whites and Luls' religion began to fade away. No Umatilla carries it on today. All of Luls' followers went over to the Presbyterians, but they still carry on the root feast. They call for the minister to pray for the new crop. They still use the old time drums and songs."

Ruth Jacobs (Umatilla) — "If you doubted the sacredness of what Luls said and walked in front of him, you would fall over unconscious. His ordinary services were held in the living lodge. On Sundays he chose seven girls. They were dressed in buckskin with beads and wore eagle feathers in their hair [cf. Feather cult ritual]. The drums were on the right hand end of the tipi. He had four men to beat the drums while the girls danced. The girls used to dance so hard they wore themselves out. They circled the lodge. All the others stood in place and kept time by waving their right arms. The songs were very inspiring. At the end of each song, they raised their right arm and said *ai*. The men were on the side to the right of the door and the women were to the left. Luis stood in the center. He had a long string hung from cross poles. On the end was a golden heart. As long as he talked it spun. [b]

"This dance took place on Sunday. Saturday night they gathered just to sing. Luls did not use flags."

Hununwe and Nukshai

Albert Barnhart (Umatilla) — "An old woman died at Cayuse on Umatilla reservation. Her husband was a Walla Walla. In four days she woke up. She had been a Washani ever since she was a little girl. She was about sixty-five years old when she got sick. She died and lay in the house for four days. They were going to bury her on the next day. She woke up at about eight o'clock in the morning. There were many Indians there and I was among them. They had her in her coffin and it was closed. They opened it up and she was well and natural. She had told them when she died to keep her five days before burying her. She got up out of the coffin and said, 'God made this country just for the Indians to live in. God gave them leaders whose spirits lead them in the Washani. Everybody is to join in this Washani religion. If they take care of it, if they are clean, the spirit will go home to God's place. The body will go back to the ground. Many people who have already died are up with God. It is a very nice country up in heaven. It is light and shiny and there are flowers; it is nice. Men and women who are bad can't go there. I thought I had done everything as I should in this country, but when I got there he showed me my name and some writing. Once an Indian woman went with me to bathe in the river. She took off her belt and two dollars dropped out of her bag. I picked up those two dollars and tied them in my handkerchief. I stole that. That is why I have come back to this country. I forgot to tell [confess] this when I was sick. In my religion, you must not steal. So I won't steal any more. I will stay in this country for four more years and then I shall go home. You must tell your friends. There are many bad ones left. Members of the old Smohalla church are honest. You have to join it. But I have nothing against the other churches.'

"For four years Hununwe led the Washani religion at Cayuse. Then she died without getting sick. She called the people and said she would die before sun-up. All were there dancing. She was dressed up nice, painted, etc. She danced the Washani all night. Just at sun-up she went to her bed and lay down and died. She said the sun was her wagon and would take her to heaven. That was in 1893.

"Her husband (Nukshai) lived four years leading the religion after his wife died. In the fall, he got sick. He just lay there until early spring in about April. He was all bony, but he was conscious and his mind was clear. He told me, 'If I die, keep me five days.' He had four handkerchiefs spread out on the floor. He confessed himself, laying down a stick on the [14] handkerchiefs for each sin. He said, 'I fished and killed salmon on Sunday; broke the law that you should work for six days and rest on the seventh.' He went on confessing himself for two or three hours. Those who did wrong never went to heaven. Once he had stolen moccasins. God sees you do these things and puts them in a book. When you die you can see it for yourself.

"Nukshai said, 'If I die, God might send me back.' About five o'clock that afternoon he died. I washed him and dressed him. On the fourth day at about nine o'clock in the morning, Nukshai woke up. There were many Indians there that day.

Nukshai spoke in the same way as Hununwe. He lived for five years giving religious dances. Finally in 1902 he died for good.

"The Walla Walla are all Washani people. Jim Kanine is their chief. His mother's mother was Hununwe. He gives dances every Sunday morning at Cayuse. Hardly any of the Walla Walla ever joined the Catholics."

Tommy Squimkin (Waiem) — "Hununwe was a woman from the Waiem tribe who went to live on Umatilla reservation. She was one of the best preachers anywhere around. She came after Smohalla. She died about 1890. She was instructed not to wear cloth dresses to church, but to wear buckskin. Every one in her longhouse had to do that. They followed her word in Wishram too."

Allen Padawa (Umatilla) — "Just before the allotments were given out, Hununwe died and came to. She told about the same things as Smohalla and Luls. She used to say at meeting, 'I saw lots of people in the holy place. They told me to do these things, so I am doing this for a few days. (She meant thereby a few years.) Then I shall die again and live with these holy people.' A vision like this makes a per son head preacher. She used to sing a song which meant, 'They are having a Joyous time and it is light for them but we don't hear them unless we join in with them.' Everyone used lots of red and yellow paint in Hununwe's dance."

Shramaia (Skin)

Martin Spidish (Wishram) — "Shramaia died and came back to life. After that he was minister at Skin. When a person has had an experience like that, he usually be comes the leader. He came after Smohalla." Smohalla, Lishwailait and Shramaia were the only Washani dreamers known to the informant.

Elizabeth Lindsay (Tenino-Umatilla) — "At Skin they circled and danced around the image of a bird on a pole. The Wishram and all the up-river people as far as

Smohalla's tribe gathered there for dances. Shramaia and his relatives lived in the house where they danced. The pole with the bird on it was outside their house. They met inside. When the meeting was [b] over, they came out, stood in a circle, raised their right arms and said *ai*. They met every Sunday. They had drums and a bell. A drum and bell were sounded together to call the people to meetings. The men were on one side of the house, the women on the other. Sometimes they were two or three rows deep. One special man was assigned to keep the lodge clean. It was a religion to give thanks for abundance."

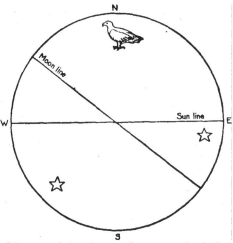

Fig. 2. Sketch of Shramaia's drum, from verbal description. Eastern star, white; western star, blue; bird, blue.

Jo Hunt (Klikitat) — "Shramaia was the one who put up a bird pole at Skin. He was shown a vision. The whites were living there then. It came to him in his sleep. He said that the white man was bringing an other law from the east to rule us. He told all which was to happen. He was shown four roads in his dream. One was a white road for the whites (English-American); one was yellow for the Catholics (French); one was blue line for the Methodists; and one was red for my race. They ran not east but north and south. Whatever the white man planned for us, could not be changed. He was going to build a church, a court, and a jail. He was going to turn against the Indian. Those buildings would require money. Shramaia told all these things. He went to The Dalles, to Portland, to Salem. He preached this to the people when he came back. Then he made a pole and a flag. People all gathered at Skin. I myself attended. He said these things. He interpreted the four roads. He erected a flag pole of cedar because it is the best wood. The house was made of cedar bark. On top of the pole was a round earth with a diameter from east to west. At the west came the Pacific Ocean [Fig. 2]. Beneath the drum was a flag with a sun and stars on it." [15]

A Wishram Prophet [15]

John Williams (Molalla-Mexican) — "There was a man who belonged to the Smohallas. He had a boy and a girl. The girl died. He was very sorry, he wondered a lot; he didn't know why he had lost his daughter. He wondered if he was wrong about something. He wished something would happen to him. He got sick. He lay on his bed and had a vision that he was not to die but would visit the other land. He told his wife and children not to bury him. So when he died they put him to one side. Every night they sang praising the Lord that he would come back. Sunday morning he talked to them. They didn't understand him. He talked in tongues. Then he laughed and said in his own language to clean out the house. They were going to have a service and tell the words to his people which he had brought back from heaven.

"He took a small dinner bell and went around the house five times ringing it. He said that God went around the world once every year. He rings that bell but you can't hear it. This man could read the promised land and all who had died. He saw them all, but he was not allowed to mix with them. He was kept separate from them all the time he was there. They showed him where there was hell, and where the innocent were. They stood in lines the way they do in the Smohalla services and in the center God sat and they had a council. Some would say the time had arrived, and others would say, 'No, there are many more innocents coming up and we must wait for them.' For us [i.e. the living] a year is a long time, but for them it is just a few days.

"The man preached all this. He said that this council happens once a year. He said they were all happy up there. It was glory. He said he was not there to stay long, just five days. But he means five years. After five years he died. He said, 'Now I am leaving you for good. Don't forsake your God.'

"This man was a Wishram. He has a daughter still living. He was living at Wishram when this happened. It must have been in about 1880.

"After this man the Smohalla took up the bell, a small one, and still use it to day. They ring it before and after a sermon.

"He was also the man who told the people that a woman in Hood River had been caught, and sure enough in a few days word came that she had gone crazy. So he sent some people to catch her. She was married to a man with two wives and she had gotten jealous of the other wife. She was angry because she had to do all the wood-carrying. She wished something would happen to the other wife. One day when she tried to lift a load of wood, she couldn't do it. [b] She looked around and saw a man laughing. He said he would grant her wish. So she wished the wood would be easy to carry. He told her he would do what she wished if she would do his will. She tied the wood and he made it roll home of its own accord. He gave her a song to whistle and as you know, Indians very seldom whistle. She got to running around like mad. It took many men to tie her down and take her to his house. She screamed and hollered. He [the prophet] took this dinner bell, walked around her five times ringing it. She fell asleep and woke up all right. The devil goes around twice a year and tries to get all he can on his side. It was the devil who had gotten hold of this woman. That man told the people to be careful not to l obey things that are not true."

Kutaiaxen

Charlie Selatkrine — "Kutaiaxen was a Yakima [?] Indian living at Parker on Yakima reservation. He started his religion a short time before we heard of Smohalla. He used to be a great gambler and a very bad man. People began to notice that Kutaiaxen was not himself at times. He would wander from home and lie around. While he was out some place the Washani faith came to him. He heard a voice telling him to praise the Lord in song and dance on Sundays. Sometimes they would find him lying in a coma as though he were dead. He had his biggest meetings in mid winter. People came to them from all over the reservation. The Washani religion seems to have died down. Kutaiaxen and Smohalla brought it back again."

When informants were asked for names of outstanding Washani leaders, many were se cured about whom there was little associated information. Some of the leading men in the minds of the Indians were probably only preachers or leaders who had no supernatural experiences comparable to the more outstanding prophets who have just been discussed. A list of these less well known persons is included to furnish some idea of the number of minor prophets or of preachers which can be secured. Also, this list may be of assistance in some future and more detailed inquiry.

Kwiumps — Husum Klikitat; probably only a preacher. Built special long house for Washani meetings. Died ca. 1900.

Jim Silatsi — Wishram preacher; have dreamed songs. Noted drummer.

Jo Kalaxam — Wishram prophet who died and returned to life (?). Held Sunday meetings. Died ca. 1l899.

Xanapo — Rock Creek preacher.

Tiawit — Yakima prophet subsequent to Smohalla. Held meeting at Satus on Yakima reservation. Congregation danced in turn with a plate. If person were evil, a dark [16] spot appeared on it.

Wolsa — Warm Springs prophet or preacher. Died ca. 1880's (?).

Kwiapama — Tenino preacher.

Laupash — Walla Walla prophet who died and returned to life prior to Smohalla.

Sutkwewat — Walla Walla preacher from Walula. Contemporary with Smohalla.

Wiyetrinawit — Umatilla dreamer. Contemporary with Luls and Smohalla. May have been only a shaman.

Pinapuyuset — Umatilla. Chiefly a dreamer of songs. Contemporary with Luls and Smohalla. Was last of Umatilla Washani leaders to die.

Somilpilp (Red Shirt) — Palus prophet or proselytizer contemporary with Smohalla. Brought word of religious revival to Texulzulsut, White Bird, and Chief Joseph bands of Nez Perce. Also visited Umatilla reservation.

Husiskeut (Bald Head) — Palus prophet or proselytizer. Brought word to Chief Joseph band of Nez Percé.

Mexistet (Large Lad) — Palus prophet or proselytizer. Visited all Nez Percé bands subsequent to two preceding men.

Kamaiyakin — Palus preacher or prophet.

A widely travelled Nez Percé attributed the Washani cult of the Smohalla period to the Umatilla, Walla Walla, Palus, Nez Perce, Wanapam, and Klikitat. It was denied by him for the Coeur d'Alene, Blackfoot, Flathead, Spokan, and Colville[10] reservation groups — "unless it go in there lately."

---

[10] For a detailed account of Skolaskin, another dreamer-prophet in this aeries, see V.F. Ray, The Kolaskin Cult; A Prophet Movement of 1870 in Northeastern Washington (American Anthropologist, Vol. 38, pp. 75, 1936).

"The Nez Perce and Cayuse did not dream as much as the Walla Walla and Umatilla. The people down the Columbia River were always dreaming and bringing their religion to the Nez Perce and Cayuse."

This list of dreamers or prophets is far from complete. It is given simply to indicate the number and variety of prophets who preceded and followed Smohalla. It establishes beyond doubt that within the Washani frame work there were constant recrudescences of dreamers and that Smohalla was simply one of a series.[11] Probably each prophet had his unique contributions which might account for local variations. The study of those local variations and contributions of various dreamers remains to be made." [b]

It may still be possible to disentangle the earliest ritualistic forms of the Washani religion from those of the last sixty years. No such attempt was made here.

Klikitat Prophets

Because of its bearing on the Feather cult some attention has been given in this section to the ritualism of the Washani prophets among the Klikitat during the last half of the nineteenth century. For our immediate purposes the descriptions in this section, in addition to various printed ac counts dealing with the Smohalla revival, can serve as background for the Feather cult descriptions which follow in the next chapter."

Lishwailait

Jake Hunt, the founder of the Feather cult, seems to have been directly indebted to Lishwailait for some of his ceremonial procedure. The two men belonged to the same community and seem to have been distantly related. They both were Klikitat who lived on the White Salmon River near Husum in Washington. Lishwailait's dates are not established with certainty. His life span fell within the last three-quarters of the nineteenth century, from approximately the 1820's to the 1890's. The period of his religious activities coincided approximately with those of Smohalla. To the Indians in The Dalles area, the three great religious figures of the mid-nineteenth century were Smohalla of Priest Rapids, Shramaia of Skin, and Lishwailait of White Salmon. Jake Hunt as a young man must have known of all three, but his closest contacts were with Lishwailait.

Jo Hunt (Klikitat) — "Lishwailait was a young man. His mother died. He mourned five days. Then he went to the cemetery. There he looked and suddenly saw his own mother as though she were living, not dead. She spoke to him, 'I am not dead. I have another home which surpasses yours. There is no sickness there. You are there for ever. You do not age. When you are a grown man or woman and die, you will enter this world in the same form you had here. You will be a full grown man forever. Also the food and the water is talking to this earth. Do not mourn so much. When a person dies here on earth, don't sorrow so.' His mother thus spoke to Lishwailait. Then he returned to his home. He kept this secret for several nights. Then it [the spirit of his

---

[11] Spier (op. cit., passim) gives a resume of the Smohalla literature.

mother?] appeared again on earth and interpreted to him in full how this earth originated, how the red race was planted here and how the food should be used on earth. This is the way he told it, 'I created the earth. I put food here on earth for you, food as a man [for a man [17] to procure?] and food as a woman. From the beginning the first man and the first woman have transmitted the food for all these generations. As night falls, so food comes [i.e. both are regular and cyclic]. In less than a year, Lishwailait began to preach his vision to the people. He said, 'All the fish of the rivers, the mountains covered with animals giving us meat, and roots of every description in the land, and berries of all sorts in the mountains, all that food is as a father and mother to me. It will enable my race to multiply. It has been shown to me that we must be familiar with all these foods which are as mother and father to our people.' So every year Lishwailait had a message. A song was given to him also.

"I and Laushlai[12]13 are like the children of Lishwailait. It is as though he had raised us. Every Sunday we must go through our regular prayer and beat our drum and ask forgiveness if we have wronged our people. That is the teaching of Lishwailait. He began when he was about twenty-one to preach of the drum and the religion. He was eighty-six when he died. Since I have adopted this drum I have taken his teaching. When his mother died, he saw the earth round like the drum. Also he saw this earth floating in water and surrounded by it."

Drum — "The pom-pom speaks and is valuable to the Indian race. It was discovered by Lishwailait [?]. He was the one who made the drum for the Klikitat. Before that they had never had one. The drum is the interpretation [i.e. symbol] of the earth (*titcam*), because it is round, yellow, and shiny. The sound of the drum is the sound of the earth. If the drum broke in a certain place, it shows that somewhere a portion of the earth's surface will be destroyed."

Horse — "When Indians were created there was no horse. There has always been a sabbath, however. In the east where the sun rises the horse originated. From the east, it came to the west. The horse spoke to our Indian ways. He did not come from above, but he came out of the water from the east and multiplied. He brought a wonderful song to my people. From the beginning when the horse became useful to man, our people began to enjoy its use. And then about that time, your race came to our land, and our work was chopped in two and put to one side. My people died by the thousands from then on. And today this land is barren of my race."

Regalia — "Mostly Lishwailait had white, red and blue stars on his flag. He had a sacred bird on top of a pole. It would turn and face east on Sunday morning. [b] Monday it turned west. No one turned it; it turned of itself. He had feathers tied along the underarm seams of both arms for his service costume. He had stars on his clothes; on the left front were white stars, on the right front were blue ones, in back he had red and blue ones. He wore this costume Sunday morning. His clothes and his flag were both of buckskin."

Susie Hunt Spidish (Klikitat) — "Lishwailait was related to Jake Hunt's mother, but I am not quite sure how. He performed no healing, but he was a great preacher. If

---

[12] The informant and Laushlai were half brother and sister. Jake Hunt, the founder of the Feather cult, was Laushlai's full brother. See Table 1.

you were evil, he saw you wrapped in a black blanket and wouldn't shake hands with you. Lishwailait could tell if you had stolen or murdered, even when no one else knew about it."

Laushlai Hunt (Klikitat) — "Lishwailait was having a big meeting in the Glenwood area where all were gathered to dig camass. He stood before the people, held up his hands with his palms up and said something would appear in his hands. He prayed and soon something yellow appeared in his right hand, and something blue in the other. He said, 'These will rule every thing else and we shall become slaves to these articles. They didn't know what it meant then, but now they realize it meant gold and silver. Another time he held up his hands and a white object, very white and shiny like an egg, dropped into his hand. He passed it around the group from one hand to the other. Some didn't even look to see what it was. But some of the older Hunts looked and saw it was like an egg and slippery as though it could almost pour through your hands."

Tom Bill (Klikitat) — "Lishwailait in his sleep dreamed that the Lord spoke to him and told him he must continue to pray and believe in the Lord because a different people [i.e. the whites] were coming who would make it hard for the Indians. They would not be free much longer. When the old ones all died, Lishwailait carried on the Washani. He danced on his knees. No one was allowed to smile or laugh. After he had danced on his knees for a time, the Lord lifted him to his feet. He carried on the religion strict and hard. He kept it up for over forty years. He began in about 1850 and he died in about 1890. The Washani was old in Klikitat country but it didn't come into Yakima reservation until later years [?]."

Martin Spidish (Wishram) --"Lishwailait was a Klikitat who followed Smohalla. He was later than Smohalla. The use of pom poms [tambourines] came in with the Smohalla religion. It was not used with the earlier religion imported from Ft. Vancouver. The Smohalla people took into [18] their religion the older idea of worshipping on Sundays.

"When the people had a meeting, Lishwailait used to hold up a mirror. As you entered the door, he looked into the mirror and saw your sins. After Lishwailait died no one had that power."

Sally Ann Joyce (Cascade Klikitat) — "Lishwailait was shown in his dream that he should make a flag of buckskin and have eagle feathers tied on his pole."

Ashnithlai

Ashnithlai seems to have been a Klikitat of Lishwailait's generation who had a marked conversion experience in the Washani cult. There is no evidence that he was an outstanding leader or that he had any marked influence upon Jake Hunt in ritualistic matters. However, the psychological influence which Ashnithlai may have had upon Jake is suggested in the following account which was given by one of Jake's sisters.

Susie Hunt Spidish (Klikitat) — This account is particularly interesting for the attitudes in the informant which it reveals.

"Between Lishwailat and Jake Hunt there was another man called Ashnithlai who interpreted the Washani religion. He worked above Husum. He took over the white man's ways and cultivated the land for his living. He was not at that time a strong believer in the Washani. He came home one day with long hip boots. He began to think. At this time Lishwailait was holding services for the Washani in the Glenwood district where many were gathered to get cam ass. At the noon hour, Ashnithlai said, 'How is this Washani? I am going to sing and dance just as a joke.' He started to swing his right arm and dance as he saw the others do. Before he knew it, he found himself with some unseen strength or power which lifted him off the ground and threw him quite a number of feet — Just as a child can be tossed. When he awoke he heard many people singing a Washani song. He heard his own mother and father among those who were singing. Then he began to cry. He was somewhat paralyzed and had to crawl on hands and knees. He cut a pole. He heard a voice speak to him, 'Cut a long pole. You set it up and on this pole we shall descend to you.' He did this. He looked up and saw something coming down this pole. As he looked up a round sphere [?] of reed matting appeared. People were on the mat and landed on top of the pole without breaking it. He cried. He tied part of his red blanket on the end of the pole. Then he crawled in the house. He took off his hip boots. His skin came off with the boots. It had stuck to the boots as though it had been cooked on. His foot looked cooked. The skin also peeled off of his hands. He had been a mocker of the Washani. He was now singing the song [b] which came to him when he first started to sing and dance as a joke. He kept on singing his own song. That night he kept on singing. Some of the neighbors decided they would go and see how he was getting along. That was several nights later. This was about six miles from Husum, before there were whites there. As they drew near they heard _aaaaaa aaa_ at his dwelling. They thought he was mocking them with his song and his pole and red flag. They laughed. Ashnithlai knew he had visitors coming but he was blind and unable to walk. He crawled out to greet his brothers. When they saw him he was so disfigured that he was no longer the same man. He said, 'My brothers, I want you to get on your horses and circle my home and this pole seven times. When you enter the house after that, also walk around my house seven times.' This they did. Then they shook hands with him. He told his story. 'I am as dead. I can now see how wicked I was to mock the Washani.' Ashnithlai was home alone. His wife was out with their young daughter digging camass. Men hurried to Glenwood to give the news. Ashnithlai was taken to the regular meeting Lishwailait was holding there. He was so disfigured it was a pity to see. I was just a little girl then. [Note: She said previously that she was born after Lishwailait's death, which was probably inaccurate.] Ashnithlai was never healed. Years later my brother Jake and I went with our mother to see Ashnithlai, who was our uncle, because he was to die soon. He was singing his Washani song and waving his hands back and forth. He was blind and so disfigured I was afraid. He had been that way many years. Ashnithlai called to me, 'My niece, salmon is very good food. Deer is also good. Camass is good food; also huckleberry and water. I am showing this that you must be thankful for them.' From then on I possessed those words in my heart and hold those foods to be most valuable for my people. Tomorrow is Sabbath and I must have these foods and this water each Sabbath. I must perform this act and prepare this food. This is the Washani belief and Ashnithlai's teaching. This prayer is the reason I withdrew from the Shakers. I could not use my prayer and I couldn't express myself enough without it. I first learned my Shaker prayer in Wasco. With the Shakers I could not express myself in Klikitat."

The following prayer is the one Ashnithlai taught the informant and her brother,

Jake Hunt. It is chanted:

nusux	winat	wakamo	wiwinu	tcawac
salmon	venison	camass	huckleberry	water

The prayer consists simply in chanting these five food names before and after meals. The same prayer is used by the other Hunt sisters. The proper foods accompanied by the prayer must be eaten every Sunday. These five words are the only ones which are plainly spoken. The [19] rest of the chant is composed of meaning less syllables.

Sally Ann Joyce (Cascade-Klikitat) — "Ashnithlai was a mocker of everything. Then he was given a task. He died and came to again. After that he said, 'I must have done a great wrong and an awful sin when I mocked the Washani work among my people.' He interpreted what he had seen while he was dead. 'Truly our Indian people are going to be up against something which is [b] very hard. There will be a new law which you will hear like a thunder storm. A people are coming who will take the strength of thunder. All will be metal and their power taken from thunder will be in the metal. It will carry you from one country to another.' All that prophesied auto mobiles, but it was years before we heard of automobiles. He made that statement be fore a Washani service. He foretold many other things which are here today." (Informant wept at this point.)

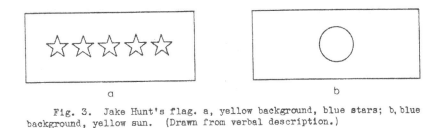

Fig. 3. Jake Hunt's flag, a, yellow background, blue stars; b, blue background, yellow sun. (Drawn from verbal description.)

Origin of the Feather Cult: Jake Hunt

The usual difficulties in getting sequential and detailed biographical data from informants of this area were encountered in attempting to secure some idea of Jake Hunt's personality prior to his conversion. Statements were fragmentary and frequently conflicting. The following accounts are a composite of the most accurate data given by a number of informants.

Biography

Jake Hunt was a Klikitat who lived in a small Indian community called *nakrepunk* where the present village of Husum is now located. It lies on the eastern bank of the White Salmon River in the first ridge of hills north of the Columbia. The country is heavily wooded and precipitous. The Klikitat were definitely a mountain rather than a river people, but since Husum is only some seven miles north of the Columbia, this particular group had close contacts with the river people.

Jake's father had two wives. By the first and older woman, there was a boy, Jo Hunt, and a girl, *Xiwili*, both of whom are still living. By the second wife, there were five girls and one son, Jake Hunt (see Table I). There appears to have been a good deal of friction and animosity between the two groups of half-siblings which still persists. Jo Hunt and his full sister never supported the Feather cult activities of their half brother, Jake.

As a child Jake Hunt seems to have led the normal restricted life of a small Indian community. Informants failed to recall any outstanding characteristics or experiences. The Hunt family were all followers of the Washani religion. They seem to have been pious in their observances, but they were not outstanding figures in the cult, although Jake's father was a respected and important figure in the community. As a youth, Jake showed no marked religious inclinations. His sister said of him, "He opposed the Washani religion because he cut his hair and wore white men's clothes." I did not gain the impression, however, that there was any rebellious bravado in his adoption of these European customs. Jake does not seem to have broken away from his environment. No one recalled that he had travelled beyond the limited confines of the food-gathering area exploited by the Husum group. Inform ants all agreed that he had been born at Husum and had always stayed in that vicinity. His contacts must have been largely limited to Indian groups since he spoke only Klikitat and jargon. He acquired a little English in later life after his conversion experience. [b] In appearance he was described as short, "only about five feet high,' but erect, unusually handsome, and of a lighter complexion than most Indians. He was careful of his personal appearance and was always well dressed. His eloquence was frequently mentioned and he "always used very polite expressions in his talk." There was no indication of an arrogant or overbearing and aggressive manner.

While Jake was still quite young, he married Annie Sloutier, daughter of the Cascade chief, John Sloutier. This seems to have been a traditional family arrangement with the customary bride price negotiations. Jake had several children by Annie, none of whom survived their infancy. He then began having relations with Annie's sister, Isabel Sloutier. Annie objected and left him. He and Isabel then lived together and there was a child from the union who also died in infancy. Jake at this time is supposed to have contracted a venereal disease from Isabel, and both were seriously ill. Shortly after this episode Jake became interested in a third woman, whereupon Isabel also left him. As one informant put it, "He was sort of restless and ran around a lot with women." His third wife was Minnie Coon, a Klikitat woman. He lived during this marriage, which lasted nine or ten years, in a small settlement between Mosier and Hood River on the southern bank of the Columbia. He seems to have been genuinely devoted to Minnie Coon and to a child from this marriage. It was at their death that his conversion experience occurred which is described in detail in the next section. A year or two after founding the Feather religion, he married a fourth time at Wishram. By this marriage there was one son who died as a youth in about 1925. During all his life, Jake and his five full sisters were very close to each other. When he travelled with his Feather religion at least one of his sisters was al ways with him. I gained the impression that his intimate contacts were with women. He seems to have had no close male associate or convert.

After an unsuccessful attempt to convert the Indians on Umatilla reservation, Jake returned to his wife's people at Spear fish (old Wishram), where he spent the last few years of his life. He seems to have suffered from a disease of the prostate glands. He is described as having large sores from which there was a discharge. The sores were said to be so deep that the bone was exposed. He was badly crippled during the last two or three years of his life and was forced to use crutches. Gossip also has it that he died from the bursting of an infected [21] prostate. The suffering was naturally intense and his activities were greatly restricted. During his years of illness, he was faithfully nursed by his fourth wife. When he died his body was taken to Husum for burial.

Since his death certain tales have grown up. It is customary along the middle Columbia to deposit corpses in death houses in isolated spots and to redress the dead once a year. Although Jake Hunt was buried, his body was exhumed for re-dressing some fifteen years ago (ca. 1919). Reports say that no decay had taken place and that the corpse appeared as natural as in life.

The dating of events in Jake Hunt's life are difficult to establish with complete accuracy. Martin Spidish, an intelligent and educated Wishram, was a brother-in-law of Jake Hunt and closely associated with him. He suggested the following dating: Cult founded and introduced in Spearfish the year in which the Spanish-American war ended, i.e. 1898; fourth marriage, 1910; illness, 1912; death, 1917. An educated and informed Shaker from Yakima reservation said that Wasco Jim's visit occurred in 1904, which would place the founding of the Feather religion in that year. We know that Jake Hunt's visit to Umatilla reservation was during the [22] period of O.C. Edwards' superintendency from October 1905 to June 1907.[13] A Klikitat interpreter said that Jake Hunt's conversion experience occurred as early as 1895. I am inclined to accept 1904 as the probable date for the origin of the Feather cult. His fourth marriage was probably about the same time and his death probably occurred between 1910-1914. Jake's age at the time of his death can only be inferred from various in determinate statements. I should judge that he was between fifty and sixty at the time, which would place his birth sometime in the decade from 1860 to 1870.

Conversion

The personal experience which led Jake Hunt to found the Feather cult resulted directly from his content with the Shakers.

The Shaker cult reached Yakima reservation in about 1890. Spier[14]15 has given a resume' of its introduction. The conversion account contained in Spier's appendix occurred in 1896 and is considered by present Yakima Shakers as the beginning of active Shaker practices on the reservation. There was at that time, as well as at present, a good deal of travel back and forth between Yakima reservation and the north

---

[13] Letter from United States Department of Interior: Office of Indian Affairs, July 20, 1935.

[14] Spier, op. cit., pp. 49-54; appendices N, 0.

bank of the Columbia River, especially during the period of salmon runs. News of the cures performed by the new Shaker church spread rapidly to the Columbia. The events which followed are intimately connected with Jake Hunt's conversion experiences.

Jake Hunt was married at the time of his conversion (ca. 1904?) to Minnie Coon, the daughter of Jack Coon. Jack Coon in turn was married to Kittie Hunt, one of Jake's sisters. All four were living on the summit of the first ridge south of the Columbia River and east of Hood River. Jake's wife, Minnie Coon, was seriously ill with tuberculosis. Their ten year old son (or daughter?) was also ill. Although no one of the Hood River and White Salmon group was a Shaker at the time, it was decided to send for Shakers on Yakima reservation whose curing powers were known. The father of Jake's first wife, Johnny Sloutier, had been converted to Shakerism and Wasco Jim (*Atsan*) had a Klikitat wife related to the Hunts. The latter was a noted Shaker on Yakima reservation. Jake Hunt invited these two men to visit him near Hood River and help his wife and child.

Prior to their visit, Wasco Jim had announced in a Shaker meeting at White Swan (Yakima reservation) that he had received a revelation to incorporate buckskin clothing and feathers into the Shaker cult. This was doubtless based on Washani precedent. When his suggestion was rejected by the group, he dropped the matter. One informant believed that Wasco Jim's vision was the source of [b] Jake Hunt's later stress upon those regalia in the Feather cult.

When the visiting Shakers arrived at Hood River, they held daily curative séances in the course of which most of the group was converted. Jake seems to have held out against adopting the new religion. Despite the efforts of the Shakers, Jake Hunt's child died a few weeks later.

The body was taken across the Columbia for burial at White Salmon. The group stood around the open grave praying. Josephine, who was the daughter of one of Jake's favorite sisters, stood with her hands raised and apart. Suddenly her hands came together as though she had grasped something. She is reported to have said, "Something has come to me in a vision and it looks awfully good." At this point Sally Ann Joyce, the sister of Jake's father-in-law (i.e. Jack Coon) and the person from whom these particular data were secured, stepped up to Josephine. "I took it from her hands myself. I looked and it became plain as a vision to me. My eyes were shut, yet it was as though a lighted match were held at night before my eyes. There was a large flat bright disk of light and in the center was a man. This circle was a piece of land (*titcam*). The man wore a buckskin shirt and trousers. In his left hand was a drum and in his right, the drum stick. At the back of his head were two eagle feathers." The informant said that Jake Hunt then took the' disk from her and claimed it as his own. Since the vision was a reality to the informant, there was no difficulty in her mind connected with its transference. She showed some resentment that the disk had been taken from her.

Table 1. Jake Hunt's Genealogy

```
1. Timák'st
   (Klikitat of
    Xatwailpom           ┌─ 4. Jo Hunt*
   = 2. Wawákun ─────────┤
         (Klikitat)      └─ 5. Xi'wilx*

                         ┌─ 6. Laushlai*
                         │     = Kwiumps
                         ├─ 7. Jake Hunt (Titcam Nashat)
                         │     = 8. Annie Sloutier
                         │
                         │     = 9. Isabel Sloutier
                         │     = 10. Minnie Coon
                         │     = 11. Mrs. Jim Kelly
                         │           (Wishram)
   = 3. Wilkú'ak ────────┤─12. Mary Hunt
         (Klikitat)      │     (Waiet)
                         │     = ♂ ? ──────────────── 18. Josephine (Yaminwai)*
                         ├─13. Kitty*
                         │     = Jack Coon (No. 22)
                         ├─14. Susie (Skẃilili)*
                         │     = 15. Silas
                         │     = 16. Martin Spidish*
                         │           (Wishram)
                         └─17. Emma (Wikstáni)*
```

```
20. John Sloutier
    (Cascade chief)           ┌─ Annie Sloutier (No. 8)
    = ♀ ? ────────────────────┤
                              └─ Isabel Sloutier (No. 9)
```

```
┌─21. Sally Ann*
│     (Cascade-Klikitat)
│     = Joyce
│
└─22. Jack Coon
      (Klikitat)
      = ♀ ? ─────────────────── Minnie Coon (No.10)
      = Kitty Hunt (No. 13)
```

```
┌─19. Mrs. Tommy Thompson*
└─    Mrs. Jim Kelly (No. 11)
```

Asterisks indicate persons still living. Indian names in parentheses follow American ones. Tribal affiliations are in parentheses below names.

The only addition which Jake seems to have made to the vision which the informant described was to identify the central figure in the disk as Lishwailait. It will be recalled that Lishwailait was a relative of Jake and the most important Washani leader among the Klikitat during the period of the Smohalla revival. Tom Bill, who was present at the time, gave substantially the same account, although he seems to have been unaware of Josephine's and Sally Ann's acquisition of the vision prior to Jake. According to his version, he was first aware of an untoward happening when Jake, who stood at his left near the head of the grave, began to shake violently. He then seemed to seize something between his upraised hands, after which he spun rapidly in place. When Jake stopped, he announced that he had Lishwailait's soul. Tom Bill, who was an ardent Shaker, answered, "I don't believe you. A person's soul goes up to heaven." This marked the beginning of a rift between the Shaker and potential Feather cultists.

After this episode, the Shaker group continued to give curing séances for Jake [23] Hunt's wife. Although many of his relatives had joined the new religion by this time, Jake was still holding aloof. Finally Wasco Jim told him that the only hope of curing Minnie Coon lay in his professing the Shaker religion. After that, Jake permitted himself to be converted.

The role of at least one of Jake's sisters in these affairs must now be considered. Susie Hunt and her husband, Silas, had at tended some of the Shaker curing séances at Hood River. Susie had apparently a marked affection for her handsome sister-in-law, Minnie Coon, and was deeply touched by her emaciated appearance. Although she and her husband went to the Shaker gathering with a skeptical attitude, Susie, at least, soon fell under the sway of the excitement. Some idea of the hectic nature of the gatherings is best conveyed by Susie's own account of her conversion hysteria. "Everyone was dancing except me, my husband and brother, Jake. I pitied my sister-in-law whom I loved. I did not see how that poor woman could be healed with all the noise of bells and stamping. I shut my eyes because I could not bear to look any longer. I had to cry. Right then and there something came into my mind and I went crazy. When they saw what had happened, they took the sick woman from the middle of the floor and worked on me. I had been all dressed up to go to the white man's dance, but now my clean clothes were half ripped off. My high heeled shoes came off. Right then and there, I got the power of the Shakers." This conversion experience of Susie occurred at about the same time that Jake joined the Shakers in the hope of saving his wife's life. It is a further indication of the rapport between the Hunt siblings.

Approximately one month after the death of her child, Minnie Coon also died despite the strenuous efforts of the Shakers. Jake's sister, Susie, professes to have foreseen this at the time that she secured her first Shaker vision. Within the course of two months, Jake lost both the wife and child to whom he had been deeply attached. His two previous marriages had been unsatisfactory and no children by his former wives had lived. It is not inexplicable that in his grief and sense of bereavement Jake should have turned against the Shakers whose noisy and costly presence he had suffered for two months. In the first throes of grief Jake secured a gun and lay in ambush to shoot Wasco Jim for whom he had developed an intense hatred. As he hid by the side of a path, he heard a supernatural voice dissuading him from violent action. Thereupon Jake put aside his gun and returned to his home in which the Shakers were still gathered. Wasco Jim was apparently aware of his hostile intent. That night as the whole group slept together in the Coon household, Wasco Jim arose and paced around the room ringing the hand bell which is so intrinsic a part of Shaker ceremonial. Jake arose, confessed his evil intentions and developed the tremor which Shakers have when "they get the power." [b]

The group of newly converted Shakers and their proselytizers from Yakima stayed together for a few days after the death of Jake's wife. The whole gathering seems to have been tense and hysterical. Susie Hunt Spidish at this time had further experiences which were significant in the light of subsequent developments. She described them as follows: "My brother's wife was like my own sister. I didn't want food. I felt as though I were sick, yet I was in my right mind. One of my sisters said I had been too long without food, so she handed me a piece of dried fish. I wanted it and asked for water. Wasco Jim handed me some in a dipper. As I reached for the water and before I could drink it, something told me, 'He is not handing this to you innocently. He likes you for your physical body. He wants to commit adultery.' My help told me the actual thoughts he had in his mind. I threw this water from me and spun around and around until I became crazy. I went to Wasco Jim and shook him until the people seized me and held me. Then I told them what had compelled me to act like this."

This significance of the drink of water spinning, and the accompanying furor will be come apparent in the subsequent description of the initiation rites of the Feather cult. It is evident that Susie, despite her Shaker convictions at the time, identified herself sufficiently with her brother to share his hostile feeling toward the Shaker leader.

Meanwhile Jake Hunt had withdrawn some what from the group gathered in the Coon household. His grief was recognized as excessive. All day he lay outside on the ground fasting and weeping. He neglected his personal appearance. He was described as being in a "filthy and pitiable condition." He seemed still to harbor resentment toward Wasco Jim and also toward Susie's husband, Silas, who was a shaman. He suspected both of them as the cause of his wife's death and threatened to kill them. His resentment was also directed toward the Shaker ceremonies. He is reported to have said, "My wife and child have both died, yet the Shakers still dance. I don't see what they can mean to me now." During this period he lay on his wife's grave and fell asleep. The dream which resulted is considered by most informants to have been the immediate stimulus to his cult activities. The content of this dream varies with different informants. His sister Susie, who was in the best position to know the details, said that his wife and child appeared to him and told him to stop grieving. He heard their voices command him to wash, resume normal activities, and abandon his plans of killing Wasco Jim and Silas. In the same dream, he recognized the voices of his ancestors commanding him to make a rawhide tambourine. He saw again a disk of light, generally called a land (*titcam*) by informants, which was brought down from the sky by an eagle. The persons who appeared to him were singing some of the old Washani songs. He was commanded to convert people in seven lands. He awoke refreshed and consoled. [24] Formerly he had not been a strong Washani believer. When he awoke, he suddenly knew all the old Washani songs of which he is sup posed to have been ignorant prior to this last dream or vision.

Accounts of this critical period varied from informant to informant. A reliable convert at Yakima said that Jake was lying out side of his house when he heard a voice command him to stop grieving and to take up a new work. A song was received at this time. Jake arose still in a trance state and went to the cemetery dancing and singing his new song. His relatives, thinking he had lost his mind, seized him and dragged him to the house. There he recovered from his trance and accused his relatives of having destroyed the full development of his powers. He claimed that had they left him alone for seven days and seven nights, he would have been able to revive the dead. Shortly after this episode, he again had a trance in which he was given the minor task of healing the sick and curing drunkards.

On Umatilla reservation several inform ants insisted that Jake had been dead for several days during which time he had visited heaven and received instructions for creating the Feather cult. This death and resurrection motif is a favorite one in the area. Their data were remarkably detailed and circumstantial, particularly in view of their inaccuracy. It offers simply another example of the manner in which thought pat terns overlay and obscure historical reality.

After the experience at his wife's grave, Jake bathed and requested clean buckskin clothing from his sisters. He then entered the house laughing and joking. The group of Shakers was about to sit down to a meal. Sally Ann Joyce rang the Shaker hand bell and all gathered about the table with their eyes closed for the customary Shaker grace. Jake stood to one side smiling. An hysterical atmosphere was still present. Wasco Jim stood beside Jake's sister Susie at the table. As she bowed her head for the grace, she saw a rattlesnake by her foot. As she moved aside, she perceived that the rattlesnake was Wasco Jim's foot. Simultaneously, Sally Ann who was praying suddenly fainted (?). Her tongue came clear out of her mouth and she circled the table putting her arms around every man and licking his face." At that point Jake raised both hands and commanded quiet. By simply waving his hands, he is reported to have upset the long, heavy dinner table. Then he said, "My brothers and sisters, you must stop. I have broken your table. Never perform this work here again. Tomorrow I am going home to my mother and father."

This seems to have definitely terminated the Shaker meetings. The next day Jake Hunt left Hood River and crossed the Columbia for his home at Husum. He is said to have made that journey in a miraculously brief time. Tom Bill ferried him across the river. As Jake left, he told Tom to inform [b] the Shakers that they need never again send for him.

Upon his return to Husum, Jake's first concern was the erection of a long house. In addition to the long house, Jake also built a log cabin. Four of his sisters soon joined him there to assist in establishing the new cult. Of these Laushlai, the eldest of the siblings, was the only one who had remained aloof from the Shaker furor at Hood River. When Susie arrived, she found her brother standing in the center of the log cabin dressed in the old style buckskin clothes heavily decorated with beads and talking aloud. "He was full of Joy." He announced that his new Indian name was to be *Titcam Nashat*. *Titcam* is the word usually used for the disk of light seen in his vision and is translated as earth or land. *Nash* at is variously translated as rumbler, groaner, roarer. Thunderer is probably the correct rendition. Thereafter Jake Hunt was always called Earth Thunderer or simply Thunderer (*Nashat*).

The first converts were in Jake's immediate family. He held meetings at Husum demonstrating his powers and strengthening his converts until he gained assurance. He then set out to convert neighboring groups. This will be described in a later section.

Clairvoyance and Miracles

Before considering the historical growth of the Feather cult, it may be desirable to continue with material on Jake Hunt's supernatural powers. There will be further discussion of these matters in sub sequent sections on shamanism and curing procedure. At this point is inserted only that testimony which bears on his miraculous and clairvoyant powers. There are many accounts of Jake's powers of pre-vision. He was believed capable of anticipating the arrival of an unannounced visitor. He could divine illness even when the patient was not present. He could read people's thoughts and gauge their moral character at a glance. On Umatilla reservation, he knew of a secret murder and secured a confession from the culprit. If intoxicants were brought into his encampment, he knew it without seeing them and could find them wherever they might be concealed. In one case of this sort, he returned with some whiskey, whereupon the malefactor's hands became rigid in an attitude of prayer until Jake released him by pouring the liquor on the fire. The colored flames resulting from this act were considered further proof of his miraculous powers. Among his supernatural gifts was his power of locating objects with his eyes closed. His location of the thunderbolt arrow point to be described later is a case in point. However, he made no specialty of finding lost objects, for which the Shakers on Yakima reservation were famous. When he made his first converts at Husum, one of his [24] tests was to toss an ordinary pin into the grass and have the new convert find it immediately. He is said to have ridden a horse down hill at the speed of lightning without even a saddle. His powers of understanding and "interpreting" all natural phenomena are discussed further in the section on shamanism.

Shamanism

The relationship of Jake Hunt's experiences to shamanistic patterns is more marked than a description of ritual implies. Most of the data concerning this subject was secured from Jo Hunt, who was himself a shaman and no sympathizer with his half brother's religious practices. His statements may be colored by his own predilections.

Jo Hunt (Klikitat) — "When Jake was a young man, before he got the Feather religion, he was on the verge of being an Indian doctor through various *tamanos* {*taaxmanawis*} [spirit familiars] which he himself did not know about. When his sister Kaimet startled him once, it aroused all the tamanos and he discovered that he possessed them. They became a light to him. Tamanos go by pairs, a brother and sister, male and female. A small doctor has one pair. A strong doctor has three pairs. Once he gets that many he can handle any number. If he can't control them, he will only kill himself. Jake had two pairs and many single tamanos which just gave him songs. One pair was eagle and grizzly bear; the other was Chinook salmon and raccoon. The grizzly bear is one of the most powerful and dangerous familiars. One of his single powers was the wind which made you spin when he blew on you. The power of the wind was in the feather he made you hold in your hand. The eagle spoke to him and told him to do this feather work."

Jake's sister, Susie Hunt Spidish, also stresses the importance of the eagle spirit in Jake's supernatural powers. She said in terminating an account of his vision experiences, "It was an eagle which commanded these things. Jake said the eagle was to be the messenger to carry your thoughts. He will bring help from the heavenly land where all our dead are when you are in sorrow. The eagle has always been a sacred being to all Indians from the beginning of this world."

Certainly these implications of an eagle familiar coincide with the accounts of an eagle "totem" given subsequently in connection with the pole and would lend added significance to the stress upon eagle feathers. A Warm Springs informant said that it was formerly customary for a man to wear some symbol of his guardian spirit. For [b] example, if he were blessed by a wolf with hunting powers, he wore a wolf pelt. The feathers are equated with the eagle, and the wind and with a messenger spirit. The degree to which these interpretations are shamanistic depend upon the bent of the informant.

In addition there is some indication of a Thunderbird familiar which was reflected in the thunderbolt arrow point which Jake kept at the foot of his flag pole and in his adoption of the name Earth Thunderer. His sister stated flatly that he had a thunderbird guardian which accounted for the adoption of his name. "There were five thunderbird brothers in the old myths. Jake had their power. He could say prayers to make it thunder and to call the wind. He raised his arms and faced in the direction from which he wanted the weather to come." When the informant was asked to explain the Thunderbird concept, she said the subject was so sacred it would make her sick to talk of it, and that her heart was already beating furiously at the mere mention of the subject.

Susie, who made extravagant claims for Jake's powers, said also that, "He could interpret any object — a dog, horse, coyote, trees, and even a dish. Once Jake heard a dish speak to him saying, 'Do not handle me roughly. Whatever you do, you must do it carefully.' These other things he did not use for healing, but just for interpreting."

In addition to this range of familiar spirits used for healing, and the variety of objects which Jake seems to have heard speaking to him and which he could "interpret" to less sensitized people, there was another point in which his powers approximated the old shamanistic pattern. In the sections on Accounts of Cures, there are references to a quivering pole in his long house. One informant reported that it shook violently when grasped by a patient in the course of a cure. This is vaguely reminiscent of the shamanistic practice in which short staffs were made "to dance" and controlled the actions of the persons who held them. Also the report from Yakima of Jake's use of a stick which patients grasped has the same implications.[15]

Jake's use of a pole on which a like ness of his guardian familiar was placed is also reminiscent of shamanistic practices (see section on Poles and Flags).

However, there is no hint that Jake followed some of these shamanistic practices of the area. I received no indication that he ever extracted disease objects by sucking, although in one account he is said to have extracted them by massage. He was never reported to have gashed himself and sucked his own blood from the wounds. [26]

Diffusion of the Feather Cult

In the preceding section it was stated that Jake Hunt's vision commanded him to carry the Feather religion to seven nations. After building a long house and making his first Klikitat converts at Husum, he set out on a series of proselytizing trips. Informants are not consistent in giving the sequence of his journeys. His first converts were among the Klikitat of his family, White Salmon and Hood River groups on the Columbia River. After that he made repeated visits to Yakima reservation and one to Warm Springs. An unsuccessful journey was made to Umatilla reservation. Each of these areas will be

---

[15] For ethnographic account of this phenomenon and further references, see Leslie Spier and Edward Sapir, Wishram Ethnography (University of Washington Publications in Anthropology, Vol. 3, No. 3, 1930), pp. 243-44. My informant identified the quivering stick as a Chinookan rather than a Sahaptin trait.

taken up in the order named — which is also the probable order of his travels.

Columbia River

During the fall of the same year in which Jake Hunt began to practice the Feather cult, he was invited to cure a young girl who was ill at Spearfish. Spearfish is the modern name for old Wishram. It is located approximately twenty-five miles up the Columbia from Husum. Jake Hunt's séances cured the girl and most of the Wishram joined the new cult. At Spearfish people had been predominantly Washani . A few had become Shakers on Yakima reservation. The resemblances between the Washani and Feather ritual in addition to its curative claims made acceptance of the new religion easy. Oscar Charlie is named as one of the few who refused to join the new cult. A long house was built at Spearfish. In front was erected an ordinary flag pole capped with a wooden sphere and from the top of which a few eagle feathers hung. Suitable regalia were made and Spearfish became one of the Feather cult centers for the duration of Jake Hunt's life. He married a woman from this community and made it one of his principal domiciles until his death. A sister of his married into the Spidish family from Spearfish. When the Spidish were converted, they destroyed most of the European furnishings in their house and returned in large part to Indian artifacts.

At present no one at Spearfish is said to practice the Feather cult. Most of the group have turned to the Shakers. A few still profess the old Washani. Jake's fourth wife has remarried and has also become a Shaker. Her sister married the present chief at Celilo, who is called Tommy Thompson. Celilo is the Waiem of aboriginal times. [b] It is on the south bank of the Columbia a few miles upstream from Spearfish. Mrs. Tommy Thompson is supposed to believe still in the Feather religion, but informants are uncertain about this. Jake Hunt never proselytized directly in this community. Both Mrs. Thompson and her husband refused to serve as informants and were hostile to any discussion of religious matters with people in Celilo. I doubt that any Feather cult practices persist among the permanent residents there.

A few months after Jake Hunt made his initial trip to Spearfish, he was invited to visit the Rock Creek group, on the north bank of the Columbia, some forty miles up stream from Spearfish. The Rock Creek Indians are the Sahaptin speaking Skin. Their conversion probably occurred in January, 1905. The principal Rock Creek convert in the minds of most informants was a woman called *Kisomxe*, who is also known as a shaman. Individuals from Fallbridge had attended meetings at Spearfish earlier in the winter. Fallbridge has recently been re-named Wishram by the whites. Its aboriginal name was Skin and its inhabitants were part of that Sahaptin subdivision to which the tribal term Skin has been applied and in which the Rock Creek are included.[16][17]

Yakima Reservation

The conversion of the Yakima reservation group was the result of repeated visits

---

[16] Melville Jacobs, A Sketch of Northern Sahaptin Grammar (University of Washington Publications Anthropology, Vol. 4, No. 2, 1931), p. 95.

by Jake Hunt. The first proselytizing trip was made shortly after the conversion of the Rock Creek group which was tentatively dated as 1905.

His first meeting was held in the Washani long house belonging to a Yakima chief, Billy Wholite, some three miles west of Toppenish. The next meeting was likewise in a Washani long house near White Swan. The third meeting was at Parker where Kutaiaxen had a long house for Washani meetings. An other of Jake's visits was a year or two after the Umatilla incident when his hair had not yet grown in fully (ca. 1908 or 1909). He remained on Yakima reservation most of that winter. He returned again two years later in ca. 1910 or 1911. That was his last visit. An informant estimated that fourteen households on the reservation were converted [27] in the course of these various visits and that most of them still adhere to this religion although meetings are held less regularly than formerly. At present the chief figures in the Feather cult on Yakima reservation are Thomas Umtuch who lives near Satus, Charlie Hultucks of White Swan, and Williams Charlie of Toppenish.

Warm Springs Reservation

Supposedly the first convert to the Feather religion on Warm Springs reservation was a woman called Sanat. On a visit to the Columbia River in about 1906, she came in contact with the new cult, became an adherent and returned to the Simnasho section of the reservation which is inhabited predominantly by Warm Springs Indians. She married Remi Sidwaller and under her influence he also joined the new religion. They may not have made converts, but at least they acquainted the community with the Feather cult ideas. The Sidwallers then moved to the southern end of the reservation, known as the *Seek seekwa* district. Here they came in contact with Paviotso and Wasco groups.

Probably in 1906, shortly after Sanat's conversion, Jake Hunt went to a Fourth of July gathering among the Warm Springs Indians on Badger Creek near Simnasho. He attended a Washani meeting which was in progress at the time. The local Washani leader, Queapama, asked Jake to address the group. "He stood up in the middle of the floor. He was dressed in yellow buckskin and even his face was painted yellow. He told about his vision. He stayed for the full two weeks of the Washani meeting. The old chief got interested and let him talk. He said openly he was not compelling people to join but they should come of their own accord. Some people tried to tempt him with drink, but he refused. Some laughed at him, but quite a few believed. He got about five members at that first meeting. Of those five, two have died; two have dropped out. Isaac McKinley is the only one of the five who still carried on the Feather religion." Of these, Isaac McKinley seems to have been the most powerful influence in the development of the movement. During the visit Jake also cured a partially paralyzed woman. This constituted Jake Hunt's only trip to Warm Springs. However, individuals travelled back and forth between Warm Springs and the Columbia River, and in this manner kept in touch with Jake Hunt. The group flourished particularly among the Simnasho Warm Springs and among the Paviotso of *Seekseekwa* whom the Sidwallers converted. The Wasco had been converted to Shakerism a year or two prior to the introduction of the Feather religion and they have remained in that faith until the present. Despite the lack of interest in the Feather religion on the part of the Wasco,

Warm Springs reservation is one of the strongest centers of this cult at present. A list of outstanding Feather cultists on Warm Springs today usually includes the following names: Isaac McKinley, Frank Winishut, Elisha Kishawa, Remi Sidwaller and [b] wife, Mac Quinn, Sally Ike, and Willie Jack. These are usually the persons who call meetings. The belief is current in Warm Springs that Jake Hunt lived only for seven years after his conversion. Seven is of course the pattern number which both the Washani and the Feather cult use. In this instance the pattern number approximates historical fact.

Umatilla Reservation

The longest trip which Jake Hunt under took was to Umatilla reservation, which is some one hundred and thirty miles to the east and south of his home at Husum. Between 1905 and 1907 he was asked to visit the reservation by a Walla Walla chief whose wife was ill. Two or three days before his arrival, he sent word that he was to come. On the day set for his appearance, "twenty-eight or thirty rigs went out to meet him and many went on foot. Everyone was excited. They brought their sick to him and followed him wherever he went." Jake Hunt had with him a group of ten young men and women among whom were his sister Waiet, his Wishram wife, and their son who died about 1925. There were also Warm Springs, Wishram, and Yakima converts. The first meeting lasted three days. It was held at Cayuse among a group of Walla Walla under the auspices of chief Newshirts. Later Jake was invited to cure a young man who lived near the Presbyterian mission of Tutuilla. The patient was a Nez Perce in the last stages of consumption. His wife, who solicited Jake's assistance, was a Umatilla. At that time Jim Kashkash was the "Indian Judge" on the reservation. Kashkash is an educated Nez Perce, proud of his Presbyterianism and intolerant of Indian practices. He and three other Indian elders of the local Presbyterian mission reported the matter to the superintendent. The Catholic element on the reservation supported the Presbyterians in their protest. On the other hand, the old chiefs of the Walla Walla, Nez Perce, and Umatilla tribes sided with Jake Hunt. O.C. Edwards was the superintendent at that time. The temper of his administration may be judged by the fact that in the presence of a crowd, he had the fire hose turned on a Yakima chief as a disciplinary measure.

It was decided to put Jake's powers as a curer to the test. That Jake consented to the proposition, attests his sincerity. He agreed that he would be willing to suffer punishment if he failed. Jim Kashkash relates that the agency physician and a doctor from Pendleton were called in to examine the patient. They gave him only twenty-four hours to live. Then Jake danced and sang over the patient, after which he predicted at least two more days of life for him. At noon of the day following the trial, the sick man died. Several hundred Indians had assembled to await the outcome. After the death of the young Nez Perce, Jake was seized by agency officials. His hair was cut short, his drums and regalia were destroyed and he was given a choice between imprisonment or [28] permanent banishment from the reservation. He chose the latter. He and his band left Umatilla reservation deeply humiliated and with seriously impaired prestige. Informants on Umatilla reservation say, "No one believed in him after that." This seems to be a reasonably accurate statement since no one could be discovered who professed to be a Feather cultist. Until approximately 1922, one person only claimed to carry on Jake's cult curings. He was an Umatilla called Billy Mackay, who accompanied the Feather group on its return to Husum. Later he went back to his own reservation where he called no meetings but did occasionally perform cures of the Feather cult type.

It is interesting that the only detailed account of Jake's supernatural experiences which I secured on Umatilla reservation was couched in terms of death and resurrection rather than a "dream" or trance which seems to be the correct version.

Also the Umatilla informants consider that his humiliation on the reservation precipitated his death. The same opinion is current on Warm Springs reservation. An informant from the latter reservation said, "Jake did not know how many years he would live after his vision. His life span was not predicted as it was for many Washani dreamers. He was told in his dream that if he didn't do right, he wouldn't live long. The cutting of his hair and the loss of his regalia at Umatilla was like doing wrong. After his property was destroyed his right leg and side became paralyzed so he had to walk with a cane. He should have saved his religious things, not have given them up so easily. His being crippled was a punishment for that. Before that time he had always been a hale and hearty man."

Jake himself is reported to have said, "Probably I have not long to live. My days will be short. They have hurt me by taking away my costume and cutting my hair."

Actually some six or seven years must have elapsed between the Umatilla fiasco and Jake's death. However, very shortly after his return to Spearfish from Umatilla, his fatal illness set in and he was incapacitated for further active proselytizing.

It is said that when Jake visited Umatilla, he planned to travel farther eastward to the Nez Perce of Lapwai. After the Umatilla fiasco this plan was abandoned. Some informants are under the impression that he actually went there. This I believe to be erroneous. However, it is said that the Billy Mackay, previously mentioned, did make an occasional visit to that reservation for curings. For all practical purposes Umatilla reservation may be considered the eastern limit of Feather cult influences.

Paviotso Converts

In the section on Warm Springs, reference was made to Paviotso converts in the southern portion of Warm Springs reservation. Most influential of these was Charlie Weewa, who died during the summer of 1934. He was instrumental in converting a Nevada Paviotso. Unfortunately Charlie died the day I arrived on the reservation which debarred not only him but his family as possible sources of information. However, the following account was secured from an able Warm Springs inform ant. It is included verbatim in the hope that field workers among the Paviotso will be able to trace the individual in question.

Frank Winishut — "A Paiute came to Warm Springs reservation. He visited all the different religions here. He went to the Shakers and Presbyterians for many Sundays. Then Charlie Weewa, a Paiute Feather man, brought him to a Feather meeting at my house. Isaac McKinley led the meeting. He knew there was a stranger there, so he preached all about the religion and Charlie Weewa translated what was said into Paiute. Then the stranger got up and made a speech saying he wanted to join and take his religion back to Nevada where he lived because his people suffered from drunkenness. He was not a drinker himself but he wanted to save his people. So we tried him out little by little to see if he was sincere. Finally he was converted. He stayed here for a time attending all the meetings. His first trip was in about 1918. He made a second in about 1921 and another the next year." The name and location of this Paviotso convert was unknown to Warm Springs informants.

Another Paviotso called Pete Polina, who lives on Klamath reservation, was converted by Charlie Weewa. Charlie with a group from Warm Springs reservation attended a Fourth of July gathering at Ft. Klamath. The inform ant stated this was thirty years ago. Probably the dating is approximately between 1907 and 1910. At that time Pete Polina was ill. Charlie said that if he joined the Feather religion he might be cured. For several nights the Warm Springs group met at Pete's house. Pete was converted, learned the prayers, songs, etc., and gradually recovered his health. Ever since then he has been a firm believer in the movement even though he has made no converts. He exercises his cultist powers chiefly in the realm of curing. Occasional Indians on Klamath reservation will go to him for treatment much as they would consult a white physician or a shaman. Since his conversion Pete has visited Charlie Weewa on Warm Springs reservation. He reported meeting at that time a Bannock convert to the cult. This may refer to the Paviotso mentioned above.

Pete Polina had a son who lived at Nixon, Nevada, on the Pyramid Lake reservation. In about 1925 or 1926 Pete visited his son and attempted to convert some of the Nevada Paviotso. According to his own report he was unsuccessful although he was asked to doctor a patient. [29]

Pete Polina was the only informant professing the Feather religion who had no knowledge, however inaccurate, concerning the origin of the cult and Jake Hunt's conversion experiences. It is possible that his inadequate background in the history and development of the cult prevented him from presenting it dramatically to potential converts. This may account in part for his lack of success as a proselytizer. [30]

Ceremonialism

Initiation

Before a person could be considered an active member of the Feather religion, he had to pass the tests of the initiation ceremony. If these were met successfully, the convert shared in the powers secured by Jake Hunt and was entitled to make converts in his own right. Informants refer most frequently to the injunction against intoxicating drinks. To a true convert, the odor of alcohol becomes repulsive. Many initiates were cured of drunkenness by this ceremony. The initiation is supposed to be most effective when a person is just sobering after a prolonged drinking bout.

The initiate is placed in the center of the room or long house, facing east. To his right, i.e. to the north, are the women; to his left, i.e. to the south, are the men.[17] The

---

[17] * Evidently this should read: "To his right, i.e. to the south, are the women; to his left, i.e. to the north, are the men." Apparently there is confusion of these directions at

three or more drummers are back of him to the west. A bell-ringer stands at one end of the line of drummers. In front of the initiate, with his back to him, stands the leader of the night's ceremony. He gazes upward into a mirror suspended above eye level. To the immediate right, left, and rear of the initiate stand three assistants to the leader. Water is heated and the leader gives the initiate three dipperfuls to drink. The water is as hot as the initiate can comfortably swallow it. Next two eagle tail feathers are taken from behind the mirror by the leader and placed in either hand of the initiate. The leader then looks into the mirror with arms raised and spread. He asks for spiritual help. To secure it, he should see the disk of light or "earth" (*titcam*) which appeared to Jake in his vision. If the leader secures the necessary vision, he goes to the initiate and drops the disk on him. This is supposed automatically to make the initiate spin violently in place. The three assistants steady him as he staggers. If the initiate is to be a true convert, the feathers which he holds will show him all his past sins. Meanwhile the members hear in the sound of the drums what is revealed to the initiate. When the seven songs which belong to this section of the ceremony are finished and if the revelation of the initiate's past life is completed, he stops spinning immediately. The leader then removes the two feathers from his hands and replaces them behind the mirror. The bell-ringer then steps forward and stands along side of the initiate. He asks only one question, [b] "What have you noticed in your spinning?" If the initiate "is to become a true member, he will confess all of the sins which he has just seen." The bell-ringer acts as interpreter. He repeats aloud those things told him by the initiate in a low tone of voice. Then the leader takes the initiate to the southeast corner of the room or lodge and gives him three more dipperfuls of warm water. The assistants meanwhile stand in the center. The initiate kneels in front of a pan while the leader presses his sides just below the floating ribs. Vomiting occurs and the initiate is considered cleansed of sins or maladies as the case may be. There will be no recurrence of his former sins. A special person, usually a woman, is appointed to empty the pan used by the initiate. No special safeguards or tabus surround the disposal of this material.

Two young men who have been appointed previously then come forward and lead the initiate three times around the room. During each circuit, they whirl around twice, once under the mirror and once in front of the drums. A final half circuit is made with a seventh spin under the mirror and the initiation is complete. Should the initiate be a woman, two girls are chosen to perform this final act. Several initiates may go through this ceremony in one night.

This procedure describes the contemporary initiation practices on Warm Springs reservation. It is possible that variations have arisen since Jake first instituted the ceremony. For instance, one of Jake's relatives stated that initiatory visions often dealt with one's dead relatives. Another informant stated that the feathers were held by simply crossing the thumb over the palm with fingers extended. Jake then spat a little water on each of the initiate's hands, whereupon they clenched convulsively over the quills. The spinning of the initiate be gins to the right and is supposed to increase in momentum. Seven young men and seven young women formed a circle to keep the

---

several points in the manuscript. Compare pages 31, 32-33, 36 and Figure 4. — Editor.

initiate from falling. Jake blew on him to increase the speed of the revolutions. Finally the initiate fell over in a trance. To arouse him, Jake once more spat water on him from a distance of a few feet. As the initiate came to, his hands relaxed, and Jake removed the feathers. A third informant claimed that the [31] feathers lifted your arms and made you feel as though you were floating. If the initiate were evil, the feathers made him spin to the left and soon weighed him down. The same informant said that Jake revived unconscious initiates by waving a feather over them. Still another informant stated that Jake had the initiate vomit before, rather than after, spinning.

When a person successfully passed through the initiation ceremony, he was given eagle wing or tail feathers and sometimes eagle down to be tied in the hair. Thereafter he is considered to share in Jake's supernatural powers.

The vomiting and spinning motifs in the initiation rites were the significant features to most informants. They seem also to have been the most original aspects. Vomiting in any other connection was denied by all informants interviewed. Among the Nez Perce, however, Curtis[18] reports that a wand was thrust down the throat to produce vomiting during the vision quest and after the contamination resulting from contact with the dead. I feel that vomiting is a different phenomenon from the oral hemorrhages of the shamanistic complex.

Personal Experiences at Initiation

Examples were secured of the type of vision which some converts experienced. They are given below preceded by the name of the person who furnished the data.

Cecelia Stowhide (Yakima) — "While my daughter was unconscious she saw a round earth come down from above with Indians wearing old time feathers and beads. They all wore orange clothes. They came down only so far. My daughter was so glad to see them, these people who died long ago, that she tried to get up on this earth. She couldn't quite make it. Then Jake brought her to. The next night she saw this very earth open up at her feet and she fell in to the chasm. This was interpreted to mean that her body would return to this earth again. She had to spin for five nights. During the next three nights she had no visions, but she felt her power in crease, and she learned the songs."

Charlie Selatkrine (Yakima) — "For two years I looked on the wonderful work which Jake performed in healing the sick and curing hopeless drunkards. I myself was impossible. I spent every cent for drinks, yet I always managed to stay where Jake was. I had become tired of not behaving myself and of being an outcast no matter how hard I tried. Worldly affairs got the better of me. I was helpless. So I went to Jake and asked to be prayed over.... He made me stand in the middle of the long house. On my left were women marvelously [b] dressed in their Indian clothes and on my right were men dressed in the same way. Jake sang a song given him by the Great Spirit. He had a little water in his mouth which he spat against my chest. Each time the water hit me, I vomited whiskey, smoke, and all the evil in me. The men and women joined in Jake's

---

[18] #18 E.S. Curtis, The North American Indian (Cambridge, Mass., Vol. 8, 1911), pp. 51, 65.

singing. The noise of the drum and singing grew louder and louder.

"Jake tied a feather on the back of my hair. I started whirling. Then I saw my self rolling around in the dirt with a bottle of whiskey in my hand. I was filthy. I realized how ugly I was under the influence of drink. I can't find words to say how horrible I looked to myself. Then I heard a high shrill _u u u_. A serpent stuck his head out of the bottle I was holding. His tongue was coming out of his mouth and he was tempting people to drink.

"Next, it seemed as though I were following a little bushy trail. I was having a terrible time struggling through the brush. Suddenly I came out in a lovely clearing. I saw myself on this earth. Long ago this must have been a lovely world with flowers, prairies, and a beautiful light on everything. Then our sins made it a dark place. It seemed as though I were travelling as I had never travelled before, because in my hand I held the feather which Jake had given me, and it was leading me on. I passed from one country to another and each became brighter than the preceding one. I went through four countries and when I came to the fifth, the land was greener and the sky was bluer than any I have ever seen. It was the land of happiness where flowers never wither and there is a plenty of all of the fruits of the earth. I saw there was a better place than this world to which we can go if we prepare for it.

"All this seemed to happen in a very short time, maybe just a few seconds. When I awoke Jake and his followers were hold ing me and trying to bring me to. I gave a worthy confession of all I had gone through while I was under the power. Jake was pleased because I had done well and was not ashamed of my sins but willing to go out into the world and show what sin can do to a person."

Jim Kanine (Walla Walla) — "When Jake was holding meetings at Cayuse on Umatilla reservation he got Kilasasomkin's wife to testify. She came up to the center and Jake said, 'It will be all right for you to see what she is going to do. You can learn a lesson from her.' Then they pinned a blanket between her legs like trousers. Jake sang his song and she began to spin. Then she fell on the ground unconscious. She acted the way she did when she committed adultery. She repeated all she had [32] said when she agreed to meet the man and acted just the way she had with him. It was Jake's spirit which made her confess these things. She was out of her mind."

Elisha Kishawa (Waiem) — "I loved to drink. My wife and many of my relatives tried to stop me but I wouldn't. I was in jail several times for drinking. Finally one Sunday Remi Sidwaller gave me water at a Feather meeting. He told me to close my eyes and think only of good things. Then he held my stomach and I vomited blood.[19] Then I went to bed for a week. When I got up I never wanted to drink again. It smells bad to me now. Then I was thin and I almost had tuberculosis, but now I am like a man. I was saved by this religion." The informant denied having visionary experiences at the time of his conversion.

Some generalized statements were made concerning conversion experiences which may be worth quoting:

"If you are an honest person, you will get a nice beautiful vision. If you are

---

[19] #19 Compare this to the oral hemorrhages reported for Klamath in Leslie Spier, Klamath Ethnography (University of California Publications in American Archaeology and Ethnology, Vol. 30, 1930), p. 126.

crooked, you will see lots of bad things."

"After you become a member, you can see people coming without looking. Souls of people travel in advance of them. The Feather people can see those souls."

"Jake made you feel as though you were way up on a height spinning on a block of ice that was too small. It made you feel as though you were falling off and you were aw fully afraid. I did not feel this way, but many who were bad felt this."

"Sometimes when people are spinning they see a great land. Sometimes they see a little round one and they are standing on it. Sometimes they see a great canyon and they are about to fall in it. Those are the sinners and they are frightened."

Ordinary Meetings

Meetings may be called by any convert who is so inclined. Sunday is considered the "holy day." Gatherings are held in mid morning and again in the evening. In addition, meetings may be held on Saturday and Friday nights. This is comparable to Washani practices. The group may gather in any type of dwelling or in a specially constructed long house. The type of building depends solely upon the facilities of the locality.

Participants enter in any order, but once within the building women seat them selves against the southern wall and men against the northern one. Members often hold an eagle feather in their right hand [b] with which they beat time to the music. The number of drummers is not fixed. They may vary from one to seven, again depending upon availability. As in the initiations, the drummers line up along the western wall of the building and on the northern end of the line is a single bell-ringer. He keeps time with the drums. The meeting begins with a set series of songs, usually seven in number. When the "third verse" of each song is ended, all members spin in place once. Non-members who may be present do not spin. A person who "wants to be helped" will stand in the center of the floor. The leader with his four assistants sprinkle him with water and fan him with their feathers. Again the leader is supposed to detect by the throb of the drums the sincerity of the person asking for help. At the end of the seven songs, two young people lead the person around the hall for three and a half circuits as described for the initiation ceremony. During the meeting the leader also exhorts the group. He tells of the history of the religion, speaks of their cult practices, urges ethical behavior, or testifies to the efficacy of the cult. Others present may also rise to preach.

This procedure again describes the con temporary practices on Warm Springs reservation. Additional data and variations were secured. One informant stated that strangers usually circled the building when they entered and shook hands in the ordinary fashion, as opposed to various Shaker types of hand clasp.[20] When the meeting was over, the men filed past the line of women and shook hands with each one before leaving. When the men have filed out, the line of women follows. As each person passes through the door, he spins once in place. The bell is rung continuously during this procedure. When all are outside of the building, a large circle is formed,

---

[20] #20 Spier, Prophet Dance, p. 68.

everyone raises his arms and shouts *ai*. The meeting is then over. This exit ceremony is precisely that which has been described for the Washani cult along the middle Columbia. It differs slightly from the Shaker exit ceremony. Among the Shakers the last woman to the left starts down the line shaking hands with each woman in turn and then with each man. After your hand has been shaken by the last person to your left, you fall in queue and make the circuit. In this fashion each person greets every other person present. In Shaker meetings, no circle is formed outside of the building.

Another informant described Jake Hunt's meetings at Spearfish. They seem to have varied considerably on the side of elaborateness from the description given for Warm Spring practices. In Jake's Sunday ceremony, all the men wore yellow or blue shirts.

The women were dressed in the *klepip* (see Clothing) {*tł'píip*}. Seven girls, dressed in yellow, stood in line in front of the drums at the [33] eastern end of the building (Fig. 4).[21] Opposite them was a line of seven boys dressed in blue. The line of girls circled the building to the south and east; the boys went to the north and west. The two lines started simultaneously. They made one circuit for each of the seven songs. When these special performers were through, they resumed their original position — the girls in front of the southwestern end of the women's line, the boys in front of the northwestern end of the men's line. Preferably there were seven drummers and each one in turn began a new song in which the others joined. Sometimes the leader gave one drummer permission to select all seven. If there were fewer than seven drummers, two or three of the drummers might initiate more than one song apiece. The bell-ringer who stood at the southwestern end of the line rang the bell rapidly at the end of each song. He was considered the "song counter." If someone wished to preach or testify, he stood in front of the drummers. When he was through speaking, he circled the room three or seven times depending upon the number of drums or songs used up to that point in the ceremony. When the person had finished his circuits, all kneeled and joined in a prayer, at the end of which all said *ai* and resumed their former position. The informant stated that this whole procedure closely resembled that of the Washani practiced at Spearfish prior to Jake Hunt.

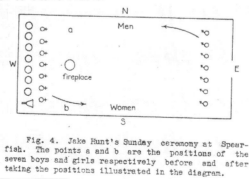

Fig. 4. Jake Hunt's Sunday ceremony at Spearfish. The points a and b are the positions of the seven boys and girls respectively before and after taking the positions illustrated in the diagram.

Fig. 4. Jake Hunt's Sunday ceremony at Spearfish. The points a and b are the positions of the seven boys and girls respectively

---

[21] * The text does not agree with Figure 4. It would seem that the girls were at the western end. — Editor.

before and after taking the positions illustrated in the diagram.

A third informant, in discussing a meeting which she attended at Husum during Jake's life time, said that everyone circled the lodge to the right upon entering and before taking a seat. Once in, no one was allowed to leave until the meeting was over. This applied even to the children. Quiet attention was demanded of everyone. People stood during the songs and hopped up and down in time. The bell-ringer in this case stood in front of the drummers, half-way down the building. After each song, when the hand [b] bell was given several rapid sharp shakes, the audience raised their right arms and said *ai*.

At dawn on Sunday, the drummers would beat their tambourines "to remind themselves of the holy day and prepare for it. They prayed to the Almighty at this time."

These data apply to the Sunday meetings. In the preliminary gatherings which were sometimes held on Saturday and Friday evenings, singing was the main object. As many tambourines as were available were given to the first group of women in the northeastern corner of the room. Each in turn began a song in which the whole audience joined. After each tambourine holder had had her opportunity to begin a song, the instruments were passed on to the next in line. In this manner the drums made a circuit of the building and ended among the men at the northeastern corner. This practice is still in vogue on Warm Springs reservation where it was supposedly introduced by Jake Hunt.

Curing Procedure

Although the ceremonial procedure of the Feather cult strongly resembles that of the Washani, two features differentiate it sharply from the older religion. The initiation with its spinning and vomiting features is one marked innovation which has al ready been described. Curing is another. Whereas the spinning and vomiting aspects of the initiation seem to be completely original with Jake Hunt, the curative functions of the cult may well be a direct borrowing from the Shaker religion. Spier[22]21 has suggested shamanistic precedents for Shaker curings. Borrowings directly from shamanism can also be detected in the Feather cult. This matter has already been discussed in connection with Jake Hunt. The point to be made at present is that the enemies of the Feather religion claim the practices are shamanistic. In the eyes of the Shakers, this is a most opprobrious accusation. The Feather cultists are not unaware of the criticism directed against them in this respect. Their chief defense is that they are evidently not "Indian doctors" since they perform cures free of charge. They warn against white doctors "who will do anything for money" but at the same time Feather cultists admit that there are illnesses which only the white physician can cure.

Curing procedure is as follows. Assistance for the patient must be requested by a member of his family. A whole group of cultists may respond to the request. If only one person is available he is often able to effect a cure alone. A group curing will be described. The patient lies in the center of the floor with his feet toward the east. [34]

---

[22] #21 Spier, Prophet Dance, pp. 52-53.

There are the customary leader and his three assistants as well as the drummers and bell ringers. The curers pray for power. The drums convey to them the nature and serious ness of the illness. If the patient is be yond hope, the family is informed and the ceremony proceeds or not, as the family de sires. If there is hope for a cure, the leader and his assistants will surround the patient and brush him off with their eagle feathers which are supposed to remove the malady. The leader may also place his hands palm to palm. The power which enters him from prayers and drumming leads the outer edges of his hands to the pain. Then his assistants also place their hands on the same spot. "When they have a good grip on the sickness," they all slowly raise their hands to draw out the illness. Then all let go at once and the illness is dissipated in to the air. It is not returned to the mountains like the older shamanistic "pains." But it is obviously similar to the Shakers who brush or draw off illness with their hands. The material just presented was given by a Warm Springs informant who went on to say that Indians had diseases unknown to the whites and the Feather cultists are particularly effective in healing this type of ill ness. The maladies peculiar to the Indians were "sicknesses through sorrow feelings. They wander around and maybe they find some thing in the hills, something which their dead relatives left. That makes them feel badly. Something turns over in them. They come home and lie down sick. Lots of Indians get that way. Then the drums will tell the Feather men what has happened. He tells the sick man, who admits that such an experience has caused his sickness. After that the patient feels better." Three nights is considered the usual period of treatment. If the patient is no better, the group leaves and returns in two or three weeks. More than one person may be treated in an evening. Between treatments, the group may sit around and chat informally. This is in contrast to the Shakers, who will work over several people at a time and for the full period of the meeting without any break in tension. In theory, all Feather converts are equally efficacious in curings, but in practice certain persons are recognized as more effective than others. Today no one pre tends to the curative powers which Jake Hunt is said to have possessed. As in other ceremonial aspects, slight changes seem to have grown up in Warm Springs for which the pre ceding description is valid. In the following section is given a series of statements dealing with Jake's cures which not only give interesting psychological material but also indicate differences in Jake's approach to treatment. His fame and the confidence he inspired rested largely on such performances.

Accounts of Cures

Susie Hunt Spidish (Klikitat) — "During Jake's healing performances, the seven young men and seven young women were the [b] only helpers he demanded. Even people with tuberculosis and other diseases like that could be healed suddenly. Vomiting was his way of cleaning the physical body. Even if you hadn't taken whiskey for several days, he could show you the whiskey you vomited. A consumptive would vomit consumptive matter. Once I was sick and Jake made me vomit an eel covered with butter that I had eaten a long time ago. That was what made me sick."

Laushlai Hunt (Klikitat) — "When my oldest girl was just a nursing baby, she got sick. The child was so sick she couldn't nurse and her eyes rolled back. She was dying. I took her to Jake's long house at Husum. It was breakfast time. The people saw that the child was dying and they could not eat breakfast. So Jake said, 'Bring her here to the center and I will work on her for a minute or two. He took the baby, said a prayer, sang a little, and then touched the baby with his finger tips. All of a sudden her sickness seemed to go. She breathed normally and fell asleep. The people went on with their breakfast and the baby got well."

Martin Spidish (Wishram) — "Jake used just his finger to cure people. It wandered around until he located the sickness. Then he seized it and threw it away. He would tell you then how you got it, how you felt. Jake didn't have to pray. He was so powerful, he could just let his finger lead him.

Isaac McKinley (Tenino) — "Jake said there were many things which could not be cured, like a broken leg and some kinds of blindness, but he healed many people. Once at Yakima, there was a little girl who was kicked by a horse on the head and chest. She was dead and they thought she would never come to. She lay that way all morning. They decided to bury her the next day. Jake came in and they told him what had happened. He said he would ask his powers that her life be spared. He laid his hand on her chest and soon she came to. That proved he had real power and many believed in him after that."

Sophie Lincoln (Umatilla) — "I had been very sick. My abdomen and limbs were swollen. Blood passed from my mouth. I could hardly eat even soup and water. I had been to white doctors, but they didn't help me. When Jake was on Umatilla reservation, he saw in his mind that I was suffering and he sent his sister to tell me to attend his meetings. But he got into trouble and had to leave before I went. So later I travelled to his place in Husum. I did not notify him that I was coming but he knew it anyhow and sent a rig to meet me. I was so sick that I had to be taken from the train on a blanket. They laid me in the middle of the floor at Jake's long house. Jake laid a feather on his open palm and it just stuck there. It led his hand to where the sickness was. Then he drew it [35] out with his hands, without actually touching me." Then the sickness came out of my chest, it almost killed me, but after that I got well."

Albert Barnhard (Umatilla) — "I saw Jake work on a nephew of his called Jo Hunt[23]" who had consumption. They had already been working three nights before I came. Jo held the pole inside the long house. Jake danced about eight or ten feet away from that pole. Everyone else joined in and danced hard. All of a sudden it looked as though an electric shock went through Jo. He shook all over. The power had entered that pole and shaken him.

After a while he stopped and they put him to bed. They worked seven nights altogether on Jo."

"When Jake worked on Alice Umtuch at Yakima, he made a stick for Alice to hold on to. Now at White Swan, Umtuch uses a stick like that for curing."

It is obvious from these accounts that Jake Hunt's curative séances were far less formalized than those which are now practiced on Warm Springs reservation. Vomiting, which was ostensibly part of the initiation rites, is considered curative by some informants. Pete Polina, who is the only practicing Feather cultist on Klamath reservation, seems to use this device in his cures. An account of one of Pete's séances

---

[23] #22. Not to be confused with Jake's half-brother of the same name.

follows.

Anthony Merritt (Klamath) — In ca. 1931 a nephew of the informant was in the early stages of consumption. Pete Polina's assistance was solicited and the patient was taken to his home. Pete's son beat the tambourine and a woman called Sarah rang a bell, but otherwise there were no feathers or special regalia of any kind. Pete began singing. Then the nephew was given as much warm water to drink as he could swallow. After this Pete kneeled on all fours, the nephew lay across his back, face downward, and Pete revolved five times, ending in the same position from which he started. The boy then vomited profusely. The same procedure was repeated for three nights in succession. Pete was paid $45 for his services.

On the other hand, Pete Polina's own account of a curing séance shows that he had a variety of procedures. He denied that he was ever paid for his work. A feast terminates each séance and he considers that his only recompense.

Pete Polina (Paviotso) — He begins a séance by singing three songs. He holds a feather which draws him to the illness which he then extracts with his hands. He spins violently to the east and dissipates into the air the intangible pain which he has drawn out. This is repeated three [b] times during the course of each of the fourteen songs used in a night. If the ill ness is severe, Pete himself vomits. To do this, he drinks water and then faces east with his back to the audience. The same procedure is optional with the patient, but it is recommended, particularly for habitual drunkards. In one instance a patient vomited of his own accord on the second night of treatment without having been given water. A small fish-like object appeared. This was considered proof that the man had been poisoned by a shaman who had sent a disease object against him. Occasionally Pete breathes into the mouth of a patient who is seriously ill. He uses the ordinary tambourine, bell, and eagle feathers, but otherwise has no regalia. He considers eagle feathers as the source of his supernatural power.

At the end of an evening's séance, a feast is prerequisite. Pete prays before the group is seated, after which everyone drinks half a cup of water. This is obviously an imitation of the Washani and Feather first food feast to be described below.

First Food Feasts

An important aspect of the Washani religion was the first food feasts. The berry, root, and salmon feasts seem to have been the most common. They were held before the seasonal food supplies might be gathered and eaten in any quantity. It was a ceremonial device for making certain foods profane and available for ordinary consumption. The custom occurred throughout the whole area under discussion among both Upper Chinookan and Sahaptin speaking people. It was an important factor in the doctrine of the Washani prophets during the last half of the nineteenth century. The ceremony was full of emotional connotation for most informants. It seemed to symbolize their whole relation ship to the landscape and to economic pursuits. Even the Christianized Umatilla, who are inclined to reject all aboriginal practices, still hold first food feasts to which the Presbyterian minister is invited to make the necessary prayers and addresses.

The Feather religion, with its roots in the Washani, not unnaturally took over the first food ceremonies without making any perceptible changes. Today the Washani and

Feather cultists on Warm Springs reservation attend each other's feasts. Sometimes members of both religions are sent out together to gather the necessary foods.

A description of the contemporary root feast on Warm Springs reservation is given. The procedure is essentially the same for salmon and berries.

At a council the group agrees to have a [36] root feast on the following Sunday. An in determinate number of men are sent out for deer and salmon. Seven women are appointed to gather roots. The designated persons then decide among themselves upon the day of departure, which is usually Thursday. They all agree to return late Saturday afternoon. When the women are in the hills, the leader places her digging stick close to the root and says, "We are about to dig roots which have been given to us to live on," or "My Creator, have mercy on me who am about to dig roots." There is probably much variation in these formulae {dicta}. Then the women all begin to dig. No one gathering the food is allowed to taste it until the feast day.

When the various providers return, each group enters the long house in turn, circles the interior from left to right and deposits the supplies on the right hand side of the entrance. This circuit is made to the accompaniments of drums and singing. The providers cook their supper in the long house and an informal dancing and singing meeting may follow. On the same evening, the roots are cleaned and all the food is prepared for cooking on the next day. Sunday morning a short singing meeting is held inside the long house. Then all leave and the food is cooked outside. While the cooks, who are the seven root gatherers, are finishing the meal, the drummers enter. Tables are set up all around the sides of the house. At each place is a cup containing about two teaspoons of water. People gather once more, taking their places at the tables with their backs to the wall. Singing continues. When the food is finished, the seven root gatherers enter, accompanied by the hunters and fishermen. All carry containers of food. These are set on the floor down the middle of the room in the following order: salmon, deer, roots, and berries (depending on foods served). Each server dishes a certain type of root or food. Then other women from the audience come down the center space, pick up individual servings, circle the long house and place the serving on the tables starting to the right of the entrance. When all of the places are supplied with food, non-ceremonial fare like bread, is placed on the tables without ritual. Meanwhile people who have been waiting outside are called in to take their places on the inner row of seats around the tables. There are one or two songs and prayers. The drums are laid aside. The bell-ringer then sounds his bell and names a particular root. Everyone in unison places a small piece of the designated food in his mouth. There is another short tap of the bell and the next food is named. In this fashion all the ceremonial foods are tasted in the order in which they were placed in the center. A sip of water and three short taps of the bell terminate this procedure. Then eating begins in earnest. When everyone has been satisfied, the meal is finished with another sip of water at the signal of the bell. Three songs are sung and the feast is over.

Feasts of this nature were given by Jake Hunt at Husum as well as by all the previous Washani leaders. The Shakers seem to have rejected this custom along with most other practices which appear aboriginal to them.

Funerals

The description of a Feather cult funeral varies hardly at all from that of a Washani or Shaker funeral. Informants are naturally quite aware of these similarities. Again the type description is drawn from the Warm Springs.

Coffins are in general use at present. Formerly the body was laid out in a long house when one was available. At present it is placed in the center of a dwelling. The corpse was formerly dressed in the yellow buckskin garment of the cult, with yellow paint on the face. Today only the face painting persists. A few people line the coffin with yellow cloth. The body is kept for only twenty-four hours. In accounts of resurrection visions of the Washani cult, however, informants often state that in former times bodies were kept five days to be sure that the person was not merely comatose. During the wake, relatives and friends sit around the wall of the room speaking hardly at all. Occasionally individuals either in the room or outside will begin to wail and others join them. When the time has come to remove the body, everyone congregates in the room. A man stands at the head of the coffin ringing a bell as everyone files by the body. Then the coffin is raised, the pall-bearers revolve in place once and then take the coffin out. The bell-ringer follows them, ringing constantly until the grave is filled. The coffin is generally placed on a truck. There is a special song for this. When the truck starts, it circles the dwelling three times, or if this is not possible, it will describe three circles before taking the road to the cemetery. The pall-bearers and bell-ringer, who are usually the immediate relatives of the deceased, ride on the truck. Those who follow sing three songs. At the end of each song, the right hand is raised and the customary *ai* is pronounced.

The grave is generally oriented east and west. The leader stands at the head of the grave, which is to the west. On his left, to the north, stand the women mourners; on his right, to the south, stand the men. The first man on the leader's right "sends up a message" which is in the nature of a prayer, confession, and credo. "They give them selves up so that their message may enter the gates of the Heavenly Father through the spirit of the dead person for whom the gates stand open." An example of these brief harangues runs as follows: "Now look with your eyes upon the dead body of this loved one which we are going to put away in the grave. My beloved people, we are also to take this very road. We ourselves are to be put away in graves. My beloved people, Do not have hard feelings toward one another, but cheer and love each other." Each man in turn from right to left makes a few remarks. Then each [37] woman makes a statement, beginning with the one on the leader's left. The leader is the last to speak. Everyone then picks up a pinch of earth which he drops on the coffin. Without further ceremony, the grave is filled.

On top of the grave are usually placed paper flowers, a hand-bell, possibly an eagle feather. Remi Sidwaller has instituted recently the custom of painting gravestones either yellow or green (blue). This is not a generalized custom of the Feather cult.

The funeral feast of the Feather and Washani religions follow the pattern of the first fruit feasts in sampling each type of food before the meal.

Morality and After Life

The most marked moral emphasis of the Feather cult was its rejection of intoxicants. No member in good standing was allowed to touch liquor. Its odor was supposed to be nauseating to true converts. The Washani religion is far less strict in this respect. The Shakers, on the contrary, are far more austere in their moral precepts although their abhorrence of intoxicants could scarcely be more pronounced. The Shakers ban smoking, and among some groups various entertainments like gambling, baseball, moving pictures, etc. The success which Jake Hunt had in reforming drunkards is generally stat ed by informants and has been adumbrated in the personal testimonies previously quoted in connection with initiation and cures. Even the Shakers with their marked hostility to the Feather cult admit his success in this respect.

The concept of after life from individual to individual varies, but certain fairly constant features appear. There follows a series of brief excerpts from informants' statements on this subject.

Laushlai Hunt — "When we die we shall go to another world where we shall be as shiny as the sun. You must be careful from day to day never to forget your prayers. Then you will be rewarded with everlasting light and your soul will enter the heavenly home."

Lucy Spidish — "Jake said if you were good you went to heaven and saw all the people there. There is a yellow sun, yellow flowers; everything smells good, looks good."

Frank Winishut — "When Jake saw the ball of light, he saw heaven behind it, a bright yellow land where our Heavenly Father lives. Jake believed he was doing on earth the same things which the dead were doing in heaven. He was told not to grieve because the dead were enjoying them selves and were united with their dear ones."

Isaac McKinley — "People enter through golden gates and at the gate is a person who is the brother of all [identified as Jesus upon questioning]. He receives and cleanses the soul before it enters the heavenly home. There is no more sickness and sorrow. You never work, never do any thing to earn your living. You get your food through God. It is already prepared." [38]

Clothing

One of Jake Hunt's first acts after his conversion was to adopt a suit of buckskin l clothing consisting of a shirt and trousers. This type of clothing reached the middle Columbia from the east slightly prior to the advent of the Lewis and dark expedition of 1805.[24] Into the buckskin was rubbed a yellow pigment. This costume is a copy of that affected by Washani leaders and members, particularly during services. In the section on Jake Hunt's conversion, it was noted that the Shaker, Wasco Jim, had had a similar vision shortly before he went to the Hood River area. This inspiration was rejected by the group, probably because it smacked of Indian customs which Shakers repudiate. The possibility of a two-fold influence on Jake Hunt in this respect must be borne in

---

[24] #23 A.B. Lewis, Tribes of the Columbia Valley and the Coast of Washington and Oregon (Memoirs, American Anthropological Association, Vol. 1, Part 2, 1906), pp. 187-88.

mind. His adoption of this costume may have been due to an immediate stimulus from Wasco Jim, but it was also a return to older patterns. Jake Hunt's clothing made a great Impression on his contemporaries, who referred tine and again to his fine yellow buckskin suits. As many converts as possible imitated his dress, at least for ceremonial purposes. Jake, however, wore buckskin clothing at all times. Today the Feather cultists no longer dress in this fashion. Instead, yellow cloth shirts are frequently substituted for the older buckskin.

The women were supposed to wear the so-called wing-dress (*klepip*),which was a cloth copy of the older buckskin dress with cape sleeves. In accordance with nineteenth century styles, these were often beaded. Figure 5 illustrates the buckskin and wing-dress patterns. Often the wing-dress was worn over other clothing simply as a sort of smock. It was three-quarter length, belted at the waist, and often yellow in color although this was not compulsory. Women were apparently far more consistent in adopting and wearing this Feather cult costume than the men were in adopting and wearing the buckskin suit. There are many older women today who still wear it over their ordinary clothing whether or not they are Feather cult members.

In keeping with the general reversion to Indian customs which the Feather cultists advocated, moccasins and long hair were considered desirable for men. The hair is wrapped with strands of fur, preferably either otter or weasel, and hung over the shoulders. Today most of the men who are sincere Feather converts adopt these styles. Moccasins are also worn by both men and women, although this again is not an exclusive Feather cult practice. Yellowed ones are much admired but not required. The religion has simply assisted in preserving the use of moccasins and long hair by lending its approval to them.

Bead wristlets and necklaces were approved by Feather cultists in contradistinction to the more austere Shakers who reject such decorations.

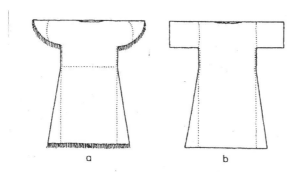

Fig. 5. Women's dresses, a, buckskin dress; b, wing-dress or *klepip* of cloth. Dotted lines indicate seams. Buckskin differs from cloth dress in shape of sleeve and fringe. In both the sleeves are not stitched together along underarm seams. Neck is slit in folded material. The gore of the buckskin dress is optional, depending on shape of hides.

Feathers

Feathers are one of the most distinguishing characteristics of this cult's regalia. Today they are generally worn in the hat bands of the men. Previously they were often attached at the base of the right hand strand of hair. Formerly women wore eagle down attached to the right shoulder seam of the wing-dress, particularly during ceremonies. Feathers which were hung down the back on a string of beads were also objects of daily wear in former times. These strings of beads were attached to a mirror pectoral described in the next section.

When a person is converted, he is entitled to own eagle tail or wing feathers. These are often held In the right hand during a meeting and waved back and forth in time to the singing. Some Washani groups [39] have the same custom, but "their feathers didn't have cleansing powers like those of the Feather religion." The feathers in possessing this power to "cleanse" had also associations which suggested that they were the seat of supernatural powers. The sections on curing reveal these properties.

There is no special eagle catcher. Any one who has caught an eagle may sell its feathers to a cultist. Today the value of a tail feather is generally placed at one dollar. One informant estimated that formerly an eagle was worth a horse. Feathers are often kept in a small parfleche type of container. This is not, however, a standardized procedure. They are more often hung on a wall of the dwelling house along side of the tambourine. Sometimes eagle down may be dyed yellow. The use of feathers on poles will also be described in the pertinent section.

The immediate origin of all the stress upon feathers lay in Jake's eagle supernatural. It will be recalled that an eagle bore the earth-disk and was supposed to be the messenger for some of Jake's revelation. We are obviously dealing here with a revival of older sacred associations with the eagle. Also, of course, the use of eagle feathers for personal adornment was old in the area since it was noted by Lewis and Clark."[25]

Mirror

The use of a mirror in initiation ceremonies has already been described. Small round pocket mirrors are the kind employed. Figure 6 is a diagram of such a mirror seen on Warm Springs reservation. The mirror is slipped into a buckskin container in which one or two holes have been cut. The buckskin is then decorated with bead work representing rainbows, sun rays or any other heavenly object. From the bottom of the container hangs a fringe of beads. From the top there is a long bead necklace which suspends the mirror at breast height. At the back of this necklace there are attached two independent strands of beads on the ends of which a bit of down is tied. These hang down to the middle of the back.

In addition to initiation rites these mirrors may be worn by participants simply as decoration. It is said that when the cult first began, people always wore them and the

---

[25] #24 Lewis, op. cit., p. 187.

eagle feathers as badges of their allegiance. Now they are used only during ceremonies. The mirrors previously worn for daily use were smaller than the ceremonial ones.

There are two antecedent uses of a mirror in connection with earlier cults. In the last statement of the section on Lishwailait, it was reported that he used a mirror for clairvoyant purposes. Very few informants [b] knew of this practice and I found no one who could, or would, elaborate on the subject. The other antecedent use of the mirror was by Jo Riddle in connection with the Shakers. Jo Riddle's particular "help" or inspiration was that he should confess people much in the manner of a Catholic priest. Jo and the person he was to confess withdrew alone to a separate tent or room. A detailed description of the confession is not pertinent at this point, but this much has some bearing. The person to be confessed gazed fixedly at a mirror in which he was supposed to see his past sins appear. This device was used by Jo Riddle probably as early as 1902. Thereafter Jo was one of the most widely travelled Shakers and it is quite possible that Jake Hunt had at least hearsay knowledge of his use of a mirror.

The symbolic significance of the mirror to the Feather cultists has not been established with complete certainty, but it is probable that it represents in their minds the bright earth-disk (*titcam*) of Jake's [40] vision. The tambourine has similar connotations. One informant identified it as a sun-symbol. Its use as an article of decoration may have some precedence in the bright metal disks used on Plains Indian clothing in post-white days.

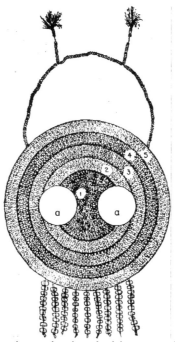

Fig. 6. Ceremonial mirror in buckskin pouch, a, holes in pouch through which reflecting surfaces show; 1, blue beads representing the earth; 2, 3, 4, 5 represent rainbow (2, deep yellow; 3, orange; 4, red; 5, light yellow).

Colors

It has been evident from preceding data that yellow is the most sacred color of the Feather cult. It is used in clothing whether of buckskin or cloth, on moccasins, drums, flags, face-paintings, both for ceremonies and burials, on tombstones, etc. It is symbolic of the light which illumes the after world and represents the brightness of the sun rays. The spirits who inhabit heaven are generally conceived as dressed in yellow clothing and wearing yellow face-paint, while heaven itself is envisaged as a round yellow land.

The other color which predominates in Feather cult decorations is blue or green. Both the Chinookan and Sahaptins fail to distinguish the two in their color terminology so that the two words were interchangeable in English statements made by informants. Generally, the second color was identified with the sky, which suggests blue. On the other hand, some informants said that the second color represented the green earth. Actually I observed more green than blue in use at present as the color complementary to yellow.

Precedent for Jake Hunt's adoption of yellow was undoubtedly Lishwailait's stress upon the same color. The Shakers lay far less stress upon color than the Feather cultists, but their garments are always in white and blue. It is possible that blue was the second color used by Jake Hunt and that he may have made further borrowings from the Shakers in this respect. I believe that the introduction of green was a secondary one, due, perhaps, to the confusion in terminology, and that the green earth symbolism was an interpretation which arose subsequent to that confusion. The doctrinal stress up on the land in the Washani cult, especially during the period of the Smohalla revival, might easily have lead to such a subsequent interpretation.

Tambourine and Bell

An ordinary hand-bell is used in Feather cult ceremonies. It is of the same type and general size as that used by the Shakers and by the Washani. Its uses have been alluded to at various times and need not be reviewed. To Feather cultists the bell has little religious significance. In this attitude they differ from the Shakers and more nearly approach the Washani. The stress upon the use of hand-bells in all three religions may be attributed, at least [b] in part, to the Catholic missionaries who summoned Indians to meetings by ringing this instrument.[26]

The tambourine on the other hand is one of the most prized pieces of paraphernalia to most male Feather cultists although it is not particularly sacred per se. Women occasionally may use a tambourine, but they seem never to own one. It usually hangs in plain sight on the wall of the dwelling and a lay person may handle it without compunction. However, a lay person is not allowed to beat it during ceremonies, a restriction which does not apply to the bell. Drummers are usually able singers.

The tambourine consists of a circle of thin wood some three to five inches wide and approximately a foot and a half in diameter. The ends of the circle are lashed

---

[26] #25 Blanchet, op. cit., passim.

together by thongs which pass through opposed holes. Over the circle of wood is stretched a piece of buckskin held taut on the under side by lacings brought radially into a central knot. The hide may in addition be laced through holes drilled in the lower edge of the wood en frame. The tambourine is beaten with a stick about one foot long, padded at one end.

The surface is usually painted yellow and decorated with symbols of heavenly phenomena like the sun, stars, etc., resembling those beaded on the mirror pouches. The drum illustrated in Figure 2 for the Washani prophet at Skin is an elaborate example of the type of decoration seen on modern Feather cult instruments. One specimen seen at Warm Springs had a red crescent moon on one edge and three five-pointed stars, also in red, on the opposite side.

To most members of the Feather religion, the drum is symbol of the shining disk which appeared in Jake Hunt's vision. In at least one account of his trance experience, he is supposed to have seen a drum, as distinct from the earth-disk.

Meeting Places

It will be recalled that one of Jake Hunt's first acts after his conversion was to build a long house at Husum. Its dimensions were approximately eighteen by twenty five feet. This was the type of oblong pole and reed mat structure used as a communal dwelling in the area. It was also the type of structure used during the later phases of the Washani religion when special "church houses" came into use. Occasionally lumber long houses were also used for the same purpose. Farther up the Columbia in the vicinity of Umatilla long oval tipis covered with canvas replaced the reed mat structure as a Washani meeting place. Doors were either in the long or short side of the building. In Jake's long house at Husum, the door faced the east on the short end of the house. [41 The same orientation of the door held for the lumber long house which he used at Spear fish and which still stands. I am under the impression that farther up the Columbia entrances were usually on the long side of the structure. Around the interior, mats were usually spread against the walls for seats. Down the center were two or three fire pits. The lodge was kept swept and clean. Jake Hunt's use of a mat house at Husum was a return to aboriginal practices which were beginning to fall into disuse. However, there seems to have been ho insistence on his part that such a structure was essential for cult ceremonies. He used Washani houses, the more easterly tipis, and any available private dwelling for his meetings. At present there exists no long house exclusively dedicated to Feather cult meetings. Those which still stand in the area are all devoted to Washani practices. The attitude of the Shakers in respect to meeting places is comparable to Jake Hunt's. Dwellings are quite acceptable, but if the religious community develops, a special oblong church structure is usually erected and its entrance is on the short eastern end. The parallel to Catholic churches is obvious.

Poles and Flags

In front of the long house entrance at Husum, Jake erected a pole some thirty feet high. This was not put up until after his return from Rock Creek, supposedly in the spring of 1905 or later. One side was painted blue, the other yellow. On top was a small flat disk about six inches in diameter. A rope was arranged to raise and lower the flag on Sundays and for funerals. At the foot of the pole was a large flint or obsidian arrowhead about three feet long. One face was painted yellow and the other blue. It was customary apparently to find arrow or spear heads about eight inches long in that area. The natives considered them the lightning bolts shot by Thunderbird. It is commonly held that an arrowhead will be found wherever lightning has struck. The one possessed by Jake was remarkable for its size and because he is supposed to have had its location revealed to him in a vision. A group of men went out to dig under the roots of a tree as he directed and the arrowhead was found. Jake told the people that the Thunderbird carried a flint of this kind under each wing and shot them at any object he wished to destroy. The connection between his Indian name, Earth Thunderer and the large arrowhead suggests that Jake may have had supernatural powers of the Thunderbird. This subject was discussed in the section on his shamanistic powers.

The flag used by Jake Hunt is illustrated in Figure 3. It was described as approximately five feet in length by two in width. This suggests affiliations with Plains banners as well as with a European prototype. At Spearfish, Jake also erected a pole with the sphere customarily used to tip [b] flag poles. From it he used to hang three eagle tail feathers. This was also a Washani custom. Jake's use of flags had precedent in the later Washani cult. Smohalla and his contemporaries certainly employed them. No other Feather cultist seems to have adopted the custom, and flags are no longer part of the cult paraphernalia.

Within Jake's long house at Husum, there seems to have been another pole. Material describing it is contradictory. One informant said it was also painted blue down one side and yellow down the other. Another informant said it was undecorated. A new convert grasped the pole in order to help fix in his mind the words of songs and prayers. It was also supposed to lead the convert's visions upward to heaven. In the section describing cures attributed to Jake, it was said to have trembled when it was grasped by the patient. One informant said that there was a stuffed eagle on the pole inside of the long house; another said it was surmounted by a carved wooden eagle; still another said there was no bird on top, but that a stuffed eagle was mounted along one of the side walls. One informant said that a stuffed eagle was mounted on the pole outside of the long house. Another said it was a wooden one. The most detailed description, though not necessarily the most trustworthy, was used as a basis for the sketch in Figure 7. Certainly there was precedent for a bird mounted on a pole in Shramaia's bird pole at Skin. This may well be based upon a shamanistic [42] procedure in the area. Spier[27] reports that Klamath shamans had painted poles on which stuffed animals were mounted and feather streamers were hung. His descriptions duplicate those for Washani practices on the middle Columbia. I suggest a common root in the shamanistic pattern. Unfortunately shamanistic data from the middle Columbia are very incomplete. Many inform ants were entirely ignorant of the question of an eagle mounted on a pole. The unusual diversity of opinion on this subject may suggest that Jake Hunt varied his procedure in this respect.

---

[27] #26 Spier, Klamath Ethnography, p. 110.

Fig. 7. Pole in front of Jake Hunt's lodge at Husum, according to verbal description. a, cedar pole; b, stuffed eagle; c, blue and yellow thongs; d, slender rod surmounted by eagle tail feather and down.

The use of a flag which seems to have so thoroughly caught the imagination of the middle Columbia region can be fairly definitely attributed at least in its more recent and intense form, to the white practice of distributing flags to the Indians. They seem to have been used in the Washani prior to Smohalla. Christian missionaries and early travellers with an imperialistic bent frequently distributed flags to Indian groups with whom they came in contact. Flags took particular hold in the 1860's and 1870's. One informant suggested that they were adopted with enthusiasm during the Smohalla era because friendly Indians who were given permission to leave the reservation during the Paiute war of 1865 and 1866 were issued small American flags as passports.

Grace and Songs

In the account of Jake Hunt's conversion, it was stated that he began by using the old Washani songs which Lishwailait had employed. He was supposed to have had no knowledge of them prior to his supernatural experiences. As his cult grew he composed new songs which were part of every ceremony. Usually a group [b] of any seven of them was selected for a meeting. I was unable to secure any precise statement on this subject. No one knows whether Jake secured his new songs through visionary or dream experiences, nor does any one claim new compositions of his own. Informants denied that songs were customarily dreamed in the Feather cult. One informant referred to the drum as the storehouse of songs. Certain songs were considered appropriate for meetings, initiations, and cures. The best and freest informant re fused to sing any of then and said that most of them had no word meanings but "are just tunes."

Grace before meals was confined primarily to the various first food feasts. On Sunday it was considered pious to eat five Indian foods: salmon, venison, camass, huckleberry, and water. Before and after meals these five names were chanted with the addition of meaningless syllables. In this Jake Hunt supposedly followed the procedure which had been taught him as a child by Ashnithlai whose conversion experiences were quoted in a previous section. On Warm Springs reservation people still pray at most meals, but particularly at those eaten during their occasional two or three day meetings. Stress is placed on taking a swallow of water before and after meals. "It is to purify your system." The bell alone usually accompanies this form of "grace."

The custom of grace before meals was part of both the Shaker and Washani religions. Both used the bell in this connection. Undoubtedly this was a borrowing from Christian practices. The sip of water, however, was Feather and Washani rite, which the Shakers did not follow. [43]

Summary

The debt of the Feather cult to the Shaker and Washani religions has been suggested throughout this paper. Table 2 summarizes the close interrelationships from the point of view of trait content. Certain additional comments might be made.

In ritual and ideology, there was little which distinguished the Feather cult from the Washani, particularly that form practiced by Jake Hunt's Klikitat predecessor, Lishwailait. From the Shakers, Jake Hunt borrowed the conversion psychology and the moralistic precepts, especially the abhorrence of drunkenness. One informant expressed with much perspicacity the differences between the Washani and the Feather cult which these two loans from Shakerism produced. "The Feathers have borrowed from the Washani and have put Spiritualism into it. The Washani are slow and respectful like the Catholics. The Feathers are all excitement and feeling like the Pentecostals."

Curing was also in large part a direct borrowing from the Shakers as far as procedure was concerned, but in the Feather cult, its supernatural sanctions seem to have been those of shamanism rather than of Christianity. In the matter of attitudes toward shamanism, the modern cultists on the middle Columbia are sharply divided. One may belong to the Feather or Washani religions and still be a practicing shaman. No conflict between the two is envisaged, although the Washani, at least, has incorporated no curative procedures. To the Shaker, however, shamanism is anathema and no more opprobrious statement can be made by them than to call a person an "Indian doctor." One of the favorite Shaker derogations of the Feather cult is just that accusation. Since the Feather cultists are curers and the Washani are not, the Shakers are far more bitter against the former than the latter. The aspect of competition for converts may enter into this enmity. Certainly there is little difference in overt practices. The conflict comes in the source of supernatural powers. On Warm Springs reservation, the Shakers in variably accuse the Feather cultists of shamanism. As a proof they say that in recent years the Feather people have taken to pounding with sticks. In former times this was a widespread custom for the accompaniment of shamanistic songs. To this the Feather people respond by saying they could not possibly be shamans since they accept no pay for their services. Some also add that their power comes from God or Jesus. This is obviously a departure from Jake's sources of super-naturalism and may result from social pressure brought to bear not only by Shakers but also by Christianized Indians. It is [b] interesting that Christianized Indians brought exactly the same charges against the Shaker religion when it was first introduced in Warm Springs and that the same denials were made. A Shaker also accused the Feather cultists of holding a winter meeting recently during which they distributed gifts "like the old time doctor meetings." In the course of these recriminations, it is often said that Jake Hunt died because of his sins in reverting to the old shamanistic practices. The fact that he was for many years a successful person although a renegade Shaker convert probably adds to the mutual antagonisms.

The whole problem of inter-religious hostility hinges on this matter of cures. Since these do not figure in the Washani, that religion is in good repute among all groups. Therefore, some informants who were defensive about Jake's activities are inclined to minimize his innovations and insist that he was simply reviving the Washani. To a certain point this is, of course, an accurate statement. It was also a procedure sanctioned by precedent and tradition, as the first part of this paper proves.

The striking characteristic of the Feather cult was its lack of originality. With the exception of spinning and vomiting in the initiation rites, every feature can be traced to some definite and prior source. Furthermore, as an attempt to revive old Indian customs, it came too late. The movement had an artificiality lacking in the Washani revivals of the 1850's to 1880's. There was already a distinct trend, and pride in the trend, toward the adoption of white customs. The Shaker church considers itself a Christian movement, one *interalia* among the quite comparable white cults which thrive in rural white communities. By the 1890's it had already begun to repudiate Indian customs although it was still proud of its Indian origins. Jake Hunt's antagonism to the Shakers threw him back upon the traditional religion of his tribe, but his re version was ill-timed and did not serve to stem the tide of acculturation. The religion spread no further than Jake's own efforts to disseminate it. He lacked forceful converts who were capable of developing the cult on their own initiative. The whole movement impresses one as a one-man affair whose force was individual, appealed to no growing social need, and was correspondingly ephemeral. (Table 2 on the following page)

Table 2. Comparison of Trait Content

Traits	Feather	Washani	Shaker
Meetings in dwelling	yes	long house type	yes
Special oblong structure for meeting	yes	yes	yes
Entrance of special structure toward east	yes	yes (?)	yes (?)
Buckskin suit for men	optional	optional	no; surplice optional
Wing dress for women	customary, optional	customary, optional	no; surplice optional
Long hair for men	preferable	preferable	no
Tambourine	yes	yes	yes
Hand bell	1	1	many
Mirror	yes	rare	rare
Ritualistic use of candles	no	no	no
Cleansing power of feather	yes	no	no
Feather worn as insignia	yes	rare	no
Color	yellow blue green	yellow, occasional	white blue
Sunday meeting (7-day week)	yes	yes	yes
Sexes separate at meetings	yes	yes	yes
Preaching at meetings by any member	yes	yes	yes
Feather waved in hand	yes	occasional	no
Circling interior as terminal ceremony	yes	yes	yes, own form
Revolving in place during ceremonies	yes	yes	yes
Initiate receives power	yes	no	yes
Vomiting	yes	no	yes
Spinning at conversion	yes	no	no
Public confession	yes	no ?	yes
Curing	yes	no	yes
Ritual number	7 3	7 3	7 3
Ecstatic vision at meetings	yes	no	yes
Songs dreamed	founder only	yes	?
Bible accepted	no, recently yes	no	some
Supreme Being	eagle	earth mother	God Jesus

DU BOIS: THE FEATHER CULT p45

Table 2. Comparison of Trait Content (concluded)

Traits	Feather	Washani	Shaker
Heaven	yes	yes	yes
Hell	not stressed	not stressed	yes
Sense of sin	yes	no ?	yes
Intoxicants forbidden	yes	optional	yes
Smoking forbidden	no	no	yes
First fruit feast	yes	yes	no
Grace before meals	occasional	occasional	yes
Sip of water before and after meals	yes	yes	no
Feather on grave	optional	no	no
Bell on grave	optional	optional	usual
Tombstone in sacred color	rare	no	no

THE YAKIMA INDIANS IN 1942
By Homer G. Barnett

Reproduced by The Department of Anthropology
University of Oregon Eugene, Oregon 1969

Table of Contents

Introduction	1
Chapter I Economic Conditions	1
The Aboriginal Base	1
Governmental Policy and the Transition	4
The Land and Its Utilization	8
Income from the Land	14
Economic Survivals	19
Indian Employees	24
Indigents and Incompetents	30
Indian Enterprise	35
Chapter II Social Conditions	37
The Indian Community	37
Tribal Government and Political Control	
Social Control	5>
Family Life	82
Health Conditions	95
Chapter III Education	101
Adult Education: an Old Policy	101
Youth Education: the New Policy and Its Difficulties	105
The Indian at School	123
Accomplishments	119
Chapter IV Conclusion	123
Tables	
Income Brackets	18
Livestock ownership by families	31
Income summary for all types of activity	
Offenses and penalties in the Indian Court	
Indian tuition, attendance, and enrollment In the White Swan school	

Introduction

When most people think of the American Indian they have a mental picture of a tall stalwart brave dressed in fringed buckskin clothing and wearing an eagle feather war bonnet. In part, this can be said to be an accident of history; but it is also a result of the fact that those Indians who fought most desperately for their homeland attracted national attention and consequently made a place for themselves in our folklore and history. Indian fighters in the early west frequently made bitter comment upon the tendency of peace commissioners to give the most consideration and award the greatest concessions to their bitterest foes, while the tribes who had taken their stand alongside their white conquerors and fought their dark skinned brothers, were given only the least tokens of gratitude. This was natural; and so it was natural, also, that the Sioux, who figured so prominently in our Indian wars, should become our popular stereotype of the red man.

In the same way the Yakimas, who are the subjects of this study; achieved a fleeting national prominence and secured their small measure of concessions through their fierce resistance to the advance of civilization. Their time of decision came earlier than for the Sioux, and its consequences were not so critical to the nation. They were not astride a vital east and west life-line; hence they never gained the distinction that some other tribes did. But they failed only by a narrow margin and were at least able to demand and get an indefinite stay of dissolution.

The people now known as the Yakima Indians reside upon a large reservation in the south central part of the State of Washington in the county [ii] that takes its name from them. On the east their land is bounded by the Yakima River; to the north and south low mountain ranges hem it in; while to the west it extends high into the Cascade Mountains. Its heart is a broad valley drained by several small rivers or creeks that flow north and eastward to join the Yakima. Much of the untilled valley floor is arid; and unproductive, yielding only a natural growth of rank grasses and hardy brush (Plate IVb). Higher up in the foothills there is good grazing land and still higher in the western mountains there are valuable stands of coniferous timber.

The occupants of this land are a composite group. Although they are called Yakimas, this name originally applied to only a small portion of them. Before the coming of the white man they were scattered in relatively all bands over the whole of the area lying west of the Cascades and in between the Yakima and Columbia Rivers. These bands were politically autonomous, but their members spoke a common language, shared common customs, and were much intermarried. There was therefore rather free intercourse between them, and even with other bands outside their boundaries.

Our knowledge of the customs of the Yakimas before they began to be affected by the white man's advance from the east is fragmentary. For long before the first Caucasian was seen in this region, the life pattern of the local Indians had undergone considerable modification as the indirect result of colonial penetration in the distant south and east. One of the principal agents of alteration was the horse. At what time the Yakimas and their neighbors first became acquainted with this new element is uncertain. It was well before the year 1800. Many changes in habits undoubtedly resulted from the introduction of the horse in this territory just as they had on [iii] the northern Great Plains. The two developments were in fact not only parallel but interrelated.

By 1800 some of the Yakima and their neighbors were in the habit of making annual expeditions to the Great Plains in search of bison, at times under the guidance of the Flatheads. There they were often forced to fight with the Blackfeet, but they also learned much about them and from them, so that by the time the first white observers went among the Yakima they resembled the tribes east of the Rocky Mountains in many respects. Like the Sioux and Blackfeet, they set great store by the horse, not only for its utility in transport, but as an item of prestige and exchange. It was the ambition of every nineteenth century Yakima to owe a herd of horses, and the greater the number owned the better. Horse stealing was common, and it was regarded in the light of a dangerous sport. Probably the Yakimas' taste for warfare and their idolization of fighters, was another result of their contacts with the warlike tribes to the east of them. Certainly the warrior — the man sensitive to affront and quick to resort to violence in vindication of his rights and honor - was a prominent figure in this region. Other traits in the familiar schoolbook pattern were current as well: scalping, buckskin clothing, the tipi, and so on.

When the white man first began to move to the west beyond the land occupied by the Yakimas the latter were undisturbed. They were off the main lines of travel which passed along the Columbi to the south of them. The first of our race to come to live among them were two Catholic priests who in 1847 established a mission on one of the creeks now within the boundaries of the reservation. They were well received; and, adapting their lives to the Indian mode, they traveled about from camp to camp converting and baptizing as the opportunity offered. The Indians were not upset by this peaceful [iv] entry into their country; they had, in fact, solicited it. The alarm came from another quarter in 1853.

In that year Lieutenant George B. McClellan arrived in Yakima territory with a body of soldiers for the purpose of exploring the passes over the Cascade Mountains in the interests of the Northern Pacific Railroad. His appearance in their country with an armed force was disturbing enough to the Yakimas, but when he told them that in the following year Mr. I.I. {Isaac} Stevens would arrive with the intention of buying their lands and making a treaty with them, their excitement ran high. Runners were sent out to inform other tribes west of the Columbia, and conferences were held between Kamaiakin {kamayakin}, the Yakima leader, and other chiefs. It was agreed that all would refuse to yield their land no matter what the price.

When Stevens appeared in the summer of 1854 he held a series of meetings with Kamaiakin and his confederates along the Yakima River and informed them that he wished to call a council of all the tribal representatives in eastern Washington the following year to arrange for their relinquishment of most of the territory in return for payments to be settled upon at that time. When told that the Indiens were not interested in the plan, he gave them to understand that it was imperative, that if they did not comply their lands would be taken anyway, and that American soldiers would be prepared to force their removal into restricted areas. His threats only served to inflame the indignation of those who heard him; and as soon as he was out of the country Kamaiakin made preparations to confer with the leading chiefs of the tribes that adjoined the Yakimas on the east. All were in accord that no treaty should be made, and to organize their resistance they urged an even wider circle of tribes to send representatives to a secret council in the Grand Ronde Valley of eastern Oregon within a month. This meeting lasted for five [v] days with an impressive array of influential warriors in attendance. They resolved to define their tribal boundaries and to assign the divisions to their leaders in such a way that no unclaimed land would be left over, hence none for sale; for all took the stand that they would refuse to accept any plan that entailed the disposal of their traditional hunting and fishing grounds.

Thus the Indiens were prepared to meet with Stevens at Walla Walla in 1855. Their confederation was of the loosest sort, and it did not survive the meeting. Their staunch declarations of a few months before dissolved under the pressures of Stevens and the renegade defection of one influential band of Nez Perce, led by the opportunistic chief called Lawyer. After much delay and parleying the treaty was reluctantly signed, but never assented to, by Kamaiakin and his supporters. In return for the land certain annuities and services were promised, and three reservations were set aside for all of the Indians of eastern Washington. Several of the supposed fourteen tribes assigned to the Yakima reservation never existed, and others were polyglot and artificial. The remainder paid no attention to orders to remove themselves from their old habitats and were never placed upon the reservation assigned to them. Even those who were required to move no great distance or not at all were resentful and did not intend to abide by the treaty. Kamaiakin and his confederates prepared to defend their country, and succeeded in involving the Indians west of the Cascades, in the conspiracy.

It was under these circumstances that the Yakima War broke out in the fall of 1855. Heedless of the ominous attitude of the Indians, and regardless of the fact that the Walla Walla treaty had not been ratified by Congress, miners on their way to the gold fields in British Columbia proceeded [vi] to cross Yakima territory. Several of these men were waylaid and killed soon after the Walla Walla meeting. But the precipitating event was the ill considered murder of Indian Agent Bolon in the fall of the same year. This unprovoked attack brought the military into action, and a number of indecisive battles were fought west of the Columbia in the succeeding twelve months. Ostensibly the Indians were subdued, but their depredations continued, and eventually all of the tribes of eastern Washington were drawn into the conflict. Hostilities did not come to a close until the latter part of 1858 when Colonel George Wright was able to dictate terms after two decisive defeats of the confederated tribes under Kamaiakin's leadership, near Four Lakes, on a southern tributary of the Spokane River. Refusing to surrender, Kamaiakin abandoned his forces to take refuge in Canada. Later he returned to the Palouse region, but he never saw his native land again. With this defeat the Yakimas gave up hope of resisting the military might of the white man. They did not fight again, although many of them were tempted to give aid to the Nez Perce under Chief Joseph in his ill-fated rebellion in 1877.

In the midst of the war, Fort Simcoe was established in the western foothills of the Yakima reservation. For three years it was in charge of the army, but in 1860 it was placed under the management of the Department of Indian Affairs, and an agent was appointed to deal with the Indians. The Reverend James H. Wilbur took over this post in 1864, and held it for nearly twenty years. He ruled the Indians with severity and with justice, according to his lights. He was a man of great strength, both physically and morally, and he applied all his energy to the task of making white men and Methodists of the Indians. He applied the lash himself to the backs of those who defied him, and with his own hands plowed the fields of those who gave their promise to go to church in return. He was unalterably opposed to Catholicism, and [vii] when the work of the priests of the mission just outside the boundaries of the reservation threatened to interfere with his plans he appealed to President Grant and obtained the exclusive right to administer to the spiritual welfare of the Yakimas. Honest and sincere, "Father Wilbur" did much good among the Indians to whom he was devoted, but the measures that he employed reveal that curious compound of compassion and cruelty that is born of bigotry.

Meanwhile other more subtle and pervasive forces were at work to civilize the Yakimas. White settlers began to move into the region even before the Indians had been pacified. In 1861 the first man took his family to live just off the northeastern edge of the reservation. Others followed him, led by their urge to live on the farthest rim of civilization, or by reports of mineral wealth, or by the attractive cattle ranges that were to be found in the foothills of the vicinity. The latter attraction was the most important. In the years that followed, this region became a great cattle country, supplying beef for the markets on the lower Columbia and for the miners in British Columbia. At one time the Indian agency itself owned several thousand head of cattle.

In 1863, Ferguson County, later called Yakima, was created by an act of the legislature, and officers were appointed. Three years later surveyors arrived to lay off several townships along the river just north of the reservation. In the following year a primitive mail service was established that crossed the Indian lands and linked these settlements with the traffic on the lower Columbia. In 1875 settlers donated their labor to construct a wagon road through the reservation and connect Yakima City with Goldendale. Some ten years later the railroad came to invade the northeastern corner of the [viii] reservation and give an impetus to the growth of the young towns in that section. With these developments it was clear that the white man had come to stay, and the Yakimas, no longer in isolation, could not fail to affect and be affected by his interests.

At present there are several towns on the reservation, the largest of which is Toppenish. A good and well-traveled highway passes through it to connect the important agricultural district around the city of Yakima with The Dalles and other points along the Columbia River. To the casual traveler on this highway there is nothing to indicate that he is in Indian country. Indeed, it is safe to say that hundreds of people pass over this route each year without knowing that they have crossed a reservation. There is more here than meets the eye, however; and that is the story that is told in the chapters that follow.

The American Indians have stimulated a wide variety of interests. For the artist and poet they have always had an appeal. Their ideals of strength and courage; their resourcefulness, their exotic sense of beauty; and the excitement of their rugged existence have stimulated the imaginations of numerous authors. As a result a vast amount of popular literature has accumulated idealizing the Redman in the Romantic tradition of James Fenimore Cooper and Henry Wadsworth Longfellow. Ethnologists and archaeologists, on the other hand, have looked upon the Indian as an object of scientific study, and for their part have contributed a large and growing stock of objective data upon aboriginal custom and belief. Although it cannot be said that these students have shunned the spectacular aspects of their material, they have disciplined themselves in the school of detached reporting that is the ideal of pure science. For that reason, and because they are conscious that their science is [ix] in its infancy, they have characteristically held aloof from attempts to popularize their discoveries.

From the thousands of Americans who have had to associate and treat with Indians as a matter of public or private welfare comes an entirely different expression of interest. For the men who became involved in the sanguinary process of expanding our frontiers, the Indian was something quite different than for the artist or the social scientist. To them he was neither a noble child of the forest nor a suitable subject for abstract study; at worst he was a flesh and blood demon and at best an outlandish being, sometimes quite human, but at all times difficult for the white man to get along with. To the men in public life who have accepted the responsibility for defining an action program the Indian was likewise not a character out of a book, nor were there any books to tell them what to do about him in order to implement their programs. In short, to these individuals the red man was a problem, and the results of ethnological investigations offered them no guides to its solution. Administrators and frontiersmen alike therefore worked out their own trial and error solutions, which in human affairs' cannot be without a heavy admixture of tragedy.

Unfortunately, we have not advanced much beyond this pragmatic stage today. With all of our concern about the unhappy results of interracial contacts in general, and our continuing difficulties with the Indian in particular, we have not acquired a body of knowledge which can serve as a guide for men who must perforce settle upon some course of action in these situations. Much has been written upon the subject by well meaning authors, but too often partisan sentiment has discredited their premises and vitiated the usefulness of their suggestions. It is easy to become resentful of the treatment [x] that we as a conquering people have given the former occupants of our land. It can also be justified, as it was, in the conscience and outlook of the men responsible for it. In any event it does no good to go over this ground again. Our task should be to understand the nature and effects of the forces that have made the Indian what he is today and to treat these social compulsives in the same way that the physicist, for example, treats of the natural forces with which he deals; that is, as impersonal, conditional, and inexorable entities. Furthermore, it is appropriate in this connection to question the traditional reluctance of the professional student of custom to enter the field of applied science, and to suggest that since he knows at least as much about social potentials as anyone else that he consider the area of contemporary problems as a proper salient in the domain of his discourse.

The following analysis has been made in the belief that the exclusive preoccupation of the anthropologist with primitive conditions is an artificial restraint upon his knowledge, and that he has not worked himself cut of a job when he has finally gathered all that can be learned about a people who are rapidly relinquishing their old customs. The implication is, indeed, that his work has just begun — if he has the heart for it. Since this attitude has not met with general acceptance as yet it is expectable that the account that follows is not tailored to a pattern. Among professional students of society, the sociologist is more likely to find something familiar in it than the anthropologist. For one thing, it is a purely social study; for another, it presents a social situation, calls it a problem, admits that something can be done about, and makes some suggestions as to what this is. The anthropologist will be inclined to demand a more comprehensive treatment, one which includes the material as well as the social, and one which is more descriptive and less analytic than the present one. It is probable, too, that he will call [xi] for a greater emphasis upon, or at least an orientation around, the facts of historical causation.

In answer to these expectations it is sufficient to say that the aim here has been neither to write an ethnography nor to present the results of an acculturation study in the current acceptation of those terms. Most ethnographies are descriptive of static patterns; most acculturation studies, in so far as they are descriptive of processes; aim at reconstructing a sequence of integrated conditions which are the consequents of specific historical events. Regardless of the value of such accounts, the approach in the present instance has been different. The emphasis in this case has been upon the contemporary scene on the Yakima reservation with an attempt to explain it in terms of itself; that is, as the result of the complex interaction of coexistent forces. Historical factors are not ignored; they are always important, even determinative, if one wishes to insist upon it. But after this is admitted the difficulties faced and presented by the Yakima today remain and if their historical causes are the unique and unduplicated series of events that they are presumed to be by the culture historian, a knowledge of them provides an uncertain basis for suggesting future courses of action, and therefore is irrelevant to a problem analysis.

In the pages that follow the aim has been to present the result of an analysis of the social and economic conditions among the Yakima Indians in terms of their adjustment to our modern standards of living; and to suggest the nature of the remedy if not the specific instruments for its accomplishment in the areas of maladjustment. The data are specific and relate to only one tribe of Indians. The analysis, however, and the suggestions, have a larger frame of reference. In consequence of their status as dependant wards of the national government, the Yakimas have experienced an interplay of [xlii] social forces that has its counterparts among other groups similarly situated; as members of a more inclusive category of individuals who have been objects of discrimination by a dominant population they have much in common with other minority elements in the United States and elsewhere.

It is with these larger identifications in mind that the socio-economic conditions of the Yakimas are reviewed and their maladjustments highlighted. Most objective observers will probably agree that, in themselves, these conditions are unimportant. In their particularity they are interesting or disturbing but non-significant. If on the other hand, they relate to a categorical framework they fall into the picture of science and are amenable to systematic knowledge and control. If out of them some of the essentials of minority-majority relations can be distilled they take on a new meaning; and our knowledge of than provides the tools for future courses of action.

Chapter I
Economic Conditions

The Aboriginal Base

In their aboriginal condition the Yakima Indians were not an agricultural people. They did make economic use of a great variety and a vast quantity of roots, berries, and other plants; but none of these were planted or cultivated in anyway. They harvested the natural growth in its native setting, which means that at appropriate seasons of the year they went on food gathering excursions, lasting for days or weeks, at the places of greatest abundance. These plant foods were supplemented by large quantities of wild game and fish.

The Indians had no domesticated animals except the dog, hence no con trolled supply of food from this source, and no livestock encumbrances to restrict their periodic movements. The demand for meat in the diet was, in fact, a further incentive to their seasonal migrant type of economic activity. Large numbers of deer, antelope, rabbits, land birds and waterfowl were to be taken with little effort in the valleys in certain seasons; but at other times it was necessary so move up in the foothills of the Cascades to secure deer, bear, elk, and other game,

Fish too, could be taken in the streams of the valley; but the primary reliance was upon salmon, and to take this in quantity it was necessary to move to favorable locations on the larger streams at the time of the runs. The Yakima River had its share of these fish and was nearby, but even better fishing and more sociability were to be enjoyed at sites on the Columbia River several miles away. Consequently the people now known as the Yakimas were [2] in the habit of congregating with the members of many other tribes at such historic locations as Priest Rapids, Pasco, and Celilo Falls.

To exploit their food and other economic resources with the only knowledge at their disposal, the Yakimas had therefore adopted a pattern of seasonal movements from one favorable locality to another. This does not mean that they were constantly on the move, nor that they wandered aimlessly. Their winter home, from November to March or April, was in the valley of the Yakima River or on stream courses tributary to it near supplies of wood and water. There was not one village, but many small ones in sheltered spots all along the creeks in this lowland area. Some economic activity was carried on during the winter; there was a little hunting, and some household activity, mostly on the part of the women, which contributed to the stock of implements, utensils, and clothing. On the whole, however, this was a non-productive period when the people lived off their stores laid up in the summer. It was also confining and dull for the active individual so most people anxiously awaited the spring and the first ripening of fresh plant food.

With the coming of April the winter village broke up, its several family units going off separately or in company with a few others to the scattered root fields. By the time these wild root crops had been harvested and prepared for storage the early salmon runs of the latter part of May and June were demanding the attention of the men. July was a time of intensive fishing when all members of the family could help in the catching, drying, or packing of the winter's supply, so a camp was established at a favorite rendezvous. Then by August the berries were ripe in the mountains, and this required another shift of camp for the whole family. Some families preferred to stay in the uplands through September and October, gathering late fruits and nuts, and hunting; others returned to the river for the September salmon run. [3]

Whatever the individual disposition, and there were alternatives throughout most of the summer, there was considerable shifting and commingling by the various families, and the community which we may call the village was dissolved temporarily. But with the return of the cold months, its constituent family units reconvened for a period of relative inactivity is conformance with the natural wild life cycle to which Yakima economic pursuits were so intimately tied.

Habitual patterns of activity such as this become deeply ingrained in time, and they are not easy to eradicate or transform. In-breeding them in the biological sense is out of the question, but continuity between generations is established socially by a very early conditioning in the life of the child; and continued familiarity with a pattern makes it the only "logical" and "proper" one. And so it has happened that the migratory habit of the Yakimas has been the despair of administrators from the date of the establishment of the reservation until the present time. The ambition of superintendents has been to bring the Indian's way of life into congruity with the white man's, and they have realized from the beginning that this is impossible as long as the economic bases of the two cultures are not in agreement. Yet despite persistent and varied attempts to induce the Yakimas to adopt sedentary life founded upon agriculture and livestock tending only scant success has been achieved with the group as a whole. Large numbers of them still resort to the mountains for gathering activities in the spring and fall, and fishing at Celilo Falls is frequently carried on at the expense of livestock increase and farm harvest. [4]

Governmental Policy and the Transition

There were many early attempts to inculcate our ideas of private property in land and its products among the Yakimas. One of the earliest and ablest of their agents, Reverend James Wilbur, believed that they should have specific plots of land assigned to them in severalty if they were to prosper, and he accordingly gave some of the more adaptable members of the tribe unofficial title to areas chosen by them for cultivation. The fields so assigned varied from eighty to two hundred acres, depending upon the size of the family and the quality of the soil. It was also his practice, in strict conformance with a Congressional Act of 1874, to distribute annuity goods in the form of livestock, harness, wagons, and food only to those able bodied men who labored for them. He was convinced that this was the only means of instilling an idea of their value.

The system worked only within limits and in special cased. While the principle seems self-evident to us, the Indian was not prepared to accept our premises in this reasoning. He had to be convinced of the value of the goods <u>before</u> he would work for them; and in this he did not differ from other men, either then or now. It is therefore unfair to charge him, as some have done, with laziness on this score. It was a question of what was worth working for, and the issue for the Indian was clear: he was not willing to trade an entire way of life for a wagon and a field of wheat. A few saw an advantage in the offered exchange; most did not, and although they made an outward gesture of accepting our system of values, their conversion was superficial, as was soon discovered. They were eager to acquire the products of the white man's patience and industry — as long as they did not have to commit themselves [5] to the price of the same discipline. The benefits of ownership were readily recognized and capitalized upon, but the obligations which it entailed were avoided, for they infringed upon the freedoms of the old pattern. It was difficult to get men to fence their lands and to expend labor in improving and tilling them. After twenty years of unremitting labor toward this end, agent Wilbur passed the job on to his successor, General R.H. Milroy. The latter, making his first report to the Commissioner of Indian Affairs in 1883, lamented that, "About half the Indians belonging to this agency remain habitually off the reservation. Most of these have no fixed homes, but move about from one locality to another as their necessity for a supply of fish, game, roots, or berries may demand. Said supplies being precarious and often failing to satisfy their wants, they forage on and become very troublesome to white settlers, from whom I receive frequent complaints. By 1885 those who owned livestock had become so careless and prodigal of it that the authorities found it necessary to require them to get an agent's order before buying, selling, trading, or slaughtering any of it.

Nevertheless, the trend in public thinking was all toward private ownership for the Indian, and in 1887 there was passed by Congress the Dawes Severalty Act, providing for the division of reservations into individually allocated portions; the process to begin at the discretion of the President in the case of each tribe. According to its provisions each family head was to receive 160 acres of arable land (or twice that in grazing or other land), each single person over eighteen and each orphan was to receive eighty acres, and all other persons under eighteen born prior to the allotment order were to be given forty acres. (The lands could not be lost by tax default, nor could they be sold. They were tax free and were to be held in trust by [6] the United States Government for the exclusive benefit of the Indian for a period of at least twenty-five years. The remainder of the reservation, after all living Indians had been provided for, was then to be thrown open to purchase and settlement by whites. There were later amendments to this act, the chief of which to concern us here being the provision that allowed competent Indians, upon request and examination, to obtain fee patents to their lands. This placed them upon the same footing as the white man, subject to taxation and free to dispose of their property as they saw fit.

There was strong opposition to this measure on the Yakima reservation. It was inaugurated by Agent Lynch, the first allotments being made in 1892. The chief of the tribe opposed the division on the grounds that it would destroy the unity of thought and action by his peoples there were some conflicting claims which aggravated the problem of distribution; and some Individuals obstructed the surveyors' work by pulling up boundary stakes and wrecking instruments. The process nonetheless proceeded apace. By the beginning of 1912 three thousand one hundred and sixty allotments had been made. In 1914 the allotment rolls were closed, four thousand five hundred and six individuals having been granted a total of 440,000 acres. Indians born since that date are without original assignments of land and if they own any at all they have inherited it. Even before that time good land was scarce, those who entered a claim subsequent to 1908 or 1910 being able to receive only marginal plots, or grazing lands, or timbered areas in the mountains.

As might be expected, it was the more adaptable individuals, those who had embraced the white man's ideals, who were foresighted enough to take advantage of the new plan. The conservatives held back, reluctantly accepted what was given than, and fared badly — a circumstance which has further [7] contributed to their recalcitrance and has perpetuated their backwardness to the present day. First and foremost among those who accepted the new way of life and capitalized upon it were the half castes and a number of women who had married white men. The parents of a good proportion of individuals in these categories did not aboriginally belong to the Yakima tribe, and according to the views of present day conservatives did not have a right to be granted land here in the first place. Further cause for complaint by some dissatisfied individuals lies in the fact that these aliens and half-castes obviously took their allotment with the intent of selling to whites, and hence they are regarded as conspirators and renegades.

There can be no doubt that the opening up of the reservation was in large measure due to these alien elements. Previous to 1887 the center of reservation life was at the agency offices established at Fort Simcoe in a western corner of the valley. The more progressive Indians had their farms in this immediate vicinity; the rest of the area was a wasteland of sagebrush and rye grass. Up until that time, too, the Indians took advantage of their treaty rights and made violent objection to any white men living within the reservation's boundaries; and they were able to secure the eviction of all but two or three who were married to Indian women. Even the railroad, cutting across the reservation in 1884, did not alter this exclusionist stand. But with the passage of the Dawes Act, and the subsequent measure relating to competency, the way was open for a radical alteration in the relations of whites and Indians. The members of five Indian and part-Indian families in particular envisioned the possibilities and seized upon locations near the railroad depot for the allotments when these were first assigned, for several years they rented their lands to enterprising whites, and upon [8] fee patents in 1905 and 1906 they platted them and sold them for townsite lots. The town of Toppenish boomed, and by 1907 when the need for incorporation became apparent it had a population of eight hundred, a bank; hotels, restaurants, a newspaper, and a variety of mercantile and service establishments. Today it has a population of 3,628 and is the hub of reservation life. Other places, such as Barker, Wapato; Harrah and White Swan, have had similar histories. Apart from their presentation of urban patterns for the good or ill of the surrounding native population, the affect of these several towns has been to shift the focus of interest and activity from the western to the eastern part of the reservation. The change has been a pronounced and rapid, even in the eyes of the Indian, that by 1915 the position of the agency at Fort Simcoe was felt to be too remote from the main current of Indian affairs, and in 1922 the administrative offices were moved to Toppenish.

The Land and Its Utilization

All the above mentioned towns except White Swan lie close to the Yakima River, which flows along the northeastern margin of the reservation. The development in this section has not been fortuitous. Its commerce is accommodated by the railroad which takes a northward swing at this point, and its fields are supplied by the necessary water from the adjacent river. During the first years of its growth this rich agricultural region had to rely upon crude rock diversion dams in the river and upon certain natural channels to distribute its water. Beginning in 1906, Congress began to make a number of appropriations, totalling approximately $2,000,000, for the development of a comprehensive irrigation system known as the Wapato Project. [9]

It ramifies from a dam built in 1917 at the northeastern corner of the reservation. Augmented by pumping units, its twenty-six miles of main canals and seven hundred and thirty-five miles of laterals embrace an irrigable area of over 140,000 acres and directly benefit about nine hundred Indian and one thousand white farm units. An immediately feasible extension in the Mabton region is in prospect and will add another twenty sections of land to the total. A more distant possibility is the projected diversion of the Klickitat River from near its headwaters into the northwestern section of the reservation. This would put some 30,000 additional acres of fertile soil into production, but it would require several million dollars to complete it, and the assurance of a return on electric power sales to liquidate the indebtedness. Since the introduction of cheaper power from larger dams on the Columbia the likelihood of this development seems more remote.

Some attempt to salvage the entire western end of the reservation valley from its semi-desert condition must be made, however, if the Indians who hold allotments in that section are to prosper as farmers. The Wapato project skirts the eastern margin of the White Swan district and does not supply its higher levels with irrigation water. Two or three small streams wind down in irregular courses through this arid upland from their sources in the western foothills, but the water flow is scanty and frequently dries up entirely during the hot months. It is not sufficient to irrigate the few patches of farming land that now exist. One incomplete and inadequate system in the southwestern part of the area permitted a crop acreage of only 1,988 in 1942. Below the limited area served by this unit, habitation and cultivation is practically confined to the narrow beds of the creeks, small patches of corn, hay, and grain appearing in irregular natural embayments and depressed areas [10] adjacent to them (See Plate IVc). The White Swan vicinity, eighteen miles to the west of Toppenish, stands in marked contrast to the greener lands nourished by water from the Wapato irrigation unit, and there is no denying that farming here is a struggle for either the Indian or the white man (Compare Plate IV a and b),

The Irrigation projects are under the direction of the US Indian Irrigation Service, capital for them having been provided in part directly by Congress and in part from Yakima tribal funds. Since 1916 charges for the use of water from the system constitute a lien against the irrigated property, and in the case of Indian allotments are collectible at the agency. Not all the land embraced by the system is under cultivation. The total acreage in production within the Wapato unit in 1942 was 109,152, an increase of 834 acres over the previous year. The two other smaller units added 1,988 and 4,719 making a total of 115,858 acres of productive land provided for by the system in 1942. To this should be added an estimated 4,000 acres cultivated by individuals in various spots on creek beds outside of the reclamation areas. This represents the total area of land under cultivation by both whites and Indians on the reservation at the present time.

The effects of these reclamation projects upon Indian life have been far reaching. They have completely altered the aspect of the valley, changing its vegetation type, rendering it infinitely more valuable and attractive to white men, and contributing to the growth of commercial and residential centers. Today a variety of crops can be grown and numbers of dairying and beef livestock raised. The leading crop, as in the past, is alfalfa; in places three cuttings can be made of this in a year, with a yield of five tons per acre, and a fall pasture provided for cattle or sheep. Other prominent crops include sugar beets, potatoes, barley and corn. [11]

In connection with the development of valuable lands and towns on the reservation, problems in the management of Indian and white relations were certain to become more complicated. Far from creating a basis for more harmonious relations between the two races, the allotment act of 1887 only made Indian administration more difficult. The consequences of this measure were disillusioning to those of its sponsors who had the well-being of the Indian in mind. The abuses that it permitted soon became manifest and inspired several special Congressional acts to control them. In addition, agency superintendents were impelled to impose restrictions upon their charges. In general, Indians were not interested in the land and the labor involved in putting it into production; whenever they could, they sold it, and often to unscrupulous white men. By 1911 forty-five patents in fee had been issued and two hundred ninety land sales had been made covering most of the patents, naturally in the areas made valuable by irrigation improvements. The prices received ranged from a few dollars to $150.00 an acre for improved farms. The Indian was not allowed to handle the money; it went into depositories held in trust by the departmental officials and was paid out only upon their authorization. The Indian could not incur valid debts against his deposits Non-competent Indians, incapacitated by age or disease, were permitted to sell portions of their allotments to get funds for the necessities of life; and those who were in good health could sell a part of their land to get funds for improvements on the retained portion, but only in special cases. There were fewer restrictions placed on the sale of inherited lands; but even then the heir had to show that the sale was for good reasons.

Since that time the restrictions upon relinquishment of titles have been increased. There is no law against the sale of their lands by Indians, [12] and they can still get fee patents. But as a matter of policy the present Indian administration is opposed to releasing land from its trust. So is the Yakima tribal council, and likewise most of the Indians. They prize their prerogatives as non-taxpayers and realize that they would succumb under present conditions if they had to pay a land tax. Perhaps it would be more accurate to say that the Office Of Indian Affairs is opposed to land sales; it will agree to them only in exceptional cases; and its authority is requisite for such transactions. The result is that only a very few Indians hold patents in fee and pay taxes on their lands.

The official attitude curbing land sales is a reaction against past tendencies which have operated to dispossess the Indian and leave him homeless. Of the original reservation comprising well over a million and a quarter acres, the present jurisdiction of the Department of Indian Affairs has been reduced to 1,112,792 acres. Before the forces of restraint came into operation, 86,814 acres had been alienated by sale and patents, and 26,953 acres conveyed in public land patents to white homesteaders who entered in accordance with a general act approved by Congress but prior to the final Yakima boundary adjustment. The loss would undoubtedly have been greater had the so-called policy patent plan of 1916-17 gone unchallenged. The administration of that period decided to declare whole groups of Indians competent without their individual petitions, and proceeded to bestow fee parents upon theme. Many Indians objected and the case was brought before the Supreme Court. Its decision was that the

Secretary of the Interior had exceeded his authority in waiving the twenty-five year stipulation of the Dawes Act and that the Indians who had been required to pay land taxes as a result of his action should be reimbursed — a decision which worked considerable hardship on several counties and caused some ill feeling. [13]

Land loss in terms of acres has not been serious for the Yakimas; but the demand by white farmers has naturally been for the choice locations, and it is in the most productive areas that the Indian has foolishly relinquished his holdings. In the irrigated sections the white man owns thirty-four percent of the land, and he leases another fifty-seven percent, leaving the Indian with only a nine percent direct interest in the preferred locations. Administrators regard this and other aspects of the land question as the paramount problem. The first requirement, they feel, is to assure the individual Indian of enough land to take care of his needs. He is to be made economically self-sufficient through land use. On some reservations this policy has necessitated the repurchase of alienated lands to provide homes for those who have been improvident (or whose fathers have been), or for those who have been born too late to be allotted. There are some Yakimas in this predicament, and many others who have fallen heir to such small portions of allotments that no good is to be derived from them. Heirships grow more complicated each year; and intra-family squabbles render the effective utilization of some lands impossible. The Yakima tribe has accumulated a fund of approximately $200,000 and the council has been considering the advisability of using part of this for the repurchase of alienated lands and complicated heirships, either for tribal benefit or to be purchased on time by some of the deserving younger Indians who have never had allotments. Nothing has come of this proposal as yet.

Probably every needy Yakima could still be given enough land. Of the 1,112,792 acres still under jurisdiction only 353,585, or about one third, has ever been allotted. There remains 759,207 acres of tribal land; but official policy is opposed to the apportionment of this, even in cases where [14] the land is good for faming or pasture. The Indian Office inclines toward the concept of community property for the Indian, presumably believing that the native's wishes are being met by this; but the Yakimas vigorously rejected the idea on a test a few years ago. They now want land, and they want it individually owned; though this its not to say that they either cherish it as a possession or want to labor on it.

Income from the land

This introduces another matter which has added to the complexity and the expense of the administration of Indian lands; namely, the practice of leasing. Almost from the beginning of individual allotment holdings it has been possible for the trust patented Indian to rent his land to others, which means, usually, to white tenants. Applicants for leasing privilege must make a formal bid on the property and the acceptance or rejection of this is up to the Indian. It is possible for him to give the agent power of attorney in this matter, but few Indians like to do this; they prefer to pass judgement upon the lessee themselves. Also, the practice of demanding "side money" or bribe for signing the lease is current, since rent payments on all so-called incompetent leases (the majority) are not paid to the lessor directly but through the office where its cash disbursement to the improvident land owner can be regulated.

Leases are let for from one to five years, most of them covering a three year period with a practical certainty of renewal if all agreements have been met and the lessee is satisfactory to the Indian. Most leases stipulate that some improvements must be made on the land, especially if they are long term grants. Many lessees have been in continuous possession of Indian property for eight to ten years, and one has been on the same [15] allotment for twenty-six years. A few of the leases each year are on a crop share basis, and a few for improvements only; but the majority are for cash. Both agricultural and grazing lands are leased. The proportions, the rental prices, and the incomes vary little from year to year. The 1940 report will therefore serve to give an idea of the scope of leasing operations.

During that year there were 1,734 leases, of which 1,197 were on agricultural land, 469 on grazing land, sixty-one on pasture land, and seven were business leases. The general acreage rental varied between $3.22 and $3.59 for the agricultural and between $.57 and $1.03 for the grazing land. The total acreage leased was 116,069, which is a little less than a third the total allotment acreage of 353,585 acres. The total cash income from this source was $257,182.00, giving an average of almost $150.00 per year per lease. This figure however, like all averages, means little in the concrete case; some individuals receive but a very few dollars a year, others are paid well over a thousand.

It is obvious that most Yakimas would rather rent their land and live off its meager returns than utilize it themselves. In contrast to the 68,000 acres which they leased for agricultural purposes in 1941, the Indians themselves farmed only 13,620 acres. Some of them find justification for this in the plea that it is sometimes difficult to work out a satisfactory agreement with co-heirs; but from the report just cited it appears that almost as many leases were signed by original allottees or single heirs as by clusters of co-heirs (344 and 869 respectively), while of the former there were more than twice as many as there were involved in a six-way partnership. Contract difficulties obviously do not play the key role in this. The same holds true for the complaint that it is not worthwhile to farm because of unproductive [16] land, for it is precisely the best land which is rented. Under the Wapato irrigation project in 1942 over seven times as much Indian owned land was farmed by whites as by Indiana; and another five-fold portion of it was white owned. Furthermore, Indians do not lease lands from their kinsmen to the degree that we might expect. The 1942 crop report shows a total of only 8,733 acres of land leased by Indians, 1,337 of it being agricultural. There were one hundred and three contracts in this category, bringing an income of $7,336.00 paid to Indians by Indians.

Officials in every department endeavor to get the Indian to assume the initiative and accept the responsibilities of his undertakings. One approach in this plan has been to encourage the private negotiation of lease contracts. The stipulations are subject to review by the superintendent, just to make certain that the Indian has not signed an invalid document; otherwise the terms are left up to him, he receives the rental money directly, and the agency assumes no legal responsibility in the matter. Few individuals are denied the privilege upon request, but most prefer to let the agency officials handle this complicated business. In 1940 somewhat less than a fifth (314 out of 1,734) of the leases were in this competent class.

Incomes from agricultural holdings belong almost entirely to the individual Indian since this kind of land is all allotted. Much of the grazing land on the other hand, has not been apportioned; it remains in the control of the tribes and its benefits and returns are group property. Any member may graze his stock upon this open range free of charge up to the limit of one hundred cattle or five hundred sheep. Over that, and for the use of any individual's land, he pays the regular fee set by the tribal council. This arrangement offers the opportunity for a few to gain at the expense of the [17] group, and although the matter has been discussed in council nothing has been done about it. At one time there was a proposal to reduce the limits of privilege and so bring greater returns to the group by surtaxing the few who manage large herds, but this was rejected. Under the circumstances leasing profits must come mainly from outsiders. In 1942 there were all told nearly 30,000 head of sheep being grazed on the reservation at the rate of $1.65 per head for nine months. At a meeting in the same year, the council decided to raise this fee to $2.05, expressing the view that the "rise in living costs makes it hard for the Indians to live on their limited incomes."

It has been said that the Yakimas have not readily accepted the implications and the responsibilities of a farming economy. Their willingness to lease their land in preference to cultivating it themselves, as is evidenced by the foregoing discussion, contributes to this conclusion. So does an analysis of the sources and amounts of their earned incomes. It is true that, in the aggregate, they produce considerable agricultural wealth; but like all group figures a summation of incomes from this source is likely to be deceptive because of an unequal distribution by families. A brief analysis of some relevant statistics is therefore to the point.

For 1941 the crop and livestock sales of all producers were valued at $412,654.00, their home grown and consumed goods at $66,610.00, their total farm and lives lock expenses at $276,382.00, and their net income at $202,881.00. The sources of their cash income fell into these major categories: cash crops $183,785.00, fruit and berry yield $5,175.00; beef sales $193,250.00; livestock products $30,444.00. The distribution of this earned income among the 222 recognized agricultural families (out of the 543 on the reservation) is shown in the following table. It will be recalled that these families farmed 13,620 acres of land. [18]

income brackets	$50 to $149	$150 to $249	$250 to $349	$350 to $449	$450 to $549	$550 to $649	$650 to $749	$750 to $849	$850 to $1000
families	10	25	60	38	39	16	13	10	15

Indians in 1941 owned several kinds of domesticated animals which were given an over-all evaluation of $483,288.00o This included 5,850 beef cattle, 651 dairy cattle, 5,540 sheep, 970 hogs, 5,724 horses and mules, 4,460 chickens, 330 turkeys, and 90 waterfowl. The numbers of families owning different sizes of herds of the more important food animals is given in the table below.

Kind	1	2	3	4-9	10-19	20-29	30-39	40-49	50-59	75-99	100-149	150-159	200-99	300-499	+500
Cattle															
Beef					11	14	25	16	10	10	1	6	3	6	2
Dairy	16	13	9	18	10	3	2		1		1				
Hogs	14	28	14	18	10	5	1	1							
Sheep					2	1									3

It will be seen from this that there were only two men with range cattle herds of over 300 head, and none with as many as 500. The general run of individuals who devote special attention to cattle raising own from twenty to forty head. Of most common occurrence is the farm with one or two milk cows and hogs; three or four horses, and a flock of chickens. It should be borne If mind however, that this generalization is far from typical of the reservation as a whole. It applies only to those Indians who keep stock of the above kinds at all; that is, to less than half (222 out of 543) of the families on the reservation, Many Indians keep no hogs, sheep, or cattle whatever, even [19] though they raise hay and grain. Milk cows and hogs are noticeably absent to one who expects farmers at the subsistence level, with little cash income, to take advantage of their opportunities to raise their own food. In this connection, it is worth remarking that agricultural reports show no home production of butter or cheese, and this bears out the writer's observations. With this impression allowance must be made for a more concentrated attention upon the western part of the valley, but there at any rate a milk cow is an anomaly. The indifferent farmers in that section own a few chickens, a team or two of work horses, perhaps a saddle horse, and very little else, as a rule. Their income, if any, apart from rentals, must come from other sources; and we may now turn our attention to these.

Economic Survivals

The traditional pattern of making hunting and gathering excursions to the mountains at appropriate seasons still survives in force among a good proportion of the population. During the month of August it was most difficult to secure informants on Indian custom, for most of those who retain a knowledge of aboriginal forms still adhere to them. Even those who have agreed to tie themselves down with stock and farm obligations still yearn for a "vacation" in the mountains and find a few days now and then to satisfy their taste for an outing and some of the old foods. As in aboriginal days, huckleberries are much sought after, and quantities are dried or canned for winter. Some are sold, but this is not an incentive in gathering them. Individual sales to the local market have been negligible. A canvass of the Toppenish stores revealed that but a few merchants buy berries from Indians, and then mostly for their own tables. Some have objections to Indian handled goods. [20]

The old root foods are much harder to get today. Sheep and other stock graze the vegetation so close that tubers and bulbs either die or cannot be found. The Indians lament this, and many of them would much rather have roots than sheep to eat. Some gathering still takes place each spring. It has not been difficult to secure specimens of aboriginally prepared plant foods during the summers in recent years; almost every household could provide them. Where they are no longer locally accessible, fish, shawls, and other items are traded for them in standard quantities, packed in native bags, from other regions.

Hunting is still a favorite activity during the winter. Several of the animal species known to older members of the tribe have vanished, but deer and bear are plentiful. Not only the meat but the skins of deer, for buckskin clothing, are widely used at the present time. Fur bearing animals such as beavers provide a cash income for some of the more energetic men. No restrictions have been placed upon hunting techniques, the quantities that can be taken, or the season when hunting can take place. This has created some problems. It is a matter of concern for not only reservation officials but others as well. Indian lands adjoin restricted areas and parks, and indiscriminate hunting in the one section practically nullifies the effects of control in others. In so far as is known Indians do not wantonly kill game, nor do they use the mass slaughtering techniques originally designed to supply meat in quantity for the village. They use guns, but they do not hesitate to kill does with fawns, and they shoot a great number of deer in winter when they are driven down from the mountains by deep snow. Not long ago the federal government, under a migratory bird act, prohibited the killing of ducks, and the Solicitor General ruled that the act applied to Indians as well as whites. [21]

Several Indians were arrested in violation and contested the validity of the prohibition, appealing to their treaty rights. The Solicitor General then reversed his position. Several attempts have been made to induce the tribal council to frame some hunting regulations for the reservation, but nothing has been done to date. It is estimated that about fifty individuals were profitably engaged in commercial hunting and trapping in 1941.

Of all wild life activities, salmon fishing continues to be the most important and the most lucrative. It attracts most of the younger and middle aged Indians and through them practically every family gets fish in some quantity. Some men spend the better part of the summer at Celilo in commercial fishing. Ordinarily they receive from one and one half cents to five cents per pound for salmon, and with luck they can make good money. Exceptional perhaps is the case of a boy of nineteen who in 1941 netted $1200.00 during the month of September; but in 1942 many fishermen earned several hundred dollars each, working for a record pack to supply government demands for the armed forces. Approximately 271 men were engaged in this commercial fishing in 1940 (the last report), either selling their catches to the cannery or free lancing and selling to wholesale fresh meat dealers on the spot. Most Indians, however, fish primarily for themselves; and families that rely upon this source for a winter food supply stock up with five hundred to six hundred pounds of salmon. This may be dried, as it was aboriginally, or canned; and recently Indians have been utilizing the frozen food lockers that are for rent in White Swan, Toppenish, and Harrah. Two or three men stored as much as a ton of fish in their lockers at White Swan in the summer of 1942.

The privileges which Indians enjoy in fishing are resented by white men, especially sportsmen, and for some time past the State of Washington has [22] refused to acknowledge certain rights claimed by them on the basis of treaty provisions. Specifically; the state has denied the Indian the right to fish commercially unless he pays for a license like anyone else. It has not denied him the privilege of fishing for his own use at any season, but has insisted that the commercial regulations must apply to everyone. This restraint was contested; and in a test case which eventually reached the Supreme Court in 1942 the Indian was vindicated, the decision voiding the state's claim but ruling that it might put reasonable restrictions upon any and all fishing for purposes of conservation. In view of this concession, agency officials do not feel that the matter is settled and they anticipate further difficulties.

The lumber resources of the reservation have never been systematically utilized. The timber as it now stands is valued at $10,000,000.00, with controlled cutting and replanting it would yield indefinitely. The question of its sale has been argued and reconsidered in council meetings for the last fifty years, but no agreement has been reached upon its disposal. The issue is perennial and is still being discussed. If the Indians could be induced to relinquish their individual claims, and could agree on a price, the tribal fund would receive the proceeds from all unallotted areas and individual allotees would benefit directly in proportion to their timber holdings.

Any Indian may now cut ten cords of wood for his owe use. If it is convenient he usually does so, but it is remarkable that many do not take advantage of this privilege; they prefer to buy their stock from the wood yards in Toppenish and elsewhere, especially if they live near these towns. Indians may also cut wood for sale in quantities over their ten cord allowance, and some do. A few sell their cuttings to the local coal and wood yards, and two or three individuals ordinarily supply white people directly in White Swan, [23] It is surprising, however, that there are not more of these individual dealers, especially in view of the high price ($11.00 per cord in 1942) for delivered firewood. Those with timber allotments pay nothing for wood at the source; only their labor and the expense of hauling have to be reckoned with. If they own no timber they may pay a basic rate of approximately $1.00 per cord, either to the tribal fund (if the cutting is on tribal land); or to other individuals. Many of those with allotments offer their timber for sale, authorizing the agent with power of attorney to dispose of it to their best interests. White men may and do secure permits on the same basis as unallotted Indians; that is, by paying the basic rate. The forestry division exercises a certain authority, indicating the trees that may be cut on the principle of sustained yield, but this is not a burdensome restriction. Other sources of wood are much farther away, and Indians could control the local market. They do not, however.

A few of the ancient handicrafts are still carried on. Buckskin is tanned by the women in the aboriginal manner while in the mountains or at home. From it clothing is made for ceremonial occasions, and also quantities of moccasins which are an item of everyday wear for both men and women among a fairly large segment of the population (Plate V b, c, d). Another characteristic feature of the woman's attire is the beaded handbag. Some plain and fancy beaded gloves are also made, although leather and cotton gloves from the store are a much more common sight in actual use. The women continue to make excellent baskets of native and commercial materials, and they prefer them to other containers for storing foods and as berry picking receptacles.

In practically every home there is to be found a product of one or more of these surviving crafts; but only a small proportion of the households make [24] any attempt to reduce the demands upon their cash outlays by such home industry. The articles are used more because they are traditional forms than because they contribute to the self-sufficiency of the family. Also, these articles bring in but little cash income or credit. Their commercial value is small; the demand for them by the larger market of whites is at a minimum. Three stores in Toppenish were found to carry a small stock of gloves (mostly), moccasins, and "trinkets"; one dry goods store takes them in on credit. Except as souvenirs they have no value to whites. Furthermore, they have mainly a sentimental value to the Indians who regard them more or less as symbols of their heritage. They are not interested in selling them, although admittedly this attitude is a function of market conditions. The principal way in which Indians realize a direct return on their handicrafts is by the uneconomic process of pawning their treasured items.

They protest against this necessity and make a show of real reluctance in parting with their heirlooms, but there thrives nonetheless a so-called trading post in Toppenish whose business it is to lend money on Indian "curios", and there is scarcely a long established mercantile house in the district which does not have a collection of unredeemed handicraft specimens taken in on credit.

Indian Employees

So far we have considered income accruing to the Yakima chiefly as a consequence of his peculiar position as a member of a privileged and protected class of citizens. He is able to maintain his statue as a landholder in most cases because he is tax exempt and cannot be duped or deprived of it in any event. He is the recipient of an unearned income with the assistance of a considerable amount of official protective machinery. He can capitalize upon [25] the wild life resources of a vast area because it has guarded borders and he ranges over it without restriction. Under competitive conditions it is a serious question whether he would survive. Even when he is expected to meet the white man's requirements of economic efficiency he shrinks away and has acquired a reputation as a lazy, unreliable ne'er-do-well. He is not a good employee by vast employer's standards.

In past years the Indian has received compensation for his labor on a variety of government projects. In its own multifaceted business the Indian Bureau makes it a matter of policy to give preference to competent Indians in hiring help. In the Yakima agency office several are employed on the regular payroll as clerks and assistants. Regular Indian employees are also in the service of the reclamation bureau on construction and maintenance crews, in the offices, and as guards at critical points in the irrigation system. Various federal assistance programs such as W.P.A., NYA, and CCC have included a good proportion of Indian beneficiaries in recent years; but in line with general national policy, the scope of these projects has been sharply reduced. In addition to its regular employees, the agency has need of men from time to time for seasonal and emergency labor in fire fighting, and on road and building maintenance. Preference is given to capable Indians on these jobs.

These paternalistic measures are designed to accommodate the Indian and to encourage him to enter the competitive labor market in the wider field of private enterprise, and also to compensate for his present inability to do so. There can be no doubt of his failure in this regard. In order to give substance to an impression to this effect, a brief survey was made of the employment possibilities for Indians in Toppenish during the summer of 1942, The [26] managers of fifty-five business houses; including stores of all kinds, warehouses, garages, hotels, and processing establishments; as well as an employment agency, were contacted. The inquiry covered the whole of the main street and, it is believed, affords a representative sampling of conditions. Three places were found to be employing Indians; no more than ten in all; with only one or two full bloods among them. As might be expected; all were unskilled laborers. It was found that in the past untrained workers have been hired on the railroad; in the produce fields of one company; and for odd jobs around a hardware store. In the service establishments; requiring sales help, the information reveals that within the recollection of present owners and managers only eleven Indians have ever been hired; and that all except two of them were fired for some kind of incompetency. The firms having had experience with native help included three grocery stores, a garage, a hardware store, a jeweler's, a paint shop, a dry goods store, a trading shop, a five and ten, and an auto parts shop. The employment agency had also made contacts for some young Indian field laborers but very seldom for any other types of wage earners; either male or female.

We do not feel that the survey misses the mark. It is true that most Indians are better adapted to job labor than to office or sales work. At the same time it must be remembered that a large number of the younger people have had a high school education, that a few have been to college; and that many have taken special vocational training. In point of preparation these younger Indians do not suffer by comparison with their white school mates. All other things being equal one would expect to find a greater number of than employed as clerks and helpers in the business enterprises of what is, geographically at least, their home towns. Their records; and the reactions of proprietors, [27] are not reassuring. The plain fact exists that there are very few Indian wage earners in Toppenish. The inference, therefore, is that all other things are not equal.

The statements of employers were monotonously the same: the Indian doesn't want to work even if he is given a job, and he doesn't apply for work. The latter part of this statement is undoubtedly true; and so is the first part in many cases; but the reasons are not so simple as is implied. The assertion of unwillingness to accept employment has a defensive ring about it. The Indian is not always at fault by any means. Many educated Indians have found to their embitterment that that technical preparation is not the only qualification for employment. They are frequently thwarted in the beginning by the prevalent tendency to lump all Indiana together into one deplorable category of undesirable men. Whites almost automatically attribute the worst that they know about any Indian to the whole group. This attitude does not further their employment possibilities. Indian graduates of local high schools, vocational schools; and even of Haskell and Carlisle, have found that although they may be competent mechanics, carpenters, plumbers, and book keepers, they are seldom wanted and always have to wage an uphill struggle against the original skepticism of their worth. The Indian community offers no outlet for their capabilities; therefore, they subside into the limbo of the aimless, discontented, unemployed reservation Indians. In other words, they "return to the blanket." Parents who have experienced this disillusionment not infrequently discourage their children's going to school or acceptance of an apprenticeship. What is the use? It is a waste of time, and unpleasant anyway.

The future offers no better prospects. In fact, now that the war has called a number of young people away from the reservation to be taught trades [28] in defense industries and be thrust into new associations with white men, there is every reason to believe that the situation will be aggravated. These young men and women in war plants and in the army will come to know, and strive to adapt themselves to our patterns of social existence. They will be imbued of necessity, to some extent at least, with our ideals and values. In our present concern for unity and cooperation in the national war effort, we want them alongside us in the ranks and in the factories, but this democratic spirit will not survive the crisis. When the war tension is over and the slackening of industry occurs, we may confidently expect that the Indian, along with the members of other minority groups, will be among the first to feel the effects of a drop in the labor market. He will be released to give way to the white man, and will, of course, return to his only refuge, the reservation. The Bureau of Indian Affairs is aware of the inevitable, and already the Commissioner is concerned about it. In the report of the Secretary of the Interior for 1941, there is a section devoted to this problem; plans are already under way to save up reservation labor projects to take care of the influx of the unemployed. But this obviously is only a stop-gap and hence does not meet the problem face to face. These men and women, rejected by the society that once accepted their services in a crisis, will return to another life in which there is no place for them either since they have outgrown it. The result will certainly be, as after the last war, more widespread unrest and discontent than exists at present.

In return to other aspects of the economic adaptation of the reservation Indian, it may be said that his rural orientation has not prepared him, particularly to accept the status of an energetic and reliable farm hand or employee. In the summer of 1942, in the face of a serious shortage of fruit [29] and vegetable pickers; with exceptionally high wages (seventy-five cents an hour) being offered, the Yakimas were not unusually interested. They were, in fact, not even considered as potential rescuers of crops which rotted in the fields for lack of help. Calls were made upon every class and age group of whites by state, national, and county officials, but the potential Indian labor pool was not touched. If they thought of it at all, officials doubtless felt that an appeal would be futile, and there is nothing in past experience to indicate the contrary. It would seem that in the past, say twenty years ago, the Yakimas were a more reliable source of farm labor than they are now. In those days orchardists and other planters were accustomed to contract with alleged chiefs to bring their bands of followers in for the harvests. The custom no longer exists, and transient white laborers have taken the place of the Indian in the orchards and vegetable fields.

The only exception to this generalization has to do with the harvesting of hops. Since 1830 Indians have been employed to pick this crop, not only in the Yakima area but in the Puget Sound district as well. In the final decades of the last century agency superintendents were annually alarmed at the general exodus from the reservations to the hop fields. Today there are many acres of hops cultivated on the reservation and Indians are sought after as pickers (Plate IVd). The basic appeal for them, however, is not the money; it is the fact that this activity, offering sociability, and a change of daily routines, is admirably suited to fit into their old scheme of seasonal movement, with its periodic convergence and dispersal. In 1942 pickers received four cents per pound, the highest ever. Some families made as much as $10.00 per day, but even this was not a compelling incentive. Hop owners found that the labor shortage was ruinous, even though many used machines. Indians were [30] noticeably absent from the fields. Quite as important as the money to then is the sociability of the occasion. Ordinarily it provides an opportunity for large gatherings to gossip, play, and gamble much after the fashion of ancient food gathering excursions. The tire shortage, a late berrying season and other diversions were in part responsible for the poor turnout of Indian hop pickers that year.

Income Summary

By way of summing up this discussion of the economic activities of the Yakima the following table is appended. It is taken from the agency report upon the income of the Indians for 1940, the last for which such statistics are available (See next page). The size of these figures is likely to give a false impression of unending prosperity for the Indian. They do not tell us the really significant thing, which is what the individual family income is. This is very difficult to get. Indians, like other people, are suspicious and reluctant to yield to an exhaustive inquiry of this sort. There are perhaps four or five families on the reservation who have an income of between $1500.00 and $2000.00. These are the most energetic of the cattlemen. A few individuals receive between $1000.00 and $1500.00 a year from all sources, but they certainly are not typical. The average income is far below this, perhaps around $450.00 per year. Even in cases where it is possible to obtain accurate figures on individual incomes they are likely to be misleading. The pooling and sharing of incomes is quite common. Sometimes a husband and his wife and even a dependent child are all recipients of rental money. Kinship obligations are strong, and indigent families of all sizes frequently live with relatives who have cash incomes, so that a knowledge of the latter provides us with no reliable cheek upon its per capita utilization. [31]

I. Income from Public Funds:

Kind of income	# individual recipients	# persons benefitting	amount~value provided
A. direct assistance	212	789	$23,299
1 Farm security	77	308	3,689
2 Social security	35	81	17,110
3 Surplus commodity	100	400	2,500
B. wages, gov't work	512	1,316	99,639
1 work projects	286	456	55,369
2 irregular service	226	860	44,000
C. gov't aid thru institutions	10	10	3,538
totals	734	2,115	$125,476

II. All Other Income:

source	money	non-money
A. agriculture, net	$222.340	$45,328
B. Other labor	$182,820	$86,276
1 own operations	55,761	66,276
a firewood consumed, sold	21,436	18,423
b wildlife activities	43,325	18,685
1 fish 450,000 lbs	30,000	15,000
2 pelts 400	4,200	
3 game birds 8000		2,400
4 big game food 6000 lbs		600
5 big game hides		60
6 wild fruits berries	125	
c arts & crafts		2,2995

d canned dried goods		26,864	
C. employment	$127,059	$20,000	
1 regular Indian service	17,059		
2 non-indian employers	100,000	20,000	
D. Unearned individual income	$263,576		
1 farming leases	202,729		
2 grazing leases	60,847		
E. group enterprise distributed to individuals	758		
1 timber sales	567		
2 leases	191		
totals	$669,494	$131,604	[32]

Indigents and Incompetents

Some Yakimas do as well economically as many white fanners. Their net profits in cash are not large, but they are by no means faced with starvation, nor can they be evicted from their homes. At the other end of the scale is a disproportionate number of families who do not till the soil or maintain their own homes, and who do not have a steady income from any source. It is difficult to understand how the majority survive. A few individuals among them are eligible for relief assistance from the state or the federal government. Welfare agencies of the two governments work hand in hand to take care of certified cases of need. The state of Washington cooperates in this matter, as in others pertaining to Indian welfare and advancement. No distinction is made between Indian and white indigents, and the state employs a social worker for full time work with the Yakimas. Her office is at the agency in Toppenish.

Indians, like whites, are entitled to several types of benefits. The federal government matches state money to provide for four categories of dependents. The aged and the infirm are provided for by old age and blind pensions. Relatives who take care of orphans or children who have been abandoned by their fathers or their mothers can obtain financial assistance through the Aid to Dependent Children organization. The Child Welfare division arranges for the support of homeless children who have been taken in as members of the household in qualified families. In addition to these federally assisted agencies there are two which are state sponsored. Their activities interlock with those of the national and local governments in relief programs. Money for General Assistance cases helps the county with its burden of taking care [33] of the poor, and under the Work Relief program those who are temporarily unable to find employment are given financial aid or are certified for public works projects.

Old age pensioners and the blind are eligible for a maximum of $40.00 per month. Any income they may have is subtracted from this sum, and a deduction of $6.00 is made for combined living arrangements. Those enjoying benefits through the Aid to Dependent Children, General Assistance, or Work Relief provisions are entitled to $28.50 per month for a single person. For household groups of individuals the relief payments are naturally scaled down; a family of six may receive as much as $43.50 per month. All of these cases are eligible for food stamps.

In 1942 about one hundred families receive one of these kinds of assistance. Approximately fifty were old age pensioners (four or five included both man and wife), eight were blind, ten received aid through General Assistance; another ten through Aid to Dependent Children, and there were twenty on work relief.

It should be stressed at this point that the government does not support the Indian. Even though the treaty with the Yakimas stipulated that, in return for the land they relinquished, compensation was to be paid in the form of goods to be distributed equally among them annually, this provision was never fully carried out. From the beginning, and up until the time the debt was considered to be extinguished, individual Indians were required by the agent to work for their annuities on the theory that they could not otherwise be made to understand the virtues of industry. It may be regretted that this policy has not borne more or better fruit, but it remains true nonetheless that the government has not in the past nor does it now subsidize its Indian [34] wards. Widely current beliefs to the contrary probably arise from the manner in which the unearned incomes of certain Indians are handled. All rental money for trust lands is paid into the agency office in Toppenish except that of Indians who are regarded as competent to make their own leases. Payments to the lessors are made by the money clerk there, but not all in the same way. Some Indians are more provident than others, and it has been found necessary to take account of this fact in disbursing rental money. Roughly, a fourfold classification has been made. For those who can look ahead and provide for themselves and their families for a year there are no restrictions; they may have their lease money for the year in a lump sum. Upon others some restrictions are placed, especially if they are in the habit of demanding large amounts for improvident expenditures. In a third class are those who cannot be relied upon to support their families; they are given only a small amount of cash each month. Some individuals receive practically no cash at all. In that event, the superintendent is obliged to give them food and clothing orders. Any merchant in town may accept these orders with the assurance that he will be paid directly by the agency; and it is this in particular which has led some townspeople to assume that the Indians are provided for by the federal government. The fourth category consists of minors. Some children have an accumulated deposit of as much as $6000.00 to $8000.00. This is held in trust for them as capital. From it they can receive only $25.00 per quarter for their subsistence while they are pre-school age minors; and even when they attain their majority they may not have the entire sum. If an investigation reveals that capital is needed to buy a house or equipment, part of the trust fund is released for the specified purpose, but not otherwise. [35]

Indian Enterprise

From the foregoing it is clear that the Yakima lives on a protested fringe of the white man's economic world. He participates in its advantages under tutelage but shies away or is excluded from the struggle for survival which keeps it going. A noteworthy instance of a lack of integration with our economic pattern is his detachment from the commercial field. The attempts that have been made to enter business are few enough to be counted as outstanding exceptions. The most remarkable instance occurred with the establishment of the American State Bank at Wapato. Both its stockholders and its officers are largely Indian, most of them from a prominent mixed blood family. The cashier, an Indian, received an education at Whittier College in Indiana and worked for a banking house in Chicago for five years. He later returned to Yakima and was bank cashier there for twenty-three years; in 1917 he entered the banking business in Wapato. The success of this enterprise has been a creditable achievement, worthy of commendation, especially so in view of its uniqueness.

In the 1830s, before there were any stores or traders on the reservation, two of the head men of the Yakimas converted their homes into small hardware and dry goods stores. Their prices were exorbitant and their stocks limited; the Indians preferred to make the long trip to Yakima to get their supplies. Later with the opening of the Toppenish townsite, two or three of the women who had married white men and whose allotment relinquishments were responsible for the foundation of the town opened hotels, boarding houses, and stores. Their children were among the first to set up blacksmith shops, livery stables, and meat market. Before long, however, these tentative efforts gave way under the pressure of white aggressiveness and domination. [36]

Indian proprietors today are unusual; none could be located in Toppenish in 1942. There did remain the recollection of a mixed blood manager of a grocery store who a few years ago conducted the business in a capable manner. In the smaller towns on the reservation there are a few men operating small establishments, such as blacksmith shops, repair shops, and gasoline stations. In the past, sporadically, there have been others, but they call for comment chiefly because of their impermanence.

To the casual observer the failure of Indians to engage in small businesses and service enterprises may be puzzling. The opportunities are multiple. In the village of White Swan (see Plate la) there are five grocery stores, all doing enough business to make a living, and some far more. One especially is thriving. All five are owned and operated by whites, but over half of the trade is Indian. A priori one might think that an Indian proprietor would be many times as successful as the white man in dealing with his own people. Add to this the special advantages of the Indian and the question becomes more insistent. Why are there no prosperous Indian fuel dealers? or dairymen? or fish marketers? The answer is not to be framed simply in economic terms; it involves far more, and we shall have to review the social setting of contemporary Yakima life before we can attempt an explanation. [37]

CHAPTER II
SOCIAL CONDITIONS

The Indian Community

No observant person can walk the streets of Toppenish for an hour and fail to note a distinct element in the population. Indian women are immediately recognizable in their shawls and moccasins; their long flowered "wing" dresses, a pattern copied from the old buckskin garment; their handbags; and leather belts, and their typical headgear, a handkerchief tied around the head. Their husbands, too, wear moccasins; and they are further set off from others in the diversified crowd by their long hair braids and tall, broad~brimed hats. These features of dress, together with other traditional standards, constitute admitted symbols of apartness, consciously and sometimes defiantly indulged in as marks of the true Indian. There is an appreciable number of these conservatives, colloquially referred to as "long hairs," and they testify to the existence of a community within a community which is distinctly Indian, albeit much attenuated and adulterated in the course of the past eighty years of white contact.

This, though; is not the entire picture. Not all people of Indian parentage dress in this manner. Some of them are not to be distinguished from Mexicans by the untrained eye, and there are still others of the mixed blood class who could pass as southern Europeans in cosmopolitan centers. A little over half of those on the agency rolls, which lists all Indian wards of the government, are mixed bloods of one degree or another. The extent of their participation in Indian life, as exemplified by those described in the first paragraph, is highly variable and is rather closely correlated with the proportions [38] of Indian and white blood in their veins. Some of them are eclectic with regard to the ideology of the conservative nucleus; that is, they are without steady conviction but are Indians only when it suits their convenience for purposes of arguments, privilege, or rationalization. Indeed, the majority have taken up a vacillating defensive stand somewhere in the ambiguous zone between the native patterns and the white simply because they can be secure in neither quarter. Others consciously strive to dissociate themselves from things Indian, and regard themselves as white men even though this view is not fully shared by those with whom they would like to be identified. To complicate matters, there are some full bloods who tend to depart from the traditional attitudes, and there is a fair number of mixed bloods who are truculently reactionary. Since neither of them is accepted by the non-progressive full blood element they are likely to veer into other recalcitrant courses.

The truth is that the Yakima are a far from homogeneous group either culturally or biologically. They do not present a united front on any issue. While they must accept their definition as Indians on racial grounds (because they cannot avoid it often times), they do not regard themselves as all the same kind of Indian. The rift between the conservatives and the progressives is the most persistent cause of discord. Typically, this resolves itself into a difference in outlook on the part of full bloods and mixed breeds; and in the latter category we must take account not only of Indian and white admixtures but also of Indian-Mexican, Indian-Negro, Indian-Japanese, and Indian-Philippine crosses, of which there is a sufficient number to be significant. From the full blood's point of view these hybrids, and especially those of Oriental or Negroid parentage, are contemptible; they use the term half-breed as a reproach and readily assign to it the worst implications. [39]

Non-racial cleavages also tend to become aligned on the progressive issue in addition to weakening Indian solidarity on their own accounts. There are, for example, two native cults on the reservation which are incompatible with each other, and, in addition, they suffer a progressive-conservative split within themselves. Group differences are also manifest at times among the descendants of the fourteen original tribes assembled on the reservation in 1856, with a noticeable tendency on the part of the indigenous tribes to be more resistant to suggestions of change. More recently developed interests come into conflict, too. Those with timbered allotments or with valuable improved lands may find their best Interests opposed or disregarded by others less favorably endowed on questions of sale, redistribution, grazing privileges, and so on.

All of this means that there is no Indian community in a social or psychological sense. For a community is something more than a concentration of population or a cluster of dwellings. The term implies a unity of thought, a group-shared ideological basis for judgment and behavior. The Yakimas have no such common denominator in their thinking. Rather, there are several communities of thought overlapping and conflicting with each other and nullifying any urge for unified action. Officials who have attempted to organize clubs and cooperative enterprises among the Yakimas, report that it is most discouraging. The people are mutually suspicious, critical, and uncooperative among themselves. This situation has been the result, in part, of deliberate policy, not malicious to be sure, but as an administrative aid in "civilizing" the Indians.

Aboriginally the people now known as the Yakima lived in a number of villages scattered along the banks of the many large and small streams tributary [40] to the Columbia River over a much greater territory than is now reserved for them. The villages varied in size from one to fifty dwellings and contained populations ranging from the extremes of a few households to 1500 persons. An average village was composed of perhaps 150 to 200 people. The dwellings were of all sizes, too, some of them being as much as sixty feet long and designed to house as many as fifty or sixty individuals. (Plate IIa). Along some streams the line of habitations was almost unbroken, but there were nodes in the string, and conceptually each village was a separate political and social entity. Each had its chief and could act independently of the others, although normally the smallest groups acted in concert with larger adjacent villages, and in times of crisis many of them voluntarily united under one common forceful leader. In any event, the circumstances were favorable for maintaining group standards. Intimate daily contact between individuals within and without the village fortified the bonds of family and community, disseminated a common fund of knowledge, kept alive the group spirit, and increased the pressure of an omniscient public opinion.

With the establishment of the reservation these important epiphenomena of community life were seriously disturbed. The administrative ideal was to break up the aboriginal village clusters by settling their constituent families upon individually assigned portions of land. The immediate objective was to introduce farming and the sedentary life. At the same time it is clear that this move was just one aspect of a more comprehensive attempt to destroy the ideological core of Indian life. The aim was not phrased in these terms, and it may be that the framers and administrators of policy in those days did not always clearly see the issue. It is certain that they did not foresee the consequences of their success in estranging individuals from the aboriginal [41] community of thought and behavior. As a result of their efforts there has been a progressive narrowing of the dimensions of the latter, a lessening of the numbers of individuals participating in it, and a growing repudiation of its ideals. But, concomitantly, there has been a crumbling of its controls and sanctions until today there is no longer an Indian society. The unity in thinking and doing, which we call custom, and the conviction of its worth, which we call sanction, have been undermined. The social cement has been dissolved, and the disintegration of the old has not been accompanied by the hoped for reconstruction or assimilation into the white man's community. The result is an aggregation of unbonded individuals without consistent ideals or direction and beyond the reaches of any effective control, Indian or white. Today family ties are weak, except when they operate to the advantage of the claimant, there is a minimum of group feeling, except when it serves to advantage in demanding special privilege or as a shibboleth to condemn the white man; knowledge of what others are doing and thinking spreads only by uncertain and faulty means; and finally, and most importantly, public opinion, the master mechanism of social control, is ineffective since there is little unity of sentiment and no techniques for expressing that which does exist.

The ultimate has not yet been reached. The disintegration of group life has not proceeded as far among the Yakimas as it has among some other tribes, such as those west of the Cascade Mountains. For one thing, the Yakimas remained in isolation much longer. For another, they have practically all memorized their treaty stipulations and are quick to point out; the everlasting guarantees contained in it. Then, finally, the Yakimas were one of the groups in the Northwest who took stubborn refuge in the tenet of a native cult which adjures them not to abandon their native customs. [42]

This cult, known as the Dreamer or PomPom religion, is the keystone of most that remains of aboriginal life. Its roots go deep into the pre-Caucasian religious beliefs of all the Indians of the upper Columbia River region. Long before the white man appeared among them, they believed in the impending destruction of the world by some great catastrophe which would usher in a new era marked by the return of dead relatives and a recasting of Indian life. From time to time men had prophetic dreams of the arrival and nature of this event, or claimed to have died and returned to life with similar revelations and exhortations to prepare for its occurrence. There were therefore periodic revivals of intense interest in the subject, and when the first glimmerings of Christianity began to seep into this region some of its consonant elements were grafted on to the older stock. This hybrid religion flourished in the third decade of the last century. Then about 1850 there came into prominence a variant form, preached with fervor and aggressiveness by one Smohalla, an Indian who lived at Priest Rapids on the middle Columbia. His prophecies were typical of the others, but a new and sinister element was added by his insistence that the whites were to be destroyed by the hoped for cataclysm; and in order to hasten the new dispensation the Indians were to reject the way of life being imposed upon them by encroaching civilization. In a dramatic speech before a group of commissioners who sought to mollify him; Smohalla said: "You ask me to plow the ground. Shall I take a knife and tear my mother's bosom? Then when I die she will not take me to her bosom to rest. You ask me to dig for a stone. Shall I dig under her skin for her bones? Then when I die I cannot enter her body to be born again. You ask me to cut the grass and make hay and sell it, and be rich like white men, but how dare I cut off my mother's hair?"[1] [43]

The Yakimas were affected by this doctrine, and it did much to encourage the Nez Perce and Bannock Wars of 1877 and after. Today, the belief in a millennium has faded; but the resistance to white dictation remains. Dreamer adherents hold meetings regularly on Sundays through most of the winter, when the people are at home, in buildings called Long Houses by the whites. (Plate Ic). There are three such buildings, one each near the towns of Toppenish, White Swan, and Wapato. Their significance is greater than appears from a glance at their uninspiring unkempt exteriors. They are one of the few remaining concrete symbols of community life. Aboriginally any large house which would accommodate a crowd was used for both secular and religious meetings; there was no distinction of type or function. But today there are no house clusters corresponding to the village; there are no Indian towns or hamlets on the reservation. The people are widely scattered on their lands over an area which extends approximately forty miles in an east and west direction and twenty-five miles to the north and south. Their home sites are interspersed with the farms of white people in an indiscriminate fashion. They cannot meet and greet their friends in daily association. But a last vestige of the ancient villages is preserved in the isolated Long Houses, and around them is centered an attenuated survival of village life. In form they are survivals of aboriginal dwellings, modified replicas in lumber of the old all-purpose mat structures (See Plate IIa). They are spoken of as churches today by the Indians, and a religious sanction has certainly been the strongest force operating to perpetuate their existences. At the same time they are the focus of other activities exclusively Indian. In them and on the camp grounds about them are held feasts, games, councils, and all manner of holiday celebrations to suit the Indian taste. These functions provide for a periodic renewal of social contacts between like-minded individuals and give emotional satisfaction and [44] support to those who are pleased to retreat into the security of the past. They are sponsored by the conservative faction, and they consolidate such unanimity of opinion and outlook as still persists within it.

It must be remembered, however, that while this group is the best organized and most effective element on the reservation it cannot claim the whole-hearted support of even the majority of the Indians. Many of the older full bloods do not go near the Long Houses; and among the younger people and the mixed bloods a large proportion have no direct knowledge of what goes on there. Their contacts with each other are more irregular, more casual; without shared purpose or emotional content. For them there is no common cause, no rallying standard or credo.

The members of the Shaker Church, another nativistic cult might claim exception to this assertion. Theoretically, one of their tenets enjoins brotherly love toward all men but the history of the church affords an example of the extent to which petty feuds, jealousies, and bickerings can flourish without completely disrupting an organization.

---

[1] Mooney, James, The Ghost-Dance Religion and the Sioux Outbreak of 1890. Bureau of American Ethnology, 14th Annual Report, Part 2, Washington, 1896, page 721.

The founders of the cult were John Slocum, who lived near Olympia, Washington, and his wife Mary. In the fall of 1881 John fell into a trance which he and his friends interpreted as the experience of death. Upon his unexpected revival he announced to his terror-stricken mourners that his soul had been transported to the gates of heaven, there to be stopped and denied entrance by an angel who told him to return to earth, repent his wickedness before God, and admonish his friends to do likewise. The Christian virtues which he preached to the Indians during the next fourteen years of his natural life had been inculcated in him through his earlier association with Protestant and Catholic missionaries; but his followers maintained that they were special dispensations ordained by God for the [45] particular needs of the illiterate Indians who could not read the Bible. According to Slocum, God also promised the Indians a "new kind of medicine" to free them from the incubus of the medicine man. And so when, a year after John's vision, his wife was overcome with a violent trembling of her arms and neck and was alleged to have cured him of an illness, it was taken as a clear sign that her shaking was a manifestation of divine healing power. Furthermore, the blessing was non-restrictive; any person who humbled himself before God might receive the power to cure himself or others. The news spread fast and in a short time there were dozens of Shaker meetings with converts from far and wide. Soon the faith spread to surrounding reservations, with a strong accent upon shaking, and a minimum of doctrine. The Yakima learned about it in 1892. Its adherents are today definitely Indian; but their quasi-Christian preachments give them no common ground for cooperation either with other believers in Christ or with the supporters of the more nativistic PomPom religion.

    The policy of village dissolution has therefore had some profound effects. Segregation upon farms has not only eliminated the outward aspects of village life; it has also destroyed its spirit by contracting the sphere of community enterprise and participation. That which remains today is severely reactionary and unappealing to most of the Yakimas. And they have not been encouraged in, nor have they developed any devices for, the consolidation of a more progressive set of ideals. There are no Indian granges, for example, nor any purely Indian trading or commercial centers on the reservation. The makeshifts that have evolved for the dissemination of news and the exchange of opinion are poor substitutes for the frequency, the intimacy, and the variety of social contacts among village members. The congregations at the summer [46] berrying and fishing grounds, the chance meetings around the agency offices in Toppenish, and the casual contacts in the city parks, pool halls, and other loafing spots in town are not calculated to create a solid body of Indian opinion of any sort.

    The emphasis upon self-sufficiency which has accompanied the policy of establishing independent family units on farms has also affected community spirit. The Yakimas are today an aggregation of individuals with an extreme diversity of interests. There is nothing which is comprehensively Indian in their mode of thought or behavior; that is, nothing typically and exclusively Indian that characterizes them all. Their exclusion from the white community throws them into an arbitrary category; but the binding force is external. It constrains; it does not unify.

    The question of racial prejudice inevitably comes up in discussing this matter of an Indian community. There are white people in daily contact with the Yakimas who will stoutly affirm that they have no prejudices against them. There is no intention here to malign their sincerity. There may be a few individuals to whom this protestation is not merely a vindication of their "broad mindedness," and who are prepared without conscious hesitation to treat the Indian on a par with their white associates. Their number cannot be large or significant. Most whites consciously exclude Indians from the category of normal human beings: they are a special brand of men of uncertain status; but clearly not members of the local civic and social world. Many whites frankly admit this attitude when it does not jeopardize their economic welfare. Others - and among them may be found the "educated" and the "intellectuals" - are sincere in their claim to impartiality; but they are easily shaken in their complacency when the question of indiscriminate social intercourse is taken off the purely verbal level and actual behavior is at issue. [47]

In the final analysis it cannot be denied that racial prejudices do exist on and about the Yakima reservation, even among whites who do not hesitate to claim true Indian friends. That the antipathy is not so marked as it is toward Negroes in the south is not to the point. The Indian and the white man are separated by a chasm of cultural cleavages, and these, no less than color, are effective barriers to unrestricted intercourse between the two races. The white community and the Indian aggregate of persons called the Yakimas are worlds apart. Each is suspicious and likely to be resentful of the other. The occasions for overt conflict have been greatly reduced, and the Indian Is cowed by white pretensions of superiority; but this has not eradicated the profound sense of difference felt by members of both groups. Both have their justifiable grievances and we are not here concerned with an adjudication of them. The fact remains that the two worlds seldom fuse or mingle, and when they do it is to the pain of both. The most distressing instances are those of Indians who attempt to bridge the cultural gap by intermarriage with white men, or more rarely with white women. They well know by experience how wide and deep it is, and because they are often sensitive and thoughtful individuals, they find little happiness in their boldness. They and their hybrid offspring straddle two ways of life, and this is not easy. Some crack under the strain to become delinquents or troublemakers, or they build and retire into a world of their own making.

It avails little to protest that the Indian has his political freedom. He can vote. All Indians were enfranchised in 1924, and the Yakimas long before that. But they do not vote except in a few distinctly unusual cases, and the reason is simple. They are not interested in what the whites do, for they feel that they have no real part in such activities, political or otherwise. [48]

The present war situation brings this out clearly. Most Indians have radios and, surprisingly, they follow the war news. But not because they believe or feel that they are a part of the whole struggle. They definitely do not. Most of the older people are outspokenly resentful of the draft and talk cynically of Japanese attacks on the Yakima valley. They are prone to regard the whole affair with the detached air of a spectator. It is a good show, but they have no part in it, or should have none. They speak not of "us" or "our side"* but of the Japs, Germans, and the Americans.

Furthermore, there is no reason to believe that this feeling will be mollified by their sons participation In the war. In fact, it is more probable that upon the termination of the conflict when men return to the reservation – as they almost certainly will in considerable numbers – indifference, where it exists, will turn to bitterness and disillusionment on the part of both the young soldiers and defense workers and their parents. A sacrifice without a reward is a vanity, and few of these men feel that they have a stake in democracy to begin with. Later they are likely to feel that they have been used, and the more so when they find that the only return from the wars for them is a return to reservation life, a pattern into which they will fit even less than before. A few years of free association approximating social equality and acclaim as a hero ill prepares a man for a lifetime of social and economic discrimination.

Tribal Government and Political Control

Under aboriginal conditions the village was theoretically the politically autonomous unit. Each village had its own chief and its members acknowledged no higher authority or any more inclusive concept of the state. The [49] chief exercised considerable power; but it was delegated to him by the unanimous consent of all his adult followers. His office was hereditary within a given family line; but since a number of lineal and collateral relatives were eligible in the choice of a successor; the selection of one of them by unanimous approval was taken to be an enduring vote of confidence in his ability as a wise leader and judge. In matters affecting individuals he therefore made decisions more or less arbitrarily; but when the issue concerned the entire village all its members were called into consultation.

Temporary alliances between villages granting the same kind of leadership over all to the chief of one of them also occurred in times of crisis. This happened during the difficulties with the whites in the 1850s; and so it came about that there were only fourteen chiefs and fourteen tribes recognized in the treaty of 1855 between the United States and the so-called Yakima Nation. This treaty further provided that one of these men should be regarded as the head chief and as the official representative of all the Indians agreeing to take up residence on the reservation. Actually, the native governmental machinery remained undisturbed, and the head chief became merely a spokes-man and an intermediary between the white officials and the several distinct local groups. Members of the latter continued to meet separately with their respective chiefs to discuss proposals affecting group policy, and their several decisions were represented in a general meeting of all the Indians by their pledged leaders. The head chief merely ascertained the predetermined wishes of the assembled groups and presented them boldly to outsiders

By the terms of the treaty the head chief was to receive a stipend from the government until a certain number of years had passed. With the expiration of this period and the demise of one strong leader in 1905, this non-essential office gradually lost its importance and ceased to play a part [50] in the administrative complex. The fundamental elements of the old system continued to function, but from an official point of view, this arrangement was unsatisfactory since it yielded only factional opinions. The Office of Indian Affairs felt the necessity of insisting upon the organization of a governing body which would represent the interests of all the Yakimas, and this proposal was made to them by their superintendent in a general meeting in 1932. At their suggestion, it was decided that a tribal council of fourteen members should be founded. Each of the fourteen councillors was to be a descendant of one of the chiefs signing the treaty of 1855. No further organization or plan of procedure could be decided upon.

This is the official administrative body on the reservation today. Its ties with the past are evident. Its members are chosen from the traditional chiefly families by the descendants of the particular bands which were recognized in the treaty. One concession is made to the modem requirement that the councillors represent the whole of the Yakimas in that all the Indians have an opportunity to vote ratification of the selections made by the fourteen bands. In some instances other nominations have been made in the general meeting, but the force of tradition is strong and the same fourteen families have always managed to maintain their privilege of providing the candidates. Presumably the councillors are elected for life. At least no provision has been made for their retirement. In the past ten years the same fourteen men have composed the council with the exception of one who resigned because of ill health and four replacements on account of deaths. Upon several occasions there have been peevish threats of resignation over some issues taken personally, but as yet nothing has come of such grumblings.

Other linkages with the past vitiate the efficiency of the council and militate against the standardization of its rules of procedures. Furthermore, [51] its status and Its legislative powers are ambiguous. In most matters affecting the tribe the council members act in accordance with their own best judgments. But upon some issues they are unwilling to take the responsibility of making a decision. Upon these occasions they prefer to call a general meeting of all the Indians. But before this takes place the different bands meet with their respective councillors, as they used to do with their chiefs, to talk the proposal over and arrive at a decision in advance. Once this has been settled upon, they all attend the general meeting to vote en bloc; and no argument will persuade them to deviate from their pre-determined stand. The meeting takes place in one of the Long Houses and is usually well attended. As in times past, it is an attractive social event lasting most of the day or night with an intermission at an appropriate time for a feast. There are no well-established rules for procedure in the deliberations. The councillors take their places at a table in the center of the large room while the rest of the tribe seat themselves along its walls. A chairman pro tem is informally chosen from among the councillors. Another is asked to serve as secretary, or for important meetings the agency superintendent is asked to provide a stenographer. An interpreter is necessary, for the discussion is carried on in both English and Yakima. The meeting is prolonged on this account; and also because anyone may speak, and many do at length. Finally a vote is taken; and again the conservatism of the controlling element in Yakima tribal affairs is manifest: the secret ballot is not tolerated, and a person must stand to have his vote counted.

It is the policy of the present federal administration to encourage initiative among the Indians. To that end the Wheeler-Howard Act was passed by Congress in 1934, enabling any Indian tribe to become autonomous by a [52] majority vote of all its members. Its acceptance gave the tribe the right to petition for charters of incorporation fore economic development of its resources, to restrict the sale of its surplus lands, to extend the trust period on allotments, to acquire additional tribal land, to participate in various loan benefits, and to establish self-government by setting up a constitution and by-laws acceptable to the majority of its adult members. The Commissioner of Indian Affairs was extremely desirous of instituting this plan on every reservation, but the

Yakimas were vigorously opposed to it, and rejected it by a two to one vote. There were various reasons for this, but chief among them were the suspicions that the act was intended to supersede the treaty of 1855 and jeopardize the rights guaranteed therein; that it provided an opening wedge for the mixed bloods and others who had lost their property rights to regain a foothold, and that the secret balloting it stipulated would abet these evils. The furor caused by the Indian bureau's drive to put the measure across culminated in an almost fanatical opposition to any kind of formal tribal, organization. The very suggestion of a "constitution and by-laws" in a meeting today is enough to disrupt it.

The result is that the tribal council of fourteen men moves informally through traditional channels to effect its ends. The agency superintendent has labored over several years to get its members to bind themselves to some clear-cut rules of procedure, jurisdiction; and organization. They now have a permanent chairman and a secretary; they also have agreed that a quorum of eight must be present to transact business; that a show of hands must be called for in making decisions, and that the majority vote prevails. Much still remains to be accomplished from an official standpoint to make the council a smoothly functioning representative body. [53]

The council meets irregularly upon the call of the chairman. During the early summer of 1942 there was a meeting almost every week. Customarily the superintendent submits a memorandum of the items calling for attention and these are introduced by the chairman; but any member may bring up a question. Discussions are carried on almost exclusively in the native tongue. The council room is adjacent to the superintendent's office and when his advice or explanation is deemed necessary an interpreter is called; likewise for any other white official or informant. The meetings are open and anyone may attend to listen. They are not supervised by the agent. A few years ago the councillors felt that he must be present before they could proceed but he has disabused them of this idea on the theory that they must be put upon their own resources, work out their own problems, and "learn by their mistakes."

The division of authority between superintendent and council is not clearly defined. He does not exorcise a privilege of veto. Perhaps he does not have the explicit authority to do so. The question has not arisen for the council looks to him for guidance and its members are, if anything, over cautious and conservative. Its decisions are subject to the approval of the Secretary of the Interior if they involve the disposition of trust property, otherwise it appears to be free to legislate on all matters affecting the tribal welfare. During the summer of 1942, it considered one proposal to establish a conscientious objectors' camp on the reservation, and another to build a telephone line across it. It also settled upon the grazing fee to be charged white stockmen. The tribal fund of approximately $250,000.00 (obtained mostly from grazing leases) is controlled by the council, with congressional approval. About $50,000.00 of this is earmarked as a loan fund for industrial purposes. It has been suggested that the remainder be spent to buy back [54-5] reservation land now in the possession of white men or land now rendered practically useless through multiple ownership by a number of heirs. With that much decided the council is in doubt as to the next step; the repurchased land may be resold or, as has been proposed, leased for ninety-nine years to worthy Indians. The trouble is that the council is faced with an almost insoluble problem on the land question; at least the federal government has not been able to solve it.

A few years ago there was an attempt to oust the council. A young full blood of respectable family connections formed a protest organization called the Junior Tribal Council. It took its stand upon a platform calling for the formulation of a constitution and by-laws to regulate the processes of tribal government. The movement was short lived; those whose opinions it sought to consolidate were phlegmatic and uncooperative. Upon an appeal to the Indian Commissioner for recognition, the leaders were told that their party must be accepted by a majority vote of the Indians it hoped to represent before it could receive official sanction. At a general meeting, attended by the aroused conservative party en masse and by a scattering of others, the proposal was defeated by a vote of 175 to 25.

Social Control

The tribal council has in effect delegated its powers of social control [56] to a Court of Indian Offenses. Specifically this means that there is an Indian Judge, assisted by two Indian policemen, who has the authority to bring Indian offenders on the reservation to justice upon properly endorsed complaints and to pass judgment upon then in accordance with the tribal code of laws. This code is comprehensive and is designed to take care of all cases not provided for by the state and national governments. It is necessary because the state and municipal authorities do not have the power to make arrests for law infractions committed on trust property by Indians — in other words, local laws binding upon white citizens do not hold for Indians while on the reservation — and because the federal courts accept jurisdiction for only the major crimes of murder, manslaughter, rape, assault with intent to kill, assault with a dangerous weapon, incest, arson, burglary, and larceny. These state and federal provisions alone leave the entire range of misdemeanors and many lesser offenses against person and property on the reservation unregulated.

The framework for the organization of Indian courts was provided for by a circular pamphlet; entitled "Law and Order Regulations Approved by the Secretary of the Interior," issued in 1935. The regulations were intended to apply to all reservations where the aboriginal controls were no longer effective and to all Indian Courts of Offenses organized to substitute for the loss. The jurisdiction of the court was to extend to any Indian offender on the reservation and to cover the offenses stipulated. With respect to these offenses its jurisdiction was to be collateral and not exclusive of state and federal court jurisdictions; i.e., the Indian court was expected to deliver offenders to the other courts upon their request or consent. It was further provided that there should be one or more chief judges, at the discretion of the [57] tribal council, whose duties were to be regular and permanent and for which compensation was to be given. There might also be two or more associate judges to be called when occasion required and to be paid per diem. Judges were to be appointed by the Commissioner, subject to confirmation by a two-thirds vote of the council, and were to serve four years. The right to challenge a judge whose competency might be impaired by a personal interest in a case, the right of trial by jury or of appeal to the full court, and the right of habeas corpus and bail ware recognized. Records were to be kept and legal formalities adhered to by the use of formal written complaints, warrants; commitments and releases. No employee of the government was to interfere with or obstruct the court proceedings.

The law to be applied in the Indian court could be "any laws of the United States that may be applicable, any authorization of the Department of the Interior, or any ordinances or customs of the tribe not prohibited by federal laws." Further, "any matters not covered by applicable federal laws and regulations shall be decided by the Court of Indian Offenses according to the laws of the state in which the matter in dispute may lie."

Certain broad powers were to be left to the discretion of the Indian court. It was to be given authority to decide paternity cases; to give judgments directing the support of illegitimate children; to determine heirs and distribute property (by custom law if this be the rule; otherwise by state law) if suit is brought by a claimant, except in the case of land and other trust property; and to review and attest the validity of wills not involving trust property if requested to do so. It was to be given jurisdiction over juvenile cases, to be heard in private at the discretion of the judge, who might, in lieu of a sentence, assign the offender on probation to some responsible person or take any other such action as night be deemed advisable. In [58] addition to sentencing, the court might further require payment in restitution for an injury inflicted upon a plaintiff and attach the defendant's trust money for this purpose and for court costs. A convicted person might be required to work for the tribal benefit, or be incarcerated; or in lieu of this, pay a $2.00 per day fine for the period of the sentence. Maximum penalties for specific offenses were established; and in applying them the court was directed to exercise restraint, to take into account the past record, the criminal intent, the desire to make amends, and the resources and the needs of the dependants of the offender. Also, the court was to give serious consideration to the merits of probation for first offenders and of parole for violators who had served one-half their sentences in good behavior. Finally, the tribal council was to decide whether custom law or state law should regulate the marriage and divorce of Indians, and if the former, to lay down rules and empower the Indian court to act upon complaints of their violation. Likewise, rules and the means of their enforcement were to be settled upon with regard to the adoption of children.

The specific offenses to be charged by the Indian court officers and the maximum penalties in days of labor or fine or both to be assessed upon conviction for each was given as follows: Assault (five days), Assault and Battery (180 days), Carrying Concealed Weapons (thirty days), Abduction (180 days), Theft (180 days), Embezzlement (180 days), Fraud (180 days), Forgery (180 days), Misbranding Stock (180 days), Receiving Stolen Property (180 days), Extortion (thirty days), Disorderly Conduct (thirty days), Reckless Driving (fifteen days and deprivation of car for six months), Drunken Driving (ninety days), Malicious Mischief (180 days), Trespass ($5.00 and damages), Injury to Tribal Property (thirty days), Maintaining a Public Nuisance (five days and removal of nuisance), Liquor Possession, Sale, Trade, Manufacture, [59] or Transport (sixty days), Cruelty to Animals (thirty days), Tribal Game Law Violation (thirty days), Gambling (thirty days), Adultery (thirty days); Illicit Cohabitation (thirty days), Prostitution (thirty days), Giving Venereal Disease to Another (ninety days and compulsory treatment), Failure to Support Dependents (ninety days for benefit of dependents), Failure to Send Children to School (ten days), Contributing to the Delinquency of a Minor (180 days), Bribery (180 days), Perjury (180 days), False Arrest (180 days), Resisting Arrest: (thirty days), Refusing to Aid an Officer (ten days), Escape

(180 days), Disobedience to Court Order ($180.00 or ninety days), and Violation of an Approved Tribal Ordinance (sentence as provided).

The Yakima Court of Indian Offenses follows this plan with some simplifications and omissions. There is one judge, appointed for four years by the superintendent as the most suitable candidate of some two or three nominated by the tribal council. He is chosen for his rectitude and also for his knowledge of his people and their customs. He holds court once a week as a rule in the council room at the agency where he passes judgment upon offenders brought before him by one of the two Indian policemen. Witnesses may testify and be subpoenaed; but legal advocates are not permitted. The sessions are quite informal, but printed forms for complaints, etc, are used, the policeman acting as clerk. The agency has an arrangement with the municipal authorities in Toppenish by which the government assumes the obligation of meeting the expense of Indian prisoners in the city jail. Often they are required to work on the grounds of the reservation sanatorium. Some of the offenses listed above as requiring action by the tribal council before they can be considered offenses have not been given this status by the Yakima council. The killing of game out of season; and gambling, for example, are not illegal; and [60] so far as could be determined, no regulations regarding custom marriage and divorce (which is recognized) have been established. Offenses in Toppenish and at other points off trust property are outside the jurisdiction of this court. So are the major crimes, which are reviewed by the US Commissioner in Yakima for indictments before a grand jury and trial in federal courts.

With this battery of legal machinery and its technical coverage of a wide area of anti-social behavior the formal means are at hand to ensure peace and security to the community. Unfortunately, these legal instruments do not answer the need. No problem is more harassing, more expensive, or seemingly more insolvable than the one of law and order among Indians on and off the reservation. No problem is more consistently ignored, precisely because it is so difficult and deep-seated and impossible to cope with effectively. This discouraging impasse is expectable when we realize that Its real cause is the almost total disorganization of Yakima society for what we call an illegal act is simply the manifestation of an anti-social attitude, and with the deterioration of social restraints the frequency of offenses against the rights and persons of others is certain to increase. In a self-sustaining society we have a right to assume that the majority of its constituent members are law abiding; if not, the society would soon dissolve and become extinct, or new patterns of control would be initiated to meet the demands of group living. But when there is no real society, as with the Yakima, yet an aggregation of individuals are nonetheless huddled together within an artificial boundary, as with the Yakima, there is no reason to assume that most individuals will conform to arbitrary social patterns — and they do not.

This is not to say that a large proportion of the Yakimas are criminals. Most of the cases which come before the Indian and the local courts are not [61] directly anti-social at all; the offender has done no harm to anyone but himself by his act, although behind his behavior may lie a record of utter disregard for the welfare of others. The situation was well summed up in a report upon law and order on the reservations in seven northwestern states in 1929: "Indian offenses are of a minor nature. Professional crime is exceptional. Homicide and other crimes of violence are usually associated with drunkenness. In the great majority of instances, the offenses of Indians are special cases of what are commonly called vices, that is, acts of low moral tone that only under certain circumstances come into conflict with the law and become recognized crimes. The last part of this statement is significant.[2] It implies, and it is a fact, the offenses which come before the courts and which can therefore be officially tallied are few as compared with the actual number which take place. They are not so important in themselves, but they are symptomatic of social strains and disruptive ferments. This is, of course, true of any people, but it is especially true of the Yakimas. In the study just cited it was found that of all the tribes visited by the investigating committee the Yakimas ranked second highest in the number of enrolled members with court records. Nine Yakimas out of every hundred during the year 1929 had been arrested for some wrongdoing.[3] Whether one considers this ratio high or not, it must be placed in conjunction with the fact that it does not adequately indicate the number of infractions of the rules of behavior presumably laid [62] down by the code of offenses previously summarized. Again, this statement does not refer to crimes of violence; it does hold for negligence and irresponsible behavior leading to the loss of peace and security of others. Field agents and others who know the Indian well have come to take adultery, illicit cohabitation, non-support, drunkenness, and disorderly conduct as a matter of course. These sub-standard situations are the regular thing, not the lapses of a few malefactors.

By far the greater number of infractions of the code coming to official notice are grounded in drunkenness. It is difficult to get statistics on the occurrence of simple over-indulgence, or on the possession or conveyance of liquor, for these acts are frequently connected with other offenses which take precedence in the charge because of their gravity. The drunkenness which gets into court results from its flagrant appearance on the highway or city streets, or as the aggravating cause for assault, sex crimes, or other serious offenses. These are the important facts from the standpoint of law enforcement; but for the social analyst the plain fact of inordinate and widespread drinking is more significant. Although the evidence is not conclusive, it appears that most drinking takes place in town, or if on the reservation, at social gatherings. The records at the police station show a far higher proportion of drinking cases than do those of the Indian court – which may, of course, be given more than one interpretation. During the three months of June, July, and August of 1942 there were 170 Indian arrests made by the Toppenish police. Of these about three-fourths or 120 cases, were for drunkenness; an average of forty a month, or well over one per day. In the 1942 annual statistical report upon the activities of the Indian Court of Offenses for the year 1941 only twenty-nine cases of drunkenness leading to arrests for disorderly conduct are listed out of a [63] total of 121 arrests made by Indian policeman on trust property. Four assault cases and one of reckless driving brings the score up to thirty-four. Part of

---

[2] Survey of Conditions of the Indians in the United States. In hearings before a Subcommittee of the Committee on Indian Affairs of the United States Senate, 72nd Congress. S. Res. 79 and 308 (70th Congress) and S. Res. 263 and 416 (71st Congress). Part 26. Washington, D.C. 1932, p. 14148.

[3] Ibid. p. 14147. First on the list were the Klamaths of Oregon, with thirteen out of every hundred.

the explanation for the different ratios in the two courts is that liquor is obtained in town and drunk there immediately, partly because a drinking Indian in town has to be an the streets if he is anywhere, and partly because drunkenness on the reservation is seldom reported unless it leads to the extreme discomfiture and annoyance of others.

The last mentioned factor is operative not only on the reservation. While Indians display a great reluctance to file formal complaints, city end state police are inclined to ignore Indian drinking and brawling so long as whites are not annoyed by its excesses or shocked at its more serious consequences. This, in fact, is the complaint of agency officials. They feel that they do not get sufficient cooperation from local authorities in enforcing liquor sale restrictions. They point to conditions a few years ago when several unscrupulous proprietors with off-premise sales permits were allegedly freely selling beer and wine to the Indians. The matter was eventually taken up with the State Liquor Control Board and these licenses were revoked. That, however, was only a minor leakage. At present Indians still have no difficulty getting whiskey, rubbing alcohol and other noxious compounds at exorbitant prices whenever they please. Police authorities do not deny this. In a frank discussion they would probably admit also that bootleggers are neither diligently sought nor vigorously prosecuted. They do reiterate that liquor traffic with the Indians is exceedingly difficult to control. And it is.

The situation is not very different from the one which faced the federal authorities during national prohibition. Arbitrary denial stimulates desire. Individuals without sympathy for the law pit their wits in a game with [64] the enforcement officers. It Is a game because the loser has nothing to lose, nothing of the real values of honor, self-respect, or prestige. The odds are all with the drinker, who has no respect for the law and who feels vindicated by his ability to circumvent it. The federal field agent appearing now and then upon the scene cannot cope with even the variety of petty bootleggers, to say nothing of the fly-by-night vagrants whom the Indians have learned to utilize as go-betweens. The game of hide and seek is not worth it.

The problem goes far deeper than mere detection and punishment. It is well appreciated by those who have to deal with these cases that jail is no deterrent to the Indian. It holds no horrors for him and incarceration does not stigmatize him. Spending a night in jail is no disgrace, and sometimes the accommodations there are more pleasant than at home, or what passes for it. The Toppenish city jail is, in fact, a minor social center for many Indians. Friends, relatives, and sweethearts drop in there while in town to pay a visit to some temporary inmate; and when they wish to find someone who has not been home for several days most Indians think at once of the likelihood of his being found, without embarrassment, in jail. There might be a twinge of remorse, but no shame.

There can be no doubt that the Indian drinks to get drunk, and this as quickly as possible. For this reason he prefers strong spirits to either wine or beer. A contributing cause is the fact that he knows that he must drink what he buys at once in order to get his money's worth and avoid arrest for possession. In other words, a slightly intoxicated Indian with a bottle of whiskey is vulnerable on two counts; drunken, he disposes of at least one of these in what he has come to regard as a normal form of recreation.

In the annual statistical report of the Indian court eighty-one cases out of the 121 were cited for disorderly conduct. This number is over and [65] above the thirty-four for which there was a special notation of drunkenness, and so presumably they did not involve drinking. This, however, is not certain, and since the citation is not further broken down we do not know what to make of it. Apart from this ambiguous category the second most common offense, as revealed by this record, is simple assault; i.e. physical violence or threat of violence to the person of another, but not of an aggravated nature and without the intent to kill or maim with a weapon. Of these there were four only (compounded with drunkenness), a very small percentage of the total. Likewise few in number were the offenses against property, there being only three cases of theft. It is significant that the more sophisticated crimes in this category such as fraud, embezzlement, forgery, and extortion do not appear. Yakima Indians have been convicted of one or another of these offenses in the past, but very rarely. When they have been they were bound over to the state courts. It seems that the normal procedure in these instances is for the Indian court to relinquish jurisdiction even when the violation occurs on the reservation. That, at any rate, is the disposition of the present judge who expresses some reluctance to deal with such cases.

The graver crimes against the person likewise do not commonly appear on the docket of the Indian court. In 1940 one case of attempted rape upon a minor was disposed of. Murder is customarily handled entirely by the county and federal authorities, although Indian policemen work in close cooperation with them. In the summer of 1942 one Indian was murdered by a drunken Mexican, another was severely stabbed by a Mexican, and another found dead under mysterious circumstances in the hills. To what extent the attacks were aggravated remained to be determined. A more uncommon case developed when five Indians on a drinking party with a white man viciously stabbed him to death. According [66] to the news release; prosecution of the case was handled by federal officers "because the Indians involved are federal wards and because the crime occurred on a federal Indian reservation." The dual basis for deciding jurisdiction is a matter to be returned to later.

The most conspicuous omissions in the Indian court records are those cases resulting from sex and domestic complications. In a court of this character, which specializes in minor offenses and which is more intimately acquainted with the violators, their outlook, and their backgrounds, and with presumably a greater concern for their welfare, one would expect to find a reflection of social conditions on the reservation. This does not seem to be the case. It needs no more than a short acquaintance with Indian family relations to corroborate the testimony of resident officials that adultery, illicit cohabitation, technical bigamy, non-support, and the transference of venereal disease are so common among the Indians as to cause no comment or embarrassment among them. The investigator must be prepared to find a bizarre variety of these technical violations in any extended family history. No count has ever been made of even those in process at the present time, and the task of doing so and of bringing violators into court would cool the reformist ardor of almost anyone. In a short time one domestic irregularity will engender another and another until such a complicated and ramifying set of relations is developed that their disentanglement would frequently create as many problems as it would solve.

A glance at the regulations approved by the Secretary of the Interior relative to the Indian court's jurisdiction (p. 58) will reveal that there is no lack of formally granted authority to prosecute these cases. Yet none of the sex (except one of attempted rape) or domestic relations offenses listed [67] in that authorization have appeared in the statistical summaries of the past two years. Two of the 1941 cases of assault were, however, charged against men for beating their common-law wives. It may be that an analysis of the individual instances of disorderly conduct (eighty-one last year) would disclose the practice of using this charge for an euphemistic or catch-all coverage of domestic cases, but there is no suggestion of this in the records. The simplest explanation, and the one which seems to hold, is that these offenses are not brought before the court in any significant numbers.

It is interesting to note that some domestic complaints are brought so the Superintendent for action. He has adjusted several non-support complaints by securing verbal agreements that a stipulated sum be deducted from the erring father's trust money for the support of his child, has advised on family disputes, and made arrangements through informal verbal agreements for the placement of neglected or unwanted children. On the whole, however, except when there is an economic pinch impelling a wronged individual, few Indians want the interference of any outside authority in their family difficulties. Either they do not care, or they resent impartial dictation. They prefer to find their own solution, which normally is to do nothing. There is no dearth of querulous complaining and recriminations. A detached acquaintance with the moral code prompts many an avowal to "do something about" an offense within the family, but these righteous protestations seldom eventuate in action. Most Indians are like their ex-policeman whose niece was abandoned by her half-breed husband for her sister three years ago without the formalities of a divorce or a remarriage. The uncle has appealed to and he "had a good idea" to bring the deserter and technical bigamist into court, but while this idea has been maturing the second niece has had two children by her erstwhile brother-in-law. [68]

In conformance with the recommendation contained in the approved framework for the operation of the Indian court, considerable leniency is shown in the punishment of offenders. The right of probation and parole is frequently exercised. The suspended sentence with a written pledge of good behavior is common, too. A brief analysis of the court's disposition of the cases appearing before it may be of interest; and since the variation from year to year is not great, the 1941 annual report may serve as a sample. A total of 114 cases are on record. Of these there were six arrests and convictions for assault. One sentence was suspended. The terms in jail imposed upon the others were five, twenty-two, one, eight, and ninety days, with two placed upon probation. Two cases of reckless driving (while drunk) brought jail sentences of eighteen days and three days, and a probation period for one of the offenders. Two jail breakers were sentenced to thirty-one days each. A case of theft was placed on probation. For one liquor law violator there was a sentence of twenty-eight days. The aforementioned case of attempted rape brought a thirty-four day term of imprisonment. All the remaining offenses come under the caption of disorderly conduct, most of which involved drinking. Out of eighty-eight arrests in this category, there were twelve dismissals; and twenty-four of those convicted ware placed on probation after signing a pledge. The jail sentences ranged between one and twenty-file days each with the mode at the lower end of the distribution; twenty-five individuals served only one day in jail, twenty each served terms of eight and nine days. There were no fines imposed upon any of the violators for this year.

One aspect of court leniency goes beyond technical bounds, but there seems to be a tacit understanding that necessity justifies it. The reference is to the conditions for probation. Theoretically, only a first offender may [69] be accorded the leniency of a suspended sentence on a pledge of good behavior, if we are to access the literal meaning of the conditions for agreement which read, "and not having been sentenced by this court for any offense, etc." There are several offenders, nonetheless, who have signed more than one such statement before the Indian court, although it may be not before the same judge.

An analysis of the social characteristics of offenders appearing before the courts is revealing. There can be no doubt from the records that the women are more law abiding than the men. Of the 170 arrests made by the Toppenish police during the summer of 1942 only about fifty were of women. Even this proportion is high if we may judge from the records of the Indian court. In them but one person in ten is a woman. We must remember, however, that the records fail to report upon the large number of sex and domestic entanglements; and in these affairs women are often of necessity co-partners in crime with the men. As with the males, the most frequent offenses among females is drunkenness and brawling. Occasionally these bouts develop into more serious breaches, as in the recent murder of a white man in Toppenish. A young woman was in the thick of the stabbing melee which resulted in his death.

An age differential among the offenders is manifest also. Very few, only about six males out of every hundred, are minors. The proportion is about twice as high for under-age females. On the other hand, a full forty per cent of all offenses are by persons in their twenties. The proportions decrease sharply thereafter with an advance in age so that a bare fifteen per cent are in their forties. These figures bear out the impression that the older Indians, as might be expected, are more settled and stable. It is from them that the familiar jeremiads upon the decadence of the modem world comes. There is evidence to show, however, that the correlation is not with the times [70] so much as it is with youth for these same righteous elders unwittingly disclose a none too restrained youth in the accounts of their own personal histories.

It is interesting to note the correlation between the degree of blood and the incidence of transgression. From townspeople and others who live and work in the midst of the Indians one hears diverse opinions contrasting the moral soundness of the mixed breeds and the full bloods. Perhaps the majority will agree with the dictum that the full bloods are more honest, reserved, and law abiding than the mixed bloods. Most merchants certainly prefer to do business with the former. There is some real basis for this view, for it seems that it is the mixed blood who most often gets himself involved in the more spectacular offences, the crimes against person, and property. He is therefore most often forced into public attention by way of the regularly constituted courts. He is likely to be more venturesome, aggressive, and conceited than a full blood; and he projects himself into situations involving the whites with greater frequency. At the same time, the full blood is often morally just as culpable, but in an unobtrusive manner; that is, in ways which do not directly concern the white man. If all of his sex delinquencies and domestic irregularities were taken into account the scales might be tipped. The full bloods tend to take the same view as the whites, and for similar reasons, and yet the very full bloods who shower anathemas upon the half-breed are likely to be fully as guilty of offenses against law and propriety. There is a possibility that the preponderance of mixed blood offenders may be the result of an age factor after all, for there are more full bloods of advanced age than mixed breeds; and, as we have seen, youth is more prone to transgress than old age. [71]

The Yakimas, like other Indians in Washington and Oregon, are inveterate visitors. In addition to their seasonal movements for fishing, hunting, and gathering, there is an almost continuous flux of various segments of the population throughout the year to fairs, rodeos, religious meetings, and family reunions. These excursions are more or less controlled in that they are timed, involve family or friendship units, and presuppose a home base. Apart from this, there is another pattern, also surviving from aboriginal times, of unmitigated vagrancy and camp-following. In the old days there were young men who had no hoses, or abandoned those they had, and gave themselves up to a life of itinerant sponging, gambling, or trading. Nothing has developed to curtail this urge at the present time. It is, in fact, encouraged by the automobile; and with the aboriginal social controls in abeyance these vagrants are conspicuous figures in the offending element. Like the criminals in our urban centers, their anonymity shields them from detection; and like the delegates to our brotherhood conventions, their status as out-of-towners exhilarates them to a measure of unconventional behavior which the social pressure at home would not allow. A retired Indian policeman pointed this out by saying that the Pendleton (Umatilla) and the Warm Springs Indians were the worst with which he had to deal. Not uncommonly a young man will run away from one of these reservations with a girl, live with her for a time among the Yakimas, and then abandon her to live with some local woman who is, as likely as not, already married. It is estimated that one-fourth of all offenders are of this transient class. Some are known to be enrolled on other reservations; but about many no definite information is available. Some of them are doubtless true vagrants with no place to call home.

An equally unmanageable element, overlapping the other categories discussed, is composed of the chronic offenders. During the calendar year of [72] 1940 there were 114 complaints on the docket of the Indian Court of Offenses. They were charged against 94 persons, making an average of 1.22 times in court per offender. To put it in what is perhaps a more socially significant way, seventeen of the offenders, or eighteen per cent of the 94, were repeaters. Fifteen of them made two appearances before the court in twelve months, one was apprehended three times, and one for a fifth time. This record, it should be recalled, is of the Indian court alone. As might be expected, upon inquiry at the Toppenish police station, it was found that the same names appeared again and again on the day book there, and others too. The police chief regards ten or twelve individuals as "steady customers." The worst of these were jailed for drunkenness and disorderly conduct five or six times during a three month period in the summer of 1942.

The record of the five-time offender on the Indian court files shows that he was arrested, with his son, on January 13, 1940 for drunkenness and creating a disturbance in the home of another Indian; and for this he served five days in jail with the balance of his sentence suspended. On March 18th he was arrested on the same charge and served eight days of a ten day sentence. On July 13th, a complaint at Celilo Falls led to his conviction on a charge of maintaining a public nuisance, for which he was sentenced to thirty days in jail. This was suspended upon his signing a pledge of good behavior for one year and a promise not to return to Celilo Falls during the summer. On August 23rd he was arrested for violating his pledge and was committed to jail to work out his sentence. Finally, on September 16th, he was again sentenced to thirty days in jail for disorderly conduct and served twenty five days.

Although this man's record is one of the worst, his son may in time equal it. He too is a repeater in both Indian and municipal courts, having in three years been twice convicted of assault and battery upon his common law wife, three years been twice convicted of drunkenness — twice in violation of pledges — [73] and finally fined $250.00 and deprived of his driving license for running down a pedestrian while intoxicated.

It would be repetitious to give further concrete data upon the careers of petty offenders and the nature of their offenses. It would be instructive to have some reliable information upon the incidence of offenses in particular families. The same family names appear with just about the same frequency in the court files as do the names of specific individuals, indicating that about twenty per cent of the families have been drawn into court by more than one of their number. Still, this gives us no idea of the proportions of consistently law abiding and law breaking families. A study of the problem from this angle would be worthwhile, but it would require a more intensive investigation of family relationships and a more careful review of individual offenses over a number of years than time would allow for the present report. The most that can be offered is an impression to the effect that among the Yakimas there are a few families who can be expected to be entangled with the law in one way or another year in and year out, a majority with disruptive potentialities manifesting themselves in indiscriminate outbreaks, and a few who never come into conflict with the forces of law and order. The plotting of this proportion on a graph would yield a "bell" distribution curve; and, if it is faithful to the facts, it signifies a departure from the theoretically normal state of a society wherein the majority of individuals fall within the no-conflict range.

The problem of the neglected, delinquent, or pre-delinquent child forces itself upon the attention of anyone studying social control. Since we have come to realize that most human behavior is conditioned behavior, not innate, and that an individual can be conditioned to contra-social attitudes even more easily than to the restraints of a social existence, it has become [74] increasingly evident that the early life of a child is all-important in pre-determining his career. All too often the family conditions into which a Yakima child is born are of such a nature as to give him no conception of restraint in moral standards. He grows up in an atmosphere of disorganized family relations; and, knowing only the rule of acting on impulse from infancy, he can hardly be expected to formulate and aspire to ideals of conduct which are alien to his parents. Even though his immediate family might be above the average in setting an example of regulated behavior, his contacts outside it are not calculated to fortify his home training. The result is a conspicuous number of wayward adolescents from whom nothing can be expected in their adult lives but a continuation of their sub-social, hedonistic failure to submit to any group restraints on conduct.

One need not be selective to find instances of uncontrolled and uncontrollable adolescents and pre-adolescents. Commonly their delinquencies include or eventuate in irregular sex relations. Within one of the small towns on the reservation in 1942 the background and consequences of delinquency were epitomized in one household: The house was owned by Mrs. X, a widow of sorts who had had two or three husbands or paramours in the course of her life. From these connections as well as from her own family, she had inherited enough property in land to provide her with a good income. During the few years previous she had supported and entertained several temporary mates who appeared and disappeared with a minimum of formality. With her lived her daughter and the man with whom the daughter cohabited. This pair had one illegitimate child; and the woman had a child ten years of age by her husband from whom she separated a few years ago. With Mrs. X also lived her seventeen year old son and his companion who was about the same age as himself. These two boys had recently brought two fourteen year old girls, E.K. and H.L. into the household [75] to live with them. This did not seem proper to Mrs. X so she complained to the field nurse, saying that the two girls should not be allowed to behave in this fashion. The irony of her protest did not appear to strike her, nor did the lack of control over her son appear to touch her personally. She had remonstrated with the boys and the girls, but none of them paid any attention to her. Her protest to the field nurse was with the hope that the nurse could take the matter up with the superintendent. When it was suggested that she herself make a complaint she replied that she did not like to talk about such matters to men.

The histories of the two girls, K.K. and M.L. are illuminating. Although they had barely turned fourteen they were already hardened by circumstances and given to self-indulgence. M.L. was the daughter of an alcoholic, a regular at the Toppenish city jail. Her mother died in childbirth, leaving M.L. and one older and one younger brother. The father turned the three children over to their grandmother and went to live with another woman, who had several children of her own. A couple of illegitimate children since then has increased his family beyond the limits of either his desire or ability to take care of it. The older brother of M.L. was much like his father. He drank to excess and was beyond the control of his grandmother, yet she supported him. The same was true of ML. Her grandmother was indulgent and provided her with money, but the girl stayed with her only when she felt like it; at other times she might be living with anyone. The year previous she had been before the juvenile court and it was decided to send her to Chemawa, the Indian boarding school near Salem, Oregon. She stayed six weeks, complained of the restrictions to her grandmother, and upon the request: of the latter was released against the advice of the authorities. She was supposed to be on parole when she took up residence in the house of Mrs X. [76] Her companion, E.K., had a similar history. Her mother died at her birth and her father practically abandoned her to his mother. He worked on a ranch off the reservation and seldom saw his daughter. He complained to the field nurse that E.K. was a "bad girl," and requested that she be sent to Chemawa, but he did not take sufficient interest in her problem either to provide her with a good *home* or to secure concrete evidence and make a formal complaint about her as he was repeatedly advised to do. E.K. received about $15.00 per month from her mother's property; and since she found it agreeable to take board and lodging with anyone who would have her, the money went for clothes and pleasure.

To round out the picture, it might be added that a third fourteen year old girl, A.R., had been reared in the same social climate and was a close associate of E.K., and M.L. She *too* lived with her mother's parents, but not because she was an orphan. Her father was dead, but her mother had given her up because "she wouldn't mind," and had gone to live, unmarried, with another man. The grandparents of the girl had no control over her. At the time these observations were made she was reported to be somewhere on the coast, ostensibly picking berries, and living with an older man. Her grandparents did not know where she was.

Cases of this kind are not infrequent. Few of them ever reach the Indian court, although the judge is technically empowered to deal with them. In 1940 only five cases of disorderly conduct by minors were disposed of by him; in 1941 there were two. His routine procedure is to parole a youth to a parent or some other allegedly responsible person on a year's probation. For violation of pledges delinquents in the past have been sent to a reservation CCC camp or to Seattle for resident training in defense work under an N.Y.A program. Another recourse in the case of incorrigibles has been to send then, to [77] Chemawa, a facile but not a recommended solution, for this is not a corrective institution and the presence of problem cases complicates its primary task of teaching Indian youths.

If the Indian judge does not feel competent to deal with a delinquency case he may, as with other offenses, bind it ever to a qualified court, in this instance to the juvenile court in Yakima. Also, if the arrest of a delinquent takes place off the reservation, this court acts in cooperation with the agency superintendent and educational director to dispose of the case. Some under-age offenders are paroled to the agency superintendent or to the Superintendent at Chemawa through this channel. For those who require more immediate supervision and more stringent control the state assumes the responsibility of institutionalizing them at the regular reformatories for white delinquents at Chehalis (for boys) and at Grand Mound (for girls). One recent case will serve to exemplify a common situation.

A fifteen year old girl, P.D., was apprehended on the streets of Yakima and brought before the juvenile court on a charge of drunkenness. She was sent to Chemawa where only the superintendent knew of her record, in accordance with the rule that is followed in such a procedure. She did well in school, and at the end of the school year she was paroled to the agency superintendent for the summer. She was supposed to be staying *at* home with her parents, but there was in reality no place for her. Both of her parents led irregular lives aid were seldom home. The father was an ex-convict and he'd spent much of his time in local jails. He was given to drink and to philandering and did not support his wife and four children. The mother, at one time in the past, decided it was easier to emulate him than to reform him and forthwith abandoned her children to live with another man. She finally tried to re-establish her family, but at the time of the return of P.D. from Chemawa [78] the household continued to be in a disrupted state. The Grand Mound parole officer could not locate the girl or any member of the family over the summer; and, although it was known that she was living with some man not her husband, nothing could be done; or was done, about it. It was not surprising, then, when her younger sister followed her over almost precisely the same course a short time later.

It seems a fair conclusion that the legal mechanisms operating to reduce and control the offenses committed by Indians are not as successful as could be hoped for. There are several reasons why this is so. Insofar as the Indian court is concerned, one of them must be regarded as personal. A frank appraisal of the men chosen to be judges compels the admission that they are often lacking in the insight, the breadth of vision, the commanding presence, and the dignity which we have come to associate with the person of an arbiter of human conflicts. Respect for the law m*eans* in great part respect for its administrators and interpreters. One gets the impression that m*ost* Indians do not respect their judges. Their reasons are various, but in the main they hinge upon the intellectual incapacities and the moral frailties of the men who, above all, should be exemplars of wisdom and ethical conduct. There can be no doubt, as the concrete evidence shows, that some Indian judges are often not above reproach in their private lives, and that they are lacking in a forthright conviction of the laws which they are presumed to be capable of administering. An impartial observer cannot fail to notice these shortcomings, regardless of his sympathies.

Even though the judge were a model of rectitude there would still remain difficulties in the way of the successful prosecution of his duties a*s we* see them. The question arises: Is not too much expected of him? He is chosen in part because of his knowledge and sympathy with Indian custom, and [79] yet the premises upon which are founded the code of laws that he administers have been evolved by whites. Can we expect a man to look both ways at once?

In other courts the attitudes of some white judges is not conducive to the impartial dispensation of justice. Many persons feel that it is both unjust and a waste of time to try to enforce our code upon the Indian: rigorous prosecution of all *cases* would only jam the courts and bewilder the offenders. Others manifest downright indifference to Indian offenses unless they infringe upon the sentiment of the white community. There is a suspicion; too, that *some* courts do not want to lower the plane of their jurisdiction to that of a domestic relations court by accepting the great number of petty cases preponderating among Indian offenders. The attitudes of some of these men flow from intelligent considerations of the Indian problem. They see the futility of punishing men and women who are not responsible for the conditions which have inured them to a life of law breaking. They regard the underlying problems of social reconstruction of more significance than the legal battle with their consequences. Not a few of these persons take the view that it would be unfair to expect more of the Indian than of the white people among whom they live, and a point is made of the scandalous behavior of many of the low class whites on the reservation.

One also hears the opinion expressed that the Indian is a federal ward, taxes are being paid to maintain an expressive "machine" to minister to him, so "let the government take care of it." Fortunately this sentiment is not widespread. The *state* and local authorities in Washington cooperate with the federal agents in an exemplary manner, but some prosecutors cannot avoid the feeling that their efforts are unavailing as long as the root conditions are under federal control, and as long as there remains some question of jurisdiction in specific cases. [80]

The matter of divided jurisdiction is especially irksome, and many issues arising from the Indian's unique position *as* a federal charge residing within the boundaries of a state have not been settled. Two variables complicate the problem: the status of the Indian as ward or freeholder and the status of the land as trust or patent in fee. In some instances there is a settled policy. Federal authority attaches *if* an Indian commits any of the major crimes already mentioned against the person or property of another Indian or any other individual if the act takes place "within the limits of an*y* Indian reservation." It is accepted also that the last phrase exempts the areas of state highways, railroad rights of way, and alienated lands, even though these are within the reservation boundaries, and that the state has jurisdiction over crimes committed in those spots even though the offender be a ward of the government; likewise of the crime is committed outside the reservation boundaries. Also, if an Indian has received a patent in fee for his land fee is subject to the civil and criminal laws of the state like anyone else; but if he has not, an offense by him on the reservation is not subject to the jurisdiction of the state unless the Indian court delegates its authority to act in such cases. A further acceptable interpretation seems to be that if the offender is a non-Indian, the injured party an Indian, and the offence committed on a reservation, then federal jurisdiction attaches. Some doubt exists, however, about jurisdiction when an unallotted Indian separates himself from the tribe for a time "to adopt the habits of civilized life," but later returns and commits a crime. In doubt too is the status of an Indian who has been issued a patent in fee for part of his lands, yet continues to hold an interest in trust property, perhaps inherited. The problem of the status of the children of parents granted patents in fee is also unsolved. [81] Even when state jurisdiction is acknowledged it is sometimes ineffectual, as in domestic cases w*hen* decrees of divorce may be granted but decisions relative to alimony or child custody cannot be enforced; or when county aid must be given a mother and child, but the father and husband cannot be prosecuted for desertion. These ambiguities are discouraging to prosecutors and entail the further evil of tending to heighten the feeling of most Indians that they are members of a specially exempted class.

There are still other difficulties to harass and dull the enthusiasm of prosecutors. These have to do with attitudes that are characteristic of the Indians. The Yakimas are reluctant to inform on each other, even in cases where there are no particular ties of blood or companionship uniting them. This *extends* even to Indian policemen. Part of this attitude may stem from a surviving fear of witchcraft; as some affirm; but more of it can be attributed to the bonding action of a spontaneous shrinking from the white man's little understood devices. Most Indians avoid formal proceedings and they are averse to the making of formal complaints. In some cases they no doubt feel that it would do no good anyway; in others, they would much rather simply talk it over with the superintendent. The atmosphere of the court room is strange and repelling, and it is not difficult for a *clever* attorney to confuse an Indian witness and cast doubt upon his testimony. Furthermore, Indians seldom display a sustained zeal in pressing a case, and the delay which characterizes our court actions can easily discourage their active support of the efforts of their legal representatives. Add to this the misunderstanding inherent in dealing with witnesses through interpreters and we are likely to conclude with some attorneys that the truth in Indian cases cannot be obtained by our routine legal procedures. [82]

Underlying all the failures at social control is the basic and unavoidable fact that typically the Indian recognizes no law, Indian or white, as his law. The aboriginal patterns of behavior and the sanctions for their control have crumbled bit by bit under the pressure to conform to the white man's standards. Some <u>individuals</u> have accepted the change; some have remained adamant; most have become vacillating and selective, making their choices from either code or accepting neither when and where it gives them the greatest personal pleasure or advantage. The consequences have been disunity and an almost complete lapse of public opinion, the absolute prerequisite for the successful functioning of any system of law and order. The harsh prosecution of a system of law may instill a fear of them, but it will not of itself bring respect for them. This requires approval by a process of spontaneous inner development.

Family Life

The integration of community life and the definition of group standards that go with it take shape within the social microcosm of the family. This is the ultimate social unit, and the abandonment of controls begins and climaxes its extensive effects here. We can appreciate this when *we* reflect upon the role of the family in perpetuating the cultural traditions of a society, especially one wherein the only means of conveying these traditions is by word of mouth. Under these conditions the only linkages between the generations are the verbal teachings, the admonitions, and the exemplary behaviors of the adult culture bearers; when these ties are repudiated the conditioning moulds of the young are broken and they are free to find their own individual, i.e. non-cultural, solution to life's problems. The Yakimas find themselves in this unmapped cultural jungle today. [83]

The emotional and ideological breach between generations is a manifest feature of contemporary Yakima life. Children generally do not respect their parents, and when they imitate them it is only to follow in their vagrant paths of individualistic self-seeking. Most parents have never disciplined themselves and hence find it difficult to discipline their children when the status of parenthood suddenly raises the issue. Some parents never accept the challenge; they do not acknowledge that they have a responsibility to or for their offspring. The detachment with which most parents regard their children and the reciprocal attitude of most children toward their parents devitalizes filial control; and no extra-familial mechanism has been devised to replace it. This does not mean that parents are callous and harsh to their children; on the contrary, they are vary "good" to them, which is to say that they are over-indulgent with them, giving them whatever they want and holding them to no accounting. But this is but one evidence of their lack of control and failure to inculcate restraint in their young. They treat, and regard, their children much as we do our pets; indulging them, expecting nothing uniquely human of them, enjoying them, but refusing to balance this selfish enjoyment with sacrifices for their future welfare. Their cruelty is the refined cruelty of a failure to prepare their little animals for an inevitable life among human beings who are equally selfish.

It is a common practice for parents to "farm out" their children when the opportunity occurs. This means that parents are in the habit of shifting the burden of caring for their children to the shoulders of anyone who will not object. Frequently they are turned over to grandparents and the mother and/or father goes on his or her way unhampered by the necessity of supporting or disciplining them. But any relative's home will serve as an unloading [84] ground, and this extends to degrees of kinship which we would not consider in enumerating family connections. These indifferent parents seldom see their children and often do not know where they are, since the children move about of their own accord from time to time. Teachers in the White Swan public school report a reciprocal practice among school children who are brought from their homes by school buses. Often they go home with other children for days or weeks at a time without notice and without causing any parental alarm. It is evident also that many parents regard boarding schools such as Chemawa, and health institutions such as the juvenile Indian tuberculosis sanatorium at Lapwai, Idaho, as convenient depositories for children whom they cannot support, control, or be bothered with. This escape device is one of the first they think of in handling their troublesome children. They do not hesitate to urge that their unruly offspring be sent to the state reformatories if their interest were capable of being sustained no doubt many more Indian children would be in these institutions. On the reservation near White Swan the Christian Church maintains a home and farm training mission for resident children. It operates at capacity even though a nominal fee is charged parents for boarding their children there. Many of its charges are orphans or children from broken houses, and there is a strong suggestion that many others are there because no one wants to give them a home.

As shocking as it may seem to us, then, a significant number of Yakima parents manifest little concern for their children and do not want to be confined and hampered by the necessity of taking care of them. If they can be institutionalized without too much trouble, they will be; if not, they are simply neglected and allowed to fend for themselves. The truth is that children are much less precious to the average Yakima than to us. Births and deaths of infants are not causes for a sustained rejoicing or a serious feeling [85] of loss. There are too many of both occurrences *to* make much of them, and in many instances another child is only an added hindrance and expense. No special effort is made to preserve an infant's life through health care, and no lessons are learned from past experiences or the experiences of others who have seen their children drop away through careless exposures, malnutrition, contagious disease, and eventual death. The philosophical acceptance of a shortened and crippled life cycle is one of the most stubborn and intangible obstacles against which doctors and nurse have to fight. It is an important aspect of parental indifference.

C. P., a full blood born around 1900, in 1923 married M.B., a full blood woman of about his own age. Previous to this marriage C.P. had had seven children by another woman. By M.B. he had nine more. In 1937 she left him and all her nine children to live will another man, by whom she has since given birth to three others, one dying as an infant of dysentery contracted in the hop field, despite the doctor's admonitions and efforts to save the child. C.P. made no attempt to support his sixteen children. He was not vicious, but was without self-respect or principle. He was, for a long time, a faithful member of a local church congregation. He was too religious to drink, but did not feel that it *was* necessary to work. While married to M.B. he lived on her property and cash income; since then, he has taken an occasional W.P.A. assignment, and now lives with and is supported by his eldest son. His children are scattered in many homes. He has tried repeatedly to get them into institutions of one kind or another. Five of them have been sent to *school* at Chemawa with trachoma infections; one of them was expelled for theft and eventually made *his* way into the state institution at Chehalis. Two others have been sent to Cushman Hospital in Tacoma where they have received treatments for malnutrition and incipient tuberculosis. One of the youngest, an [86] eight year old child, was in the Tacoma hospital in 1937 and again in 1940 on account of malnutrition. In 1941 she was sent to the sanatorium at Lapwai because of tuberculosis. In 1942 this *was* arrested and she was released, but since she had no home to receive her, she is now living with *a* distant relative under conditions of filth and disease which are likely to cause a recrudescence of her ailments and probably kill her. It is not to be expected that either her father or her mother will do anything to halt the development of this tragedy.

Parental neglect has its reward it lukewarm emotional attachments, filial neglect, and disobedience. Children are accustomed to regard their parents much as they do any other Indian; they are simply other individuals. The boomerang returns in old age when parents in their turn become burdens and drags upon a selfish life. There is nothing to repay, and the aged and the blind are treated with a callousness that approximates cruelty. The detachment with which children consider their parents is sometimes surprising. Often it is impossible to judge from a youth's manner of reference, attitude, voice inflection, or actions whether he is speaking of his father or just some other person. One frequently hears the expression "that man" in such a reference; or "that old fellow" or "the old lady." Even small children are sometimes heard to refer to their mothers and fathers quite impersonally by their first names. Unquestionably many children feel the lack of tranquility, assurance, and stability that go with a well-integrated family life. To the reservation social worker several delinquents who have spent some time in the industrial training institutions have expressed a desire to go back. There at least they knew for the first time the feeling of security which comes with a regulated and shielded life.

Our ideal of conjugal unity and fidelity is no more accepted by the average Yakima than is our concomitant ideal of filial love and loyalty. It [87] would not be accurate to say that none of the Yakimas ever experience either a feeling of romantic love or the more matured sense of admiration and dependence upon a *mate* that comes with a long continued cooperative partnership in marriage. It is certain that both sentiments are sincerely possible to them, and many examples of both can be found it marriages today. Too often, however, the sexual drive is untempered by other considerations of either beauty or propriety. Again, in this matter as in others, there are no impersonal patterns demanding conformance either in a positive or a negative sense. That is, for most people the conjugal union of a man and a woman is a simple and unadorned act of temporary mating, unleavened by formalities of negotiation, public notification, or psychological preparation; and the only restraints upon it in point of person, age, consequences, or duration are the personal ones of choice and pleasure. Men and women live together as man and wife without so much as a token gesture of marriage; they have children, dispose of then variously, and move on to another mate. Even though originally married this formality is no deterrent to future indiscriminate mating.

It must be admitted that there are many families to whom this generalization does not seem to apply. It is easy to point to stabilized unions, but of these something needs to be said in explanation. For one thing, they are to be found *almost* exclusively among the older people. This in turn generally means one of *two* things: that such cohabitations are custom marriages (contracted on the aboriginal pattern, or they are the middle-aged culminations of less orthodox unions. With an advance in age most people in most matters tend to settle down, and not infrequently a companionate mating will endure; but this *does* not absolve some of the aging conservatives from the charge of youthful philandering. Many of them have a marital history which is not above reproach. [88]

Agency officials have done all that they can to introduce sanctions into this situation, but once again we meet with the fundamental fact that external pressure to conform to an impersonal standard is a poor substitute for an inward conviction of its value, Indian policeman are instructed to see that couples who live together are brought before the proper authorities and married, but this is an onerous charge for *two* policemen among several hundred potential offenders. Many prospective brides and grooms secure marriage licenses under pressure and with these in their pockets begin their life together while evading and postponing the ceremony as long a*s* they can. They artlessly admit that they do not want to get married because the ceremony is too final; it settles their future; and divorce is too expensive, difficult, and troublesome. They are abetted in their subterfuge by the official recognition of custom marriage. Many of the older Indians have never been married by state law, but they or their parents have exchanged quantities of valuable goods in a publicly acknowledged sanction of the union and in accordance with the rigid formalities of aboriginal custom. This is custom marriage, and the government recognizes it. Barely is it practiced today, but young couples wishing to avoid the restraints of legal marriage claim its sanctions to lend the semblance of propriety to their sexual indulgences. The older Indians, and those who have "had their fling," are, as usual, quick to criticize these irregularities; but they are without influence over their children, and public opinion is moribund.

Our concept of the family revolves about the important social, biological, and economic unit of man, wife, and child. This unit was important to the Yakima aboriginally too, but it was not so exclusive, not so independent, among them as it *is* among us. Other lineal and collateral relatives, such as grandparents, uncles, aunts, and cousins; were drawn into it with greater [89] intimacy than *among* ourselves. This more extended unit often lived; worked, rejoiced, and suffered in common. The idea of cooperation, reciprocal aid, and interdependence has survived until the present time; but since there is a tendency to reject social responsibility the emphasis is now upon interdependence. That is, the psychological accent is upon taking rather than giving. A household nowadays often consists, as it did in the past, of not only the man-wife-child unit but of a dependent fringe of oddly assorted relatives and would-be relatives. Some dependents comprise family units themselves, such as sons- and daughters-in-law, or brothers- and sisters-in-law, with their children. Others are different segments of Indian families, single relatives of all degrees, or even strangers. In some instances their stay is temporary; in others, its termination is not a subject for discussion. In some cases the members of this fringe have incomes and contribute to the upkeep of the household; in others, they do not, and they make no pretense about it. It would be unthinkable to reject them, even though the help they might give the householder in his fields or at odd jobs around the farm far from compensates him for their support. In addition to these more or less perennial visitors others of uncertain relationship and destination are accustomed to drop in from time to time to share home and board with the house owner.

A specific example will give substance to this generalized picture. At one *time a* certain informant had a stead job as blacksmith's helper at the agency. He was earning $50.00 a month, and was married but without children. For a period of one year he supported in his house five other adults and two children. The father of the children was sickly and unable to do more than a few chores around the house. Asked about his or his wife's relation to the informant, the latter replied that he was not certain, "some kind of a cousin," he thought. A second married couple was a niece and her husband who had a few [90] odd jobs during the year. The seventh dependent guest *was a* woman, also of uncertain relationship to the informant. To support this conglomerate household he had to go into debt at the agency trading post. Asked why he did not revolt and turn his guests out; he said, "I couldn't do that. It's the Indian way – If I threw them out, my name would be no good."

This custom, undiminished at the present time, brings in its train two evils from an administrative standpoint. It overcrowds the living quarters, and it lowers the Indian's standards of living. It is evident from the above quotation that a Yakima is esteemed not because he has much in material wealth and the comforts of home, but because, if at all, he shares much. It is doubtful whether the word esteem is applicable even in this connection; relatives and strangers rather take a man's hospitality for granted. If his only thought is to provide for his wife and children, his friends fall away, thinking him a strange and outlandish being; if he tacitly welcomes all who come to his door, that is only to be expected. It is the natural thing to do, and no especial credit is due him. Most individuals submit to this pressure, and in consequence few of them aspire to an above-the-average standard of living. An extra bit of effort and foresight in providing for the future nets nothing more in the long run. Sharing with all the sundry smoothes out the curve of individual ambition and reduces its achievements to a common level. A higher-than-average income is an invitation to sponge and not, as we should suspect, a challenge to emulate its possessor's industry. Social standing does not depend upon the standard of living, and hence there is no incentive to raise it.

Many Yakimas begrudge the necessity of conforming to the hospitality pattern, and an atmosphere of resentment, contempt, and potential conflict pervades their households. This comes out in the callous unconcern of one co-dweller for the comfort and well-being of another, and in the uninhibited [91] tendency to discuss, criticize, and complain about relatives, even to strangers. The spirit of generosity is absent, leaving the empty shell of formal hospitality. Since parasites are without honor and have nothing to lose by insult or contempt the situation is static, bound by the traditional form that no single effort can break.

In addition to the requirements of hospitality there are other traditional survivals which contribute to a system of values at variance with the one that Americans advocate. One is the urge periodically, or on whim, to move about. This has already been discussed, and it has markedly divergent effects upon Yakima concepts of family life and home. It is nor conducive to the building up of permanent intangible relationship bonds within the conjugal family, and it provides a minimum in the way of economic roots for home development on our design. Interest in the house as the material embodiment of home association is lacking, with a consequent failure to improve it and take pride in its appointments. Sentimental devotion to a house as "home" does not enter into the thinking of most Yakima as it does with us. Home is spatially distributed over a wide area of root grounds, creeks, hills, and woods; not localized in a boarded living room. For the same reason there is a lack of interest in livestock or other property which would require continued care at one spot.

Still another value, which meshes with the preceding one, is the custom of sleeping on a low, flat, hard surface; in the old days upon the ground. This has survived today in the form of pallet sleeping. In many homes there are no beds. In fact, a fair estimate would show about one-third of the houses as without bedsteads of any kind, and another third as having only enough for a few of the inmates. The rest of the Indians; by preference, sleep an the floor on a nondescript assemblage of reed mats, blankets, and old straw [92] mattresses. That this disposition is by preference is shown by several facts. In 1941, when *the* extension agent initialed a program of mattress making among the women in an attempt to encourage the use of bedsteads, there was a disheartening response; only twenty-one women were sufficiently interested to complete their project, although several inducements were offered them. Also, it is clear that the custom is not a matter of poverty. It can be shown that some families receiving higher incomes will cling to the old custom of sleeping on the floor while others less able financially have adopted beds. Over-crowding is a consideration, for in households filled beyond capacity some individuals must go without beds. This, however, is not the critical factor, for when all the houses wherein all members sleep on the floor are taken into account it will be found that they contain, on an average, only four or five persons. That is, overcrowding or not, wealthy or not, a good proportion of the Yakimas prefer to sleep on the floor. The real determining factor is conservatism. Old people like pallets; they rationalize by saying that they are afraid they might fall out of a bed and hurt themselves. The custom is also linked intimately with the surviving custom of camping through most of the summer and with an indifferent or negative attitude toward all property which binds and hampers.

This rejection of property entanglements has other material manifestations. Indian houses evince little pride in ownership. They are seldom painted and seem to be on the verge of ruin. Steps and porch (when there is one) are likely to be sagging, window pains out and covered with cardboard, the foundation flimsy, and the roof inclined to leak. The yards are a litter of odds and ends of cast-off objects and others which may be used from time to time; they are unswept and a hazard to automobile tires despite the fact that most Indians or their visiting friends have cars. There are no lawns. The [93] houses are almost without exception old, dating in materials and architecture from the beginnings of this century: a high gable to afford an upstairs room or two with sometimes an intersecting unit of the same pattern to give an L~ shaped ground plan (see Plate II). They are drafty and, by our standards, inadequate for the winters of this area.

The furniture is bleakly utilitarian, and normally in disrepair. Cooking and heating is by wood stove. The disarray of the outside continues into the interior with little distinction. Floors, corners, beds, and tables are strewn and piled with clothing, toys, papers, and utensils, in a variegated clutter. Walls are hung with calendars, colored geographical and historical charts, and family photographs after the fashion of another day in our cultural history. A remarkable anachronism, found in most homes, is the radio. Many, too, have electric lights.

That this scene is not changed by the mere acquisition of wealth is amply demonstrated by the contrast between the unkempt houses; and the shiny newness of the late model automobiles which frequently stand beside them (Plate Vf). To put it succinctly, Indians have money — or can get it — for cars, but not for homes and their improvements.

A potent factor in this contrast is once again the deep-set appeal of a transient existence. Automobiles have admirably accommodated the urge to move since they allow of even quicker transport; and the Indian does not hesitate to take them over the most forbidding roads, just as he used to do the horse. Comparing individual incomes and the houses that they might be spent upon shows no correlation between wealth and property investment. The two scales may be divorced, and are among the Yakima; that they are intimately linked in our own culture only serves to throw the Yakima disparity into higher relief. The house of one of the most financially able even on the reservation is shown in Plate IIe. [94]

The living traditions in Yakima summer encampments are even more destitute of order and convenience; as they are among us. These resorts, with their filth, flies, and other unsanitary conditions, are the despair of doctors and nurses. The huts at Celilo Falls epitomize their concern; they are an arresting sight to the traveler along the Columbia River Highway (Plate IIIe and f) The Yakimas occupy one section of this sprawling shantytown through the summer. Even when at "home", they prefer to live camp style during this season. In almost every family cooking and eating is done outside on stoves and tables under a brush arbor (Plate III). Many sleep outside. The house is only an auxiliary convenience, mainly for winter. Some old people still insist upon living in aboriginal type constructions during the winter (Plate IIa), although they are now few in number.

Throughout this section the stress has been upon patterns of thought and action, upon systems of belief and scales of values. In some instances they have been action. patterns which have survived from aboriginal times and are in conflict with our present day demands upon the Indian to conform to our manner of life. In others, the standards are degenerate from any stand-point, whether our own or that of the aboriginal scheme. These intangible entities are the real motivating forces in any culture. The conflict between ideals poses the issue of adjustment, and the injuries to morale and the impalpable values of social existence are at the heart of the cultural stresses so manifest in Yakima life. An attempt has been made to indicate that material conditions such as poverty, overcrowding, unkept houses, lack of concern for real property, and the like are but reflections of these more fundamental value systems. It is upon these that we mu*st* focus our attention if we are to further our efforts to bring the Indian into line with our social norms. His material condition meets the eye more readily, and is more likely to draw the [95] fire of reformers; but *it* must be asserted that these are mere symptoms, not primary causes of our cultural differences, and they must be treated as such.

Health Conditions

The same thesis applies to another material manifestation; namely, disease. We, after centuries of controlled experimentation and rigorous questioning, have come to take a mundane view of disease, regarding it as a part of our experience of materialistic causes and effects. This is what we have come to call the scientific attitude. Since the causes are materialistic w*e* consider that the cures must likewise be of this nature, and we place our trust in the mechanical operation of medicines and surgery. Pre-literate man also recognizes a field of disease and cure on this plane, but it is a restricted field. Most disease causes are not understood by him, and hence he takes the view that they spring from supernatural sources. Given this premise, then, logically enough, he reasons that these supernatural causes mu*st* be counteracted by techniques which draw upon the supernatural world of spirits as curing agents. Hence, the medicine man with his claim of control over occult forces which can be brought to bear to relieve the sick and the sorely distressed.

The two systems of thought are worlds apart. They are founded upon utterly different premises. It does no good to argue with the Indian that a medicine *man* cannot suck some foreign object from his body when his own *eyes* have borne witness to the performance and, as long as his mind fails to operate along the materialistic channels that we are accustomed to from our earliest childhood. Such is the case with many of the Yakimas. Today there are several medicine men who are regularly called upon to cure the sick among a large proportion of the people. Some families will have little or nothing to do [96] with the resident physician and his aides; others admit the possibility that he may be able to help them in illness, and will skeptically give him a chance with the reservation that if he fails they will turn to the medicine man. The scant allowance that they make to his ability is weighted against his success, for they will seldom follow his directions with conviction and are all too ready to charge him with failure. They admit that he can help white men, but rationalize their beliefs by stating that Indians are different from white people, being subject to mystic forces that we cannot understand. It must not be thought that this conviction is confined to the older uneducated members; many, if not most, of the young people are frankly convinced of the powers of the medicine man even though they have been exposed to a high school education.

It is against this psychology that physicians and field nurses have to fight. To what extent they realize the character of their problem is perhaps not to the point here; it is certain that they do not attack it at its roots, and they cannot be expected to do so under existing conditions. All of their time must be devoted to stemming the tide of sickness among the already afflicted, and adequate techniques do not exist for altering native thinking on the etiology of disease. It is always a defensive struggle, and consequently health programs make little headway against the ignorance apathy, and skepticism of the Indian.

Satisfactory records upon the prevalence of disease among the Yakimas are not available. It would require a special effort and budget to make a survey of all case; chronic, unattended, and current. Many of the sick never voluntarily make an appearance before the health officer, and what little treatment they receive is under pressure of home calls by the nurses. Others of unknown number never appear on any tally sheet. The only records of statistical [97] value in an analysis of incidence and prevalence are the current reports of the activities of the doctors and field nursed. These are primarily work reports, but from them certain health data are inferable. They bear out the impression that the m*ost* prevalent diseases are syphilis, gonorrhea, tuberculosis, and trachoma in approximately that order. Over the six month period from July to December 1941 field nurses attended one hundred and three *cases* of venereal diseased, one hundred of tuberculosis, and eighty-seven of trachoma. These are the most difficult to control since they become chronic, are not too painful, and require protracted treatment for a cure. Like many white men, the Indian therefore tends to ignore then as not worth the trouble. The result is a large number of virulent carriers who spread their infection in a hopelessly ever-widening circle impossible of circumvention. Many old people have not only become blind themselves but have laid the foundation for this affliction among their children and grandchildren because they have refused to persist in treatment for *trachoma*. The eighty-seven cases noted as receiving treatments of some kind on the last semi-annual report did not represent the total number afflicted; in the White Swan district alone there were fifty-four long standing cases on file which *went* unattended and at best could be regarded as only arrested. The same apathy characterizes the Yakima's attitude toward tuberculosis and venereal diseases; they are taken to be unavoidable accompaniments of a normal life. In 1941, fifty-two new cases of venereal disease were recorded; but again this does not take into account the large number of unreported infections and the prevalence of chronic afflictions.

The ravages of these diseases are m*ost* pitiable among children, many of whom are racked and disabled before their lives are fairly begun. More vicious, perhaps, because it is more insidious, is malnutrition. The mysteries [98] of *a* balanced diet are even more incomprehensible to the Indian than are the workings of specific medicines. As elsewhere, poverty is a potent factor in the prevalence of this disorder; but the root is still psychological. Taste, not medical considerations, governs the expenditure of the grocery budget of whatever size. Arguments for a more restrained and circumspect diet are met with the usual clichés and rationalizations; and even the admitted demonstration of a connection between a wasted body and *its* continued neglect lacks force for the Yakima. Disease and death are necessary evils, everybody is subject to them, and to have syphilis or rickets is not disgraceful or abnormal.

With other diseases the doctors have more success, principally because they can be controlled by inoculation or specifies and because whole groups like school children can be treated. Regular inspections and treatments are a part of school routine for Indian children. Most of the immunizations are for smallpox and diphtheria. These were completely controlled in 1941, as were measles, scarlet fever, and meningitis. The incidence of typhoid was also very low. Chicken pox *was* epidemic. Signal achievements are being made now in the cure of trachoma by the use of sulfa drugs, but these are not usually locally applied. The practice has been to send infected children to the Chemawa school, which at the present time is able to take care of a much larger number than heretofore due to the new discoveries. Weekly roundups of young children in need of tonsillectomies and the like are also made during the summer, and they are taken to the Cushman Hospital in Tacoma for surgery. Regular tuberculin tests are also made and as many of the acute childhood cases as can be accommodated are sent to the Indian hospital in Lapwai, Idaho. Formerly, the Cushman Hospital offered limited facilities for rehabilitation cases; but the continuation of this necessary complement to a tuberculosis [99] "cure" seems doubtful. A*s* with the venereal diseases, the long period of recuperation must be left up to the Indian, and he normal treats debilitation with indifference.

The unsanitary conditions in homes thwart the efforts of the health authorities. They make little progress in curing a communicable disease where the patient lives in filth and in contact with others likewise infected. Patients in Indian homes may be treated but not segregated from others; they take pills but continue to eat, sleep, and take their pleasure as they feel like it. Multitudes of flies and dogs provide contact agents, and the virtues of sterilization go unappreciated. Nurses labor against the scourge of dysentery which appears annually in the hop fields to take the lives of babies. Mothers take their entire families there (Plate IVd) and many infants fail to survive the hazards of long days in the heat under unsanitary conditions.

The attitude of the Indian toward the offerings of our medical science is typified by his reactions at child birth. Nurses are not encouraged by policy to attend actual deliveries, and therefore their records do not normally show them in attendance at births. They do endeavor to assist *and* advise before and after, however, and chiefly on account of their own insistence they make a fairly large number of field visits to expectant and newly delivered mothers. Most Indians do not want the physician to attend them or even advise them at childbirth; or if they do, they take the precaution to appeal also to native midwives and magicians for a more certain emotional security. In 1941 the doctor's report states that a total of only thirty-six births were attended by him. We do not know how many births there were, actually, but it is certain that many fathers and mothers prefer the assurances of the special variety of native doctor whose business it is to make prognostications of the [100] of the *sex of* unborn children; their characters, and the circumstances of their birth, and to ease the pains of labor. Such men have special supernatural powers which give them clairvoyance beyond anything claimed by our physicians, and they are widely sought after to give aid and solace to expectant mothers*

Once again we must admit that the economic factor plays a part in retarding the acceptance of modern medical science by the Yakima, but only to stress that this is not the controlling influence. Indians pay their medicine men well for their services, although not as extravagantly as is sometimes claimed. Those who want scientific treatment but cannot afford it may be hospitalized at Cushman, Lapwai, or the sanitarium for adults on the reservation at government expense. Also; the county assumes its share of the burden in accepting indigent Indian patients on a par with whites. In the past the county hospital has requested some financial assistance from the government for cases involving uncommon expenses, but even this practice is declining. For the poor who need expensive services and cannot afford them the superintendent must make a special request for an individual appropriation from the Secretary of the Interior. In other words, patients must pay for their medical care themselves if they are able, and only in particular cases does the government assume financial responsibility. Tribal funds are not used for such emergencies.

It should be clear from the foregoing that the Yakima health problem is not simply economic. It is not simply anything. Physical health is but one aspect of the more general and more fundamental problem of social well-being which we have already considered. When we inquire what has been done and what is being done to remedy the total situation we turn inevitably to the subject of education. [101]

Chapter III
Education

Adult Education and Policy

There is an intensive program of adult education in process on the reservation under the auspices of the Extension Division, a collateral department of the agency with general offices in Washington, D.C. The function of this branch of the service is to im*prove* the economic conditions of the Indians through instructor and assistance in individual problems pertaining to their more extensive and effective utilization of resources. The personnel of the office on the Yakima reservation includes an Extension Agent, two Farm Agents, and a Home Demonstration Agent. These four people are in intimate contact with the Indians, spending much of their time on the farms or in the homes where they can be of the most help.

The primary objective of the farm agents in the extension service is to encourage the Indians to make more and more use of their lands. One aspect of the problem is to devise means to induce them to do the farming of their lands themselves instead of leasing them to white tenants. Definite projects are laid out to this end, such as concentrating upon selected families over a set period of time and giving them every instructional aid possible to encourage them. In 1941, for example, four families were induced to start farming for the first time, three of them with good results. Other objectives of the service center about the improvement of conditions which will make faming more lucrative and efficient and the control of ignorant and destructive practices. Agents assist in planning for improved irrigation, control of weeds and poisonous plants, control of livestock diseases and inferior strains in herds, soil conservation, crop rotation, [102] marketable planting, and in any other project for the more scientific exploitation of native resources. Fortunately, financial aid as wall as advice is available to the enterprising Yakima. The tribe maintains a loan fund of $50,000 administered by a committee which investigates its petitioners for assistance and conducts regular tours of inspection to check upon the utilization of money granted. It is the policy of this committee not to *subsidize* chronic pleaders such as those who would make annual requests for seeds. In 1941, 35 loans *were* made, totaling $8,782, of which 59% was for teams and equipment; 26% for building material, 9% for livestock, and 5% for seed.

One of the most successful projects instituted by the Extension Division was the formation of a cooperative Indian Cattleman's Association in 1931. The stock was, and is "loaned" from a government pool, repayments to be made in kind; but today, due to branding and other complications resulting from this method; there is a movement on foot to substitute money payments. Roundups and sales are engaged in cooperatively, but each man owns his own stock. Acting as an association; the group is able to bring buyers to local stock pens and secure better prices than otherwise. In 1942, there *were* 98 members operating 3,543 head of cattle out of the total of 6,501 reported for the reservation. The year before they sold 747 head for $49,168. There was also a Junior Stockmen's Association whose 41 members were each issued 5 yearling heifers five years before. In 1942, 31 of them had more than 5 head; 25 had more than 7, and 10 had over 10 head each. During 1941 four more families were started with cattle. Sheep do not appeal to the Yakima and they cannot be induced to raise them, a familiar antipathy which can be appreciated by other cattlemen. [103]

The Home Demonstration Agent endeavors to improve the economic conditions of the Indian home through introducing and encouraging *new* techniques in household management. Her plan, like that of the farm agents, has been to establish certain goals over a given period. Lately she has been concentrating upon gardening, food preservation, and nutrition. She has organized five clubs in different sections of the reservation and has 65 women enrolled. For the year 1941 she was able to report upon several projects and accomplishments, the whole of which the following will convey an idea: Twenty-seven well planted gardens were being tended, and were growing an average of 11 different vegetables. Forty-two families were encouraged to can 18,239 quarts of fruit, vegetables and meat; fourteen families canning their winter's supply of vegetables for the first time. Three new pressure cookers were purchased by Indian women, making a total of fourteen on record. Club members remodeled 23 of their dresses, and 65 made new ones; a local dress revue was held, and two of the women exhibited and won prizes for their dressed at the state fair in Yakima. A project was initiated, to stimulate the use of mattresses in the home through having the women, assisted by their husbands, make their own under supervision. As a result of much publicity given it, 63 applications were received, 58 were granted, and 21 of the applicants completed their mattresses.

4~H club work is also carried on under the auspices of the Extension Division. In 1941 eleven boys were encouraged to undertake the care of gardens of their own; and all of the 35 girl members were engaged in sewing and clothes making projects.

Although it is handled by a special teacher in the public school and is not a part of the program or division being discussed, we should not fail to note the similar work undertaken among young people, Indian and white, [104] under the Smith~Hughes plan. Boys in high school receive classroom instruction in farm management, and must in addition carry on supervised projects at home for credit. Girls, under a similarly sponsored plan, have class work in household economics and are also responsible for home projects. These programs are in effect in the reservation high schools.

The difficulties and the discouragements which tend to dull the enthusiasm of workers in adult Indian education are numerous and persistent. The Extension Division personnel is continually thwarted in its efforts at club formation by the lack of community feeling among the Yakimas. They do not feel any tribal solidarity, and when this is added to the excessive number of personal feuds and dislikes, the difficulties in the way of forming cooperative enterprises among them are almost insuperable. This is an old evil on this reservation and in the past has vitiated group unity with respect to tribal council, church membership, and clubs of a social or economic character, even including the cattlemen's association. Still other obstacles balk the conscientious efforts of the extension service. Quite apart from the apathy of the Yakima - which is fundamental — there are such deterrents to the success of the farm agents' plans as the demand for leases on good irrigated land by whites, the inadequate irrigation facilities on some allotments and the involved inheritance claims on others. The advances that are made in one year in converting some of the Indians to the sedentary life are frequently nullified by as many losses in other quarters. For example, in 1940 there were 226 families rated as farmers on the reservation, tilling 13,347 acres;

whereas in 1941, despite the 4 new ones added, there were only 222 such families with 13,620 acres under cultivation, the increase in [105] acreage being due mainly to added pasture lands.[1]

It is difficult to build much hope on this kind of a program. It is not a scatter of securing able or conscientious agents in the field; the service has these. The disheartening feature of it is that it has been tried for so long and has produced so little in the way of tangible results. The reports of conscientious Indian agents to the Commissioner of Indian Affairs in Washington from 1855 until the present contain abundant proof that the same hopes and methods have prevailed over these many years. In 1865, and for many years thereafter, an agency farm was maintained and operated by students at the boarding school for their benefit and instruction; a knowledge of soap making, harness and wagon making; blacksmithing, tanning, home management, and clothes making was likewise imparted under even more favorable conditions than now exist. In addition, there was even an "extension" service, though under other names: the government farmer, miller, sawyer, and carpenter helped the Indian to break, fence, and plant his ground, to harvest and mill his grain, to saw his logs for lumber, and to build his house. At the same time, women, who were usually the wives of employees, introduced stoves, lamps, and sewing machines into such homes as they could. The ideals, compromises, and failures of present day field workers have an unhappy familiarity for one who has read these early documents carefully and made some incisive inquiries among the older Indians who remember the conditions of thirty to fifty years ago.

Youth Education, the New Policy, and Its Difficulties

In one respect, however, there has been a marked deviation from the older [106] approaches. This concerns the education of Indian youth. In times past it was believed by m*any* administrators, including the agents at Fort Simcoe, that the only way to secure lasting benefit to the Indian child under instruction was to remove him as much as possible from his home surroundings, for these inevitably degraded him. Then too, under rural conditions in the past it was often difficult if not impossible to provide daily transportation to and from the child's home and the distant school house. Boarding schools were therefore established by many reservations, and some of these, together with other types of off reservation institutions, exist today, but the emphasis now is upon day schools and more particularly upon utilizing the facilities and advantages of the public school for the benefit of the Indian. The policy of the present administration relative to this matter is contained in the following excerpt:

"In reducing the numbers in boarding schools, the aim has been to place the younger pupils in local schools so that they may live at home. Notwithstanding the pressure upon boarding schools during the past years due to the economic situation, the total numbers have decreased and pupils in advanced grades now far outnumber

---

[1] Figures from the reclamation office on the reservation actually show a decrease in acreage, but according to the Extension Division's reckoning this does not take into account new land outside the irrigation projects.

those in the lower grades. In the fall of 1932, there were approximately 2,000 fewer boys and girls in Government boarding schools than there were the previous year. The whole tendency is to save these additional opportunities as long as they are needed for special types of work that Indian boys and girls, particularly those of a considerable degree of Indian blood, could not get in their own localities or with the resources they have.

"Another item contained in the announced policy of the Secretary says that Indian schools should only be provided if it is not possible to merge the training of the Indian into the school system of the States. In so far as it is possible, scholarships in the institutions of higher learning of the country shall be provided for those Indian boys and girls who are capable of going beyond the ordinary high school training.

"Referring to the education of Indian youth in institutions of higher learning, it was possible to obtain in the 1933 appropriation act, for the first time, authorization to use funds for the tuition of Indian pupils attending higher educational institutions, under such rules and regulations as the Secretary of the Interior may prescribe.

"The elimination of pupils in boarding schools has naturally reflected a large increase in the amount to be expended for tuition of Indian children [107] enrolled in the local public schools, and Congress has provided both for the present and the next fiscal year increases in appropriations to meet these charges, though it is significant that even with these increases the total cost of schooling for Indians has been materially reduced."[2]5

The success of this policy of conversion from Federal school to local public school obviously depends upon the cooperation which the state and district educational boards are willing to tender the federal agencies. No more than a brief analysis is needed, however, to show that something more ingenious than mere cooperativeness is called for if the problems raised by the plan are to be solved.

To instrument the plan of conversion, public school authorities in the State of Washington very early agreed to undertake the education of all local Indian students not otherwise provided for, so that by the date of the above statement of policy there were already 1,951 native pupils enrolled in the public schools of the state and none were being accommodated in federal boarding schools on the reservations within it.[3] On the Yakima reservation 425 were being taken care of. In return for the assumption of this burden the national government agreed to reimburse the local districts, on the basis of the computed average cost per pupil per day in attendance at each school. Arrangements were made between the local school districts and the agencies whose

---

[2] Indian Administration Since July 1, 1929. Mimeographed Pamphlet, United States Department of the Interior. Office of Indian Affairs, Washington, D.C., March 3, 1933. pp.47-49.

[3] There were other pupils provided for in other institutions. A summary for the state for the year 1933 is as follows: Total children 6-18 years inclusive, 2,946; total enrolled 2,490; enrolled in public schools 1,951; enrolled in Federal non-reservation boarding schools 180; enrolled in mission, state, and private boarding schools 203; enrolled in sanatoria 156; no definite information 196; not enrolled in any school 260.

wards were served by them. Payments were made three times a year directly to [108] the public school by the superintendent whose agency benefited from the service. Only children of one-quarter degree of Indian blood or more were provided for by this measure. Of necessity the financial adjustments between the federal agency and the district board had to conform to local conditions: in some instances special services, such as hot lunches or transportation by bus, were provided by the school; in others, there was a demand for more class room space, vocational training, or an accredited high school to accommodate the increase in enrollment. As a result, there was a considerable disparity in the per capita payments to the different public schools, even on the same reservation. Over the state in 1934, this ranged from twenty cents to seventy-five cents per Indian pupil per day, and within the Yakima reservation from the same low figure for the Wapato district to fifty cents for the White Swan district. This disparity, together with other embarrassments, was sometimes a source of considerable dissatisfaction and discord between local and federal administrators of the program. Furthermore, it was understood that the federal government had, by its elimination of the boarding school, effected an appreciable saving of its former education costs, and the feeling was quite general that the public schools, not the government, should benefit by the change, especially in view of the poverty of many school districts. This opinion was fortified by the conviction held by many that the government is responsible for the impoverished condition of some districts through its policy of withholding Indian lands from taxation, a matter to be referred to later.

In an effort to give greater security and consistency to the program of cooperation the Johnson-O'Malley Bill was passed in 1934. This authorized the Secretary of the Interior to contract directly with the state. The State Superintendent of Public Instruction was likewise empowered to negotiate, with the advice of the Attorney General, and in 1935 the contract was signed. By [109] its terms the State of Washington agreed to provide adequate "education in public elementary schools, public secondary schools, colleges, special schools, and vocational or trade schools to all Indian children residents of the State of Washington upon the same terms and under the same conditions as to any other citizens of the State and to provide, in so far as funds transferred in accordance with the terms of this contract by the party of the first part (the federal government) will permit, transportation of Indian pupils to and from schools where necessary, school lunches for Indian pupils when needed, required text books and school supplies, and school medical and dental service," as well as to meet special educational demands of the Indian and to maintain standards of teacher training, school supplies, equipment, and sanitation "not lower than the highest maintained by the State of Washington. A Superintendent of Indian Education was also provided for whose duty it became, in cooperation with the State Superintendent of Public Instruction, to determine the tuition rate for the various public schools and to disburse the apportioned sums from the central office in Olympia.

That this measure has not met with complete success is attested by the following quotation from a manuscript by Clifton A. Crook, Superintendent of Schools in the White Swan district on the Yakima reservation:

"The State contract, in many ways, has created nearly as many problems as it has eliminated. The schools are receiving less reimbursement now in return for services rendered to the Indian pupil than they received prior to the contract agreement.

It would be somewhat premature to say that the present system, under the State contract method, is a complete success. Much work remains to be done before an equitable method for the payment of tuition moneys can be worked out for each school district concerned. In certain instances prior to the introduction of the State contract certain districts had agreed to furnish transportation, develop vocational classes, arrange a service of free text books, serve free hot lunches, and render various other services to its Indian pupils. In return, for this service, agreements were made with the local agencies whereby certain specified tuition rates would be given. These tuition moneys would help defray the added financial burdens assumed by the district in attempting to pay for its busses and other extra costs thus incurred wholly or in part for the Indian pupils. The State contract [110] apparently abrogates these prior agreements. Unless due consideration be given under the new method of tuition payment, these above mentioned districts will suffer financially.

"In certain instances special allotments of funds for libraries, hot lunches, and scholarships have, in part, helped compensate certain districts for the decrease in tuition rates. There has been an attempt to adjust these problems amicably and fairly to the best knowledge of the Indian Office. However, the successful operation of the State contract plan remains yet to be demonstrated to the satisfaction of the school boards and school administrators who have schools located upon Indian reservations in the State."[4]

The general problem referred to by Mr. Crook is epitomized in his own district where a rather steady increase in Indian enrollment since 1930 has been accompanied by a decrease in tuition receipts from the federal treasury. Some idea of the resulting pinch can be obtained from the following table, keeping in mind that days in attendance and not the simple fact of Indian enrollment is the basis for reckoning reimbursement:

Indian Tuition, Attendance, and Enrollment[5]

Year	Indians Attendance	Enrolled	District Total Attendance	Enrolled	Tuition Receipts
1931-32	?	?	?	?	$10,366.75
1932-33	24,919	147	46,977	36l	9,235.75
1933-34	19,960	148	50,595	374	9,268.10
1934-35	20.354	168	54.832	415	9,196.51
1935-36	24,294	186	62,087	468	7,757.13
1936-37	23,105	184	62,446	489	6,038.20
1937-38	27,162	209	70,000	522	6,766.00

As these figures show, over a six year period from 1932 to 1938, there has been

---

[4] Crook, Clifton A. A Study of Indian Education in Washington. Manuscript Thesis submitted for the degree of Master of Arts, University of Washington, 1938. p. 2.
[5] Ibid. Adapted from table, p. ?

a reduction of over twenty-six per cent in tuition receipts, and over [111] the same period an increase of nine per cent in Indian attendance in the White Swan district, the discrepancy resulting from a reduction of the per day per capita payments from fifty cents to thirty-four cents. There may be more economic justice in this adjustment than appears in the bald presentation of the figures; only a more exhaustive analysis than is here called for would warrant a decision. It seems that we can conclude, however, that most school authorities are not attracted by a program which is likely to yield them less rather than more for assuming added responsibilities, especially when, as many believe, these obligations more properly belong to the national government.

Also, it is apparent that tuition payments, no matter how liberal, as long as they are for operating costs only, cannot take care of the demand for additional buildings and equipment to accommodate the increases in enrollment. A few districts in the state have been able to get special consideration from the government for capital outlays; others have not. The White Swan district, in 1935, received a $50,000 loan for the specific purpose of building a high school, to be repaid over a period of thirty years at the interest rate of three per cent per annum. The Wapato district on the same reservation, unable to bond itself for new high school buildings to meet overcrowded conditions, failed to secure such relief.

At the root of the difficulty of accommodating an increasing enrollment in public schools on reservations is the dearth of taxable land to support the systems. Indian land, whether it is *allotted to* individuals or reserved in the name of the tribe, is held in trust for the Indian, is inalienable except in singular cases, and cannot be taxed. This remains true even though, as is usually the case with valuable land, the Indian leases to a white tenant. Neither individual is liable to a land tax, and the white lessee not infrequently has a minimum of personal property from which revenue can be [112] Derived. Some land which was formerly hold in trust has in the past been deeded to the Indian and a good part of this sold to white men. All such deeded property, whether in the hands of whites or natives, is taxable; but there is comparatively little of this in Yakima county. It is estimated that there are 2,734,720 acres in the county, but the 1,112,792 acres of trust land under the jurisdiction of the Indian agency is exempted from taxation, as is the 503,000 acres of the Columbia and Snoqualmie National Forests. In the case of the forests, however, the county is compensated at the rate of twenty five per cent of the yield from lumbering, grazing, and other operations, plus a ten per cent investment on improvements. On the Yakima reservation the total acreage under cultivation is in the neighborhood of 120,000 acres. According to the school report just cited, over half of this land in 1942 was leased by whites who paid no tax, and yet whose children constituted one-third of the school population; about 40,000 acres of the total crop-producing land was assessable for the support of the remaining sixty-six per cent. The White Swan district contains 763 sections of land, or 488,320 acres; but of this only 45,974 acres are patented, i.e. taxable. Thus only one-tenth of the potential land values are capitalized upon for the maintenance of the public school, the benefits of which are shared not only by Indian children but also by the children of many lessees from whom no support is forthcoming.

These difficulties are not peculiar to the Yakima reservation. In other places there is an even greater proportion of restricted land. Schools located in these areas in many cases face a real problem of survival. They must receive enough tuition from their Indian enrollment, assisted by the state, to make up for the loss in local taxes; and sometimes this is not a solution which will meet the demands of local conditions. If the policy of the Office of [113] Indian Affairs called for the continued isolation of the Indian and the exclusion of whites from the reservation then we might feel that public schools were intruders and must accept the consequences. As it is, with a federal unit seeking to utilize local district facilities and obtaining cooperation under stringent handicaps, it would seem that the next move should be with the government. The Indian Office is sensible of the difficulties of the program and is conscientiously trying to alleviate the financial distress of school districts; but this can only mean larger appropriations from Congress.

The Indian at School

There are six school districts on the reservation; namely, Toppenish, Wapato, White Swan, Parker, Harrah, and Granger. Only three of these maintain a high school, of which the one in White Swan is the most recent, having been accredited in 1933. The Toppenish schools serve an urban population as well as students from its rural environs. Wapato is next in town size. White Swan has a clustered population of only 321; therefore most of its 500 students are carried to and from school by busses, and from distances up to ten or twelve miles. To it also falls the task of attempting to educate a major part of the most conservative block of Indians on the reservation.

Theoretically, all Indian children of appropriate age and sound health are required to attend school, but the difficulties of enforcing this regulation on the Yakima reservation are apparent to all concerned. For one thing, there is no marked desire for an education either on the part of the child or his parents. Some of the latter are even antagonistic toward the idea. At best, many of the others are indifferent, so that if a child acquires a liking for school it generally comes from fortuitous circumstances external to the family. [114]

The complaints that one hears against schooling are various and testify mainly to a simple and unreasoned dislike of the whole idea. Some declare that the children learn nothing but bad habits, others that they should be taught farming and household management instead of arithmetic, geography, and English, while still others protest against the discipline and the various regulations necessary to any smoothly functioning institution of the kind. So unimportant do most parents, particularly those of the conservative group colloquially known as "long hairs," consider an education that children are kept out of school (or rather, not encouraged to go) on the slightest pretext; and they make a regular practice of taking them away to the fishing grounds or the Columbia early in the spring before school is over, and of keeping them out through September for hop picking, or for any one of a variety of reasons which exist for going to the mountains in the late summer and fall.[6]

---

[6] The belated and curtailed school year of the Indian is well shown by the 1940-41 monthly enrollment figures at White Swan: September 111, October 175, November 190, December 190, January 192, February 189, March 182, April 183, May and June 165. It is noticeable that the high school enrollment remained almost

This unconcern has its effects upon the children. Even though a child were to develop a taste for learning under such circumstances the retardation he is bound to suffer as a result of frequent absences would have unfortunate psychological consequences. Unquestionably this factor has been a critical one in causing the pronounced decrease in Indian enrollment in the higher grades at White Swan. In this district there is a grade school, a high school with a manual training shop, and a separate building for remedial work with handicapped students. For the school year of 1941-42, which we may take as representative of other years, there was a total enrollment of 380 students [115] in the elementary grades and 121 in high school. The 150 Indian grade school pupils constituted a little less than half the total, while in high school white children outnumbered Indians about five to one.[7] As far as could be learned this ratio has been rather constant through several successive years, indicating a rather high Indian "mortality" in the education process. Very few Indians have graduated from high school in the eight years that this has been possible, and a significant number of the few have been mixed breeds, some to such a degree as to challenge classification as an Indian. The records reveal that in the first graduating class in 1933 two out of ten were of Indian blood; in 1934 four out of ten; in 1935 two out of twelve; in 1936 eight out of twenty-one; in 1937 five out of seventeen; in 1938 two out of nine; in 1939 five out of nineteen; in 1940 seven out of thirty; in 1941 six out of nineteen; and in 1942 three out of twenty-one.

Another factor which doubtless has an effect in estranging the Indian child from the school situation is his linguistic handicap.[8] Teachers report that almost every child appearing at school for the first time speaks English. This is expectable since elementary school teachers are not prepared to cope with the Yakima language, nor would an Indian family so confirmed in its native ways as not to teach its children English be likely to send them to school. Still, the facility with the English language achieved by most children of six in the White Swan district is by no means of the kind to put them upon a basis of equality with white children. White people generally are not sufficiently [116] indulgent of this handicap with the Indian of any age; they have little to gain from indulging him, are brusque, and expect him to face their demands of efficiency in conversation. Teachers naturally are more considerate since this id a part of their business; but in spite of all their patience there remains an unbridgeable gulf between any two people neither of whom knows the native language of the other. The Indian, as a member of a minority group, is the one to suffer. The disadvantage is aggravated by the fact that the Indian child is normally in daily contact with parents and associates who use the native tongue, and so must he, at least to the point of understanding it.

---

constant, varying only from 21 to 26 over this period, while of the younger children only 90 were in attendance in September and 142 in May and June.

[7] On an average. Monthly enrollment varies. The highest Indian enrollment any month was grade school 167, high school 26.

[8] Allied to this, and even more fundamental, is the seldom appreciated fact that the Indian's thought categories are frequently quite different from those of his white teacher.

In some homes parents deliberately speak the Yakima language to their children so that they will not forget it. One girl who has been two years to college comes from such a home. Like many other young people who have had a high school education, she understands the Yakima language but either does not speak it at all or has difficulty in doing so. Even her facility with our language is not impressive; with those who speak Yakima fluently the results are worse. In by far the greater number of cases the bilingual high school graduate is lacking in the ability to express himself in English, and his comprehension of it in conversation is markedly limited. The writer has attempted to use some of these young people as interpreters, but with discouraging results. The school teacher, even in high school, therefore, has a persistent problem, and one which must be borne in mind if her efforts are to meet with more than nominal success.

Another source of uneasiness for the Indian beginner is the strangeness of the school community. In the rural districts Indian children seldom if ever have white playmates, and they are remarkably shy of adult white strangers. As time goes on some of the tension is lessened, and perhaps for the [117] majority of students after a few years no direct evidence of it remains. However, one teacher in the White Swan grade school who has had several years experience has found that Indian pupils as a group are more reticent and timid than whites. In every class or room, he says, there are Indians who will not volunteer to recite or answer questions, and some who, even when asked and know the answer, will reply that they do not knew. Also, it is difficult to get them to participate in group activities except in games and sports. In the latter they do well, and are sought after in the choosing of teams in club activities, however, they fall short of what could be expected, all other factors being considered equal.

Once again the question of racial discrimination obtrudes itself, this time with respect to the school community. It obviously is not relevant to teacher-pupil relationships, but it is pertinent to inquire whether white and Indian children display any feelings of racial differences. This is a very delicate subject to investigate. Not everyone *is* capable of forming a reliable opinion about it. Conscious observation is called for, as well as a refined appreciation of what constitutes the feeling of difference, and a knowledge of the subtle ways it can manifest itself. From all that can be learned from a question and answer survey it appears that there is no conscious recognition of racial differences in the White Swan school, either on the part of Indians or whites. Indian pupils do not give expression to any feelings of resentment, frustration, or dislike of what they experience there. Teachers assert that there are no play group cleavages along racial lines, no "name-calling," no aloofness on the part of whites. From the same sources, it appears that boys of both races fraternize more noticeably than do the girls, possibly because of their more extensive cooperation in games. [118]

On the other hand, interracial school ground romances are decidedly rare. It would seem also that cross-racial friendships are nominally superficial, and are confined, moreover, to the school grounds. The few that are not are striking enough to occasion comment. In addition, there are evidences of Indian caution and sensitivity. In making their tours of inspection and treatment, field nurses have learned that they get only a reluctant response when they use the adjective "Indian" in summoning their charges out of school rooms.

Without long and casual familiarity with the district it is impossible to say what undercurrents of antipathy flew beneath the relations of whites and Indians either on or off the school ground. Latent antagonisms are certainly bred along the way somewhere, somehow. One observer had occasion to verify the existence of a smoldering resentment among a group of ten-year-old boys. They were playing nearby while he eat alone at some distance watching a ceremony of gift distribution after a funeral. Resenting his presence, they laid out a rather realistic schema to drive him away, all agreeing to the pronouncement of one that "White people do not allow Indians to go to their affairs, so Indians should kick white men out." It would be interesting to check the conclusion of one grade school teacher to the effect that there are no evidences of suspicion and aloofness in the youngest Indian children who come under his observation, but that there comes a development of this with time.

Teachers are agreed that the intelligence of their Indian pupils is not inferior to that of their white children. Some Indians do not appear for first grade training until they are nine, and some are held over two years in this class. But the causes for this relate to factors external to their native intelligences. The remedial school contains about equal numbers of Indian and white children. One thoughtful teacher has come to the conclusion that Indians excel as students in the botanical and other "outdoor" sciences because [119] they are better observers; that they are not so capable in the physical sciences which call for an aptitude in abstractions and thought configurations. This implies a lack of interest in academic training and learning for its own sake, a generalization which will hold for the vast majority of white high school students as well, especially from the lower middle class stratum of our society. Adequate data are not available for verifying impressions on racial differences of interests and aptitudes.

Accomplishments

Without attempting to make any statistical or other interracial comparisons it can be said that there have been very few Indians in the past who have taken advantage of their opportunities for higher education. A review of the White Swan graduates from 1933 on discloses that there have been only nine who have taken some kind of advanced work in institutions off the reservation. From the first two graduating classes, in 1933 and 1934, there were two boys each year who went to Haskell Institute (for Indians) in Kansas. In the 1935 class there was one girl who took training as a beauty shop operator, and who has since been employed in Portland. In 1936 another girl helped to pay her own way to attend Washington State College, but completed only two years there. In 1937 another girl graduate obtained a scholarship for a four year course at Washington State Normal at Ellensburg, but did not finish. Finally, two girls of the class of 1939 attended business schools, and *so* far as is known both have successfully completed their training and are working at present.

It is to be remembered that this is not the complete story. There are [120] two other high schools on the reservation;[9] but it is felt that the White Swan summary provides a fair sample of the appeal of post-high school training. When inquiry is made

---

[9] Both, however, have a smaller Indian enrollment. A comparison of the highest enrollment any month for the these schools shows White Swan l67 grade, 26 high, Toppenish 100 grade, 21 high; Wapato 67 grade, l6 high.

among students to account for the small number a common answer is that low grades render then ineligible to take the entrance requirements of colleges. That, however, is obviously only the immediate and formal reason. Opportunities for the ambitious are not wanting. In posted bulletins from the education office, interested students are urged to take advantage of one of several means of intellectual advancement; Indian scholarships, educational grants and loans by the government, university loans and grants, national defense vocational training, state employment service, N.Y.A. in colleges and vocational schools, industrial loans by the government, and training in the armed forces.

The Indian scholarships mentioned are available from three sources. The federal government will provide funds to worthy students upon application and recommendation of the local superintendent; the State of Washington Department of Education also offers a certain number of scholarships each year to Indians of one-quarter degree or more as one item in the federal assistance contract; and finally, the loan committee of the Yakima tribal council will consider applications for educational assistance, drawing upon tribal money for the benefit of deserving students. The requirements are not stringent, but the applicants are few. In 1942 one student from the Yakima jurisdiction was granted a scholarship for a four year course of study in civil engineering at Washington State College. He was one of four in the state receiving state awards. [121]

From the circumstances here reviewed it can hardly be maintained that the Indian is convinced of the value of an education, and this despite the preachments that he has been subjected to for decades. Stirring appeals for educational facilities and inspiring claims for successes in bringing Indian children out of savagery have charged the pages of Indian agents' reports all through the early years of the reservation's existence. We do not believe that these enthusiasms were intended to deceive, but it does seem that they were ill-advised and premature. Something more fundamental than the integrity and industry of administrators is involved.

The bald truth is that, despite the claims of educators, an education is not worth the effort to the Indian. Generation after generation he has discovered to his disillusionment that learning how to read and write, or even to keep books and repair machines, does not solve his problem. It does not make him a white man. It does not *give* him a job in Toppenish or Yakima. It does not make him an eligible candidate for the district attorney's office. It does not open the doors of the social leaders to him. Even if it makes him a more successful farmer he is still an Indian farmer. This is the crux of the Indian's problem, and the issue which we will do well to face.

Quite apart from these facts — and their importance must not be underestimated — there remains the signal truth that cultural evolution of whatever kind does not take place as a result of formal, academic education. That we have gone on the assumption that it does has been our mistake. Formal education is a relatively rare phenomenon among peoples taken the world over, and it is a comparatively recent development in our own cultural history. Yet the world and its peoples have changed customs in an unending kaleidoscopic fashion for millennia. And today, before our eyes, history is m*ade* and customs change [122] in spite of our teachings to the contrary, and in the face of our reluctance to admit the need for new patterns of behavior. Grammarians continue to teach the "proper" forms of speech and moralists to deplore the loss of feminine reserve while the populace goes on as ever; to set up its own standards of speech and ladylike behavior. Somehow this obvious certainty has escaped us in our preoccupation with the magic of formal learning. We have seen its revolutionizing effects upon individuals, and upon nations, and we know what a disadvantage it entails to both to be without it. And yet it would seem that it is time that we accept the fact that education, as we commonly use the term, has definite limitations. It is not the panacea that we think it is. It will not, of itself, solve our social problems.

This is not to say that education has had no effect upon the Indian. It definitely has; but what we fail to take into account in practice is that it has been able to produce its effects only after the way has been prepared by other equally determinative influences. So far these other forces have eluded control — they have even escaped adequate detection and delineation — and consequently the efforts to apply our techniques of instruction have been thwarted, buffeted, and misdirected. We operate on an unsteady base and with unknown potentials. Without any controlled knowledge of the part education plays in the whole process of custom change — and that is our aim in educating the Indian — we do not know just how to make the most of our techniques or what the results will be. All that we are sure of is that some results will be apparent in time if our efforts are prolonged and intensive enough. Pedagogy has been our only device; hence we cling to it in hope and desperation rather than with conviction and assurance in its efficacy. In other words; our attitude toward education is more properly a part of faith than of science. [123]

CHAPTER V
CONCLUSIONS

Our conclusions must be that the Yakimas have neither fully adjusted themselves to our way of life nor retained intact the virtues and ideals of their aboriginal culture. They live an in-between existence of tag ends and uncertainties. On the one hand, they cling to certain survivals of their ancient habits; odd bits of custom and belief which immediately set them apart from their white neighbors. They preserve not a few material items out of the past such as moccasins, baby cradles, tipis, and a ceremonial regalia which is the embalmed secular dress of old. More important is their retention of aboriginal forms of behavior which vitally affect the character of their live today. Among these may be mentioned the preference for outdoor living in mountain or river camps during the summer; their migratory habits, their concept of hospitality, their adherence *to* native kinship reckoning frameworks; their reactionary views upon group leadership, their perseverance in native religious cults, and their rejection of modern medical science in favor of native practitioners.

All these things are not only sources of friction with the whites; they are not even completely satisfying to the Indian, for they are in themselves anachronistic and incomplete. They are fragments of the old cultural fabric; frayed ends and weak seams in an out-moded garment. They do not satisfy for emotional warmth because they are no longer integrated one with another in a master pattern. For any given individual, one habit or idea does not presuppose the others; and he is never quite curtain how his fellow men are going to react with respect to its observance. He is not secure in his world of multiple courses, conflicting principles; and personal options. His friends, even [124] his closest relatives, are enigmas, unpredictable in their reactions. This is brought out when one attempts to find out whether some expected event is to take place; such as a move to the mountains, or whether some appropriate native ritual is to be carried out. It is irritating but illuminating to discover that no one knows until a few hours before the actual occurrence — if it does indeed transpire.

While some customs have therefore been preserved to the confusion of both whites and Indians, others equally vital to the old way of life have faded and lost their appeal. We need not dwell at this point upon the numerous items in their material culture which the Indians have abandoned in favor of the technological advantages which our science has brought to them. This is an important topic, but we are concerned for the moment with those customs which have vanished and for which no substitutes have been accepted. Chief among these are the devices for social control, and in that sense they are the negative values of the old culture. They are the "don'ts" and the "musts" of aboriginal life, the formalized procedures and the avoidances that gave a well-defined form and a certain uniqueness to the Yakimas as a people. It is only necessary to recall what has been said of the failure of public opinion, the relaxation of marriage restrictions, the demise of constituted authority, the avoidance of economic compulsions, and the emasculation of parental authority, to appreciate to what lengths this process of abandonment of controls can go.

The sum and substance of this conclusion is that the Yakima are without faith or independence. They are men without a whole culture, which in anthropological parlance is the organized self-perpetuating totality of a particular peoples' customs and beliefs irrespective of their degree of refinement. Bereft of anchors and stays, they are bewildered and irresponsible. Deprived [125] of their own system of social control, they lack conviction in the one that has been imposed upon them. Without a coordinated system of belief and behavior, they vacillate and dissipate their energies in conflict. In a world of the white man's making, they have nothing that they can be proud of and nothing that they can defend. It is ironical that in spite of all our efforts to civilize them we have only succeeded in desocializing them.

The essence social living is that it embodies a system of privileges and obligations. In any human society worthy of the name there are rules of behavior, some things which can, and other things which cannot be done, acts that are appropriate and acts that are improper. These specified ways of doing things and thinking about them are what we call the social forms of a given people. They are artificial phenomena in that they modify and redirect the drives and demands that motivate human beings. They at once provide for satisfactions and place restraints on impulse and passion in ways that make human life something entirely different from that of dogs or cats, for example. When the man-made controlling devices are abandoned or ignored a people lose their social balance, and if they survive as a group at all they do so under tutelage and protection with controls being imposed from the outside. That is the position in which the Yakima find themselves today. They have lost the initiative to maintain themselves as a self-contained society.

The absence of self-discipline is evident on every side. As has been noted, the Yakima commonly avoid the restraints that marriage imposes and elude the responsibility of child support. They repudiate parental and community authority. They maintain only those forms which give them pleasure and disavow the restricting patterns. Their physical wants are given free play, as is evident in their mating, whenever and with whomever they please, in their eating whatever they want whenever they want it, in their relaxation from labor when [126] they tire or get bored, in their careless overindulgence in liquor, and in their disposition to allow children to behave as they see fit. In their world the necessity for food and clothing does not imply the necessity to submit to discipline; they want little of either and for many that little can be obtained with no labor by sponging or by desultory and relaxing efforts at hunting and fishing. Labor for others, which involves a stipulated amount of service at a given place and time, is irksome because it is confining. Even in their play this diffuse attitude of irresponsibility is apparent. Every society makes provision for the relaxation and refreshment of its members, but, again, these <u>are</u> provisions, and in a real sense they are rewards for good behavior. There are certified rules and places as well as accepted forms of play. There are rules and proprieties to every game. Culturally approved relaxation is <u>controlled</u> play. For most of the Yakimas self-indulgence knows no rules of time or place or duration. It can intervene at any point in the business of making a living. Men leave their haying to go to a rodeo, to go on a "vacation" to the mountains, to go to the agency or to town to meet their friends; and there is no certainty about when they will return.

The net result of all of this is that the Yakimas are an aggregate of people who do not act with unison. They are not a true society. They have no group sentiment. They are a conglomeration of individualists, each one seeking his private satisfactions in his own way regardless of the effects upon others. In part, the inability of the Yakimas to get along among themselves is due to their disparate origins in several tribes, but fully as much comes from their decultured condition. As a group they simply have nothing in common with each other.

It is a commonly observed fact that men in all lands tend to turn to religion for aid and comfort in time of personal crisis. A social crisis is [127] not the same as a personal crisis, although the former frequently is the underlying cause of the latter. If the two were synonymous we should expect to find all the Yakimas earnestly praying for salvation. As a matter of fact, most of them are not; and the reason is that the social chaos in which they live does not distress them individually. As has already been pointed out, this de-structured condition is an ideal setting for unrestrained personal satisfactions. True enough, a hedonistic pursuit of personal benefit is not satisfying to many people for it has ifs unpleasant consequences; and the older most men become the truer this is for them. The Yakimas are no different from other human beings and so we should expect to find, and do find, many who lament the consequences of social disorder but do nothing about it. It is only a minority who feel the pinches and stings so acutely that they have need for active relief and who turn to religion to find it. Yet even in this resort it is obvious that the Yakima satisfactions are purely personal. Both of the native cults make protestations of charity and brotherly love, but the actual manifestations of these virtues are rare. Cult members practice their rituals and prayers for the emotional releases that they derive from them. They come away purged and refreshed but no better citizens.

That this incomplete life pattern is the business of the Indians and not ours is a short-sighted contention. Apart from the purely academic and humanitarian issues involved, the Indian's problems are definitely our problems. The conditions under which they live vitally affects our socio-economic interests. With their lack of attention to their own health they endanger our own. With their disregard of law and order they impose upon our legal system. Their privileged economic position brings complaints from wild life conservationists, commercial competitors, and public institutions supported by local taxation. They do not maintain a self-sustaining society; they are expensive wards [128] living on the fringes of our culture, producing little and that little only because of the paternalistic supervision of our government. Without this prop most Yakimas would succumb.

However much some people might resent this situation, the fact is that the Indian is with us. Nor is he "our vanishing American." Contrary to popular opinion the linden population is not decreasing but increasing at a rate even exceeding that of our national figure. There was a serious decline up to 1900, but at the present time Indians are increasing at the rate of one per cent per year as against the .7 per cent of our general population. In the United States in 1901 there were 269,388 Indians; in 1936 there were 337,336; in 1940 there were 361,816; and some statisticians estimate one-half million by 1960. Furthermore, these citizens control several million acres of land with its natural wealth, and some of them need more then they have. The Yakima themselves hold well over a million acres and an untouched timber stand valued at $10,000,000 at a minimum. Nor must we forget that it is the policy of the present administrators of Indian affairs to make the natives economically secure on a land base. In many cases to do this It is necessary to acquire addition holdings by purchase or legislation.

With all this in the balance it is obvious that we have a stake in the Indian's future whether we like it or not. As humanitarians we owe him a debt. As practical business men we owe it to ourselves to make of it a mutually satisfactory investment. It behooves us to give serious consideration to the Indian problem because it is our problem, if for no more lofty reason.

In June, 1943, there appeared a report of a Senate Sub-Committee which recommended a series of drastic revisions in our Indian policy. Among other things it proposed the release of Indian property from federal control and the [129] placing of it on local tax rolls, the closure of Indian day schools, the abandonment of Indian forests, the release of Indian forests to the Department of Agriculture, and the distribution of tribal funds per capita to individual members. If followed, these recommendations would initiate a harsh new order for our 350,000 unprepared citizens. Doubtless many of them would not survive its rigor. There are some individuals who can view this prospect with complacency, and others who are inclined to agree with the spirit of the report and assert that the Indian is weakened rather than strengthened by our present official policy. At the same time, it is neither fair nor wise to again toss the Indian football into the political arena to be scrimmaged over by representatives of opposing ideologies. This has happened too often already.

If we are to make a real contribution toward the solution of our common problems we must understand the historical background of the Indian's plight. We must appreciate the circumstances which have made him what he is, and the part that we as his teacher and policeman have played in this. At bottom, the difficulty has been this: we have, by means of exhortation and pressures of various sorts, succeeded in causing the Indian to abandon many of his old habits, such as purchasing wives and worshipping strange gods, yet have not succeeded in devising a means to induce him to adopt our habits instead. We have shattered his old system of values and have failed to inculcate a new one.

One of the first steps in the disintegrative process was the early attempt by the agency officials to get the Yakimas to abandon their aboriginal economic base and to adopt farming. Favors were dispensed to those who were adaptable, they were estranged from their fellow members, and the basis of chiefly pre-emence and control was udermined. The agent became the law, replacing the chief and public opinion. Men with property bestowed by the agent, [130] i.e. amenable men, became the important men; but they were not admired for their wisdom or acknowledged as leaders in place of the old chiefs. Contributing to the process was the policy of establishing individually owned house-holds and lands — in effect, at least, a program of "divide and rule," for a division of interest was effected thereby and the ties of family and community were weakened. The intimate knowledge of the affairs of others, the aboriginal controls over children by a village disciplinarian, the sociability of village gatherings, the story telling and the moral instruction by elders at campfire congregations, the centralization of interests in village affairs — all these were dissipated by the breakup of the village.

Equally potent were the effects of thie uprooting of most of the tribes from their old homeland soil and their transportation to the reservation. They felt like strangers and never settled into their former channels; they were at loose ends in a new land crowded with new neighbors. In this connection it is a remarkable fact that the indigenous inhabitants of the reservation area are still the most conservative Indians.

Members of other tribes are more like white men.

For another factor contributing to the abandonment of native social controls we must look to our own ideals. As Americans we have always prided ourselves upon our individuality, self-sufficiency, resourcefulness, and personal worth, regardless of family background. Traditions are not sacred to us as they are to many other peoples. We flout conventions and are proud of it. A man's personal worth is the most important thing, and we admire ruggedness in personality. These characteristics make up the ideal man for us, and there were many men with these traits to spare in pioneer western life. It would be surprising if the Indian had not absorbed some of the recklessness and [131] unconventionality of our forefathers, or the cynicism of our modern youth. Indian boys and girls today will answer a reproof for their conduct with the familiar, "I can take care of myself." Can we blame them?

Although these are important causes of Yakima cultural collapse, by far the most important has been our faulty approach to the cure. It was long ago recognized by educators that adults are much more difficult to teach than children. It is not easy to teach an old dog new tricks, and reservation officials early appreciated that the same applies to old Indians. They therefore felt that the salvation of the native with his strange customs lay in isolating his children and imbuing them with our cultural ideals. There can be no denying that the principle is sound and also that it has achieved some success in its application. But this is not the end of the matter. There are important consequences to the procedure which surely were not envisioned in the beginning, and even today for the most part are not recognized as effects of the educational process. Nevertheless, a moments reflection will show that much of the unruliness of Indian children can be laid at the educator's door. For these young people are taught to admire and give credence to our ideals and to be skeptical of and condemn those taught them by their fathers. They are taught that the Indian customs are wrong, immortal, or fantastic and that they spring from ignorance, stupidity, and fear.

All of this may be true, but it does not inspire a child with an admiration for his father and mother to be told, in effect, that they are ignorant savages. And without respect for their wisdom, and experience, the child is not likely to value their advice or submit to their discipline. It is more probable that the children will turn out to be irreverent savages themselves, confused, torn between two contrary sets of priorities. In any case, they do not obey [132] their parents and the structure of the serial order is destroyed at its base, that is, within the family. Education has been effective then; indeed; too effective. It has destroyed something more valuable than that which it has to offer, namely, peace, security, and the foundation of social stability.

In addition to understanding the weaknesses of our past and present approaches to the Indian problem we must also be aware of the forces against which any new program must contend. Conservatism is most pronounced in persons of middle or advanced age; and in Indians of full blood. Most people who deal intimately with the Yakima say that they prefer to deal with this combination of traits, for their possessors are more honest and reliable. It seems to be a fact that mixed bloods are more unpredictable; and the reason is that they are at odds with both the white and Indian way of life. They are misfits and unhappy because of it. Rejected by both groups they load a groping, frustrated existence and are likely to be more extravagant and unprincipled in their behavior because they have nothing to lose by such irresponsibility.

By the same token they are more easily brought into the white man's camp — if they are invited. The aged are more conservative for several reasons. One is that they have participated more completely in the social values of the old life and in consequence are more disciplined and conscientious. Another is that they have not been much affected by the social and moral confusion of onrushing events in the modern world. Also, they have not been subjected to so many contacts with whites as their children. Then, finally; there is the seeming fact that with the advance of age there comes a marked regression in the thinking of most Yakimas. This is more than a crystallization of the viewpoints of adult life. It is not a mere stabilization of thinking as mature individuals. It seems to be a nostalgic return into the past. In all probability this retrogression is occasioned by disillusionment: the life that was promised them through [133] cooperation with the white man's regime has not materialized and they retire into a disgruntled advocacy of the Indian's ideals. It is a defense and a psychological refuge that they conjure for themselves.

We have to reckon not only with these differences in personal background; the kinds of habits which Americans seem dedicated to change reveal varying degrees of resistance to alteration. Other factors being equal the material objects used by a people are more easily eliminated or replaced by newly introduced ones than are new habits or thought or behavior; and this is especially true if the new thing, such as an iron knife, is demonstrably more efficient than the native object, such as a stone knife. But certain customs, such as these which constrain and hamper the forthright expression of impulses or passions, can also be readily eliminated, other things being equal. Contrariwise, it is difficult to substitute features which interpose additional obstacles to the direct expression of a physical want, as knives and forks do for the Indian who is accustomed to eating his food by the more direct mode of using his fingers.

The pressure of group opinion, whether of family, associates, or the community at large, enters to complicate the problem facing the reformer. In the case of newly introduced material objects this element has a minimum effect, and this is one important reason why they are more readily accepted. They involve only one person, the user, and an inert object, and so only his wishes are relevant. If he wants to adopt a new <u>thing</u>, such as the white man's axe or his coat, that is generally his business alone. He may suffer some ridicule for his poor taste, but he does not thereby infringe upon the rights or deny his obligations to other people; therefore, they are less concerned. They take a non-personal interest in his vagary and so leave him more to his own desires. It id otherwise with social patterns, for these personally affect other members of the [134] group; and the Indian who proposes to junk old social customs for new ones introduced by the white man is in for a bad time of it. That is why it has been so difficult to effect a change to our notions of private property and generosity. The Indian who refuses indiscriminate hospitality or who rejects communal living and perennial visiting offers a personal affront to his fellows, and he receives the full measure of their scorn. It Is no longer up to him alone to accept or reject the white man's offerings.

If we would change the Indians we must realise, too, that with them as with us certain persons and things develop into symbols of their distinctness and that in time these come to constitute hard-shelled cores of resistance, difficult to crack. The chief is such a person. To the extent that he is recognized he represents the people, is the embodiment of their ideals and becomes the symbol of their unity and distinctness.

Even though he might have a personal preference for the white man's ways — and this is not normally true — the pressure of his followers upon him to continue to be an Indian is far greater than for ordinary men who lack positions of public, trust and responsibility. Long hair braids for men, buckskin clothing, the medicine man, and the Long Houses have taken on the same symbolic significance for some of the Yakimas. So have the native religious cults. The Shaker Cult is militantly and exclusively Indian. The PomPom religion is the leaven for much of the ferment resisting further progress of the adjustment process. It is the rallying point of the die-hard conservatives.

It is futile to say that the process of adaptation "takes time." If time were the critical factor in effecting change, and if progress in the past can afford us any criterion for the future, then we could look forward to at least another century of wardship for the Indian. But we need not accept this [135] cliché. Those who plead for time to remodel the Indian into a white man argue on a fallacy. It is easy to demonstrate that custom is not a biological matter. It is not instinctive and it is not inbred in the biological sense. It does not need to be, and in fact, it cannot be, bred out of a population as can a physical trait such as skin color. It can be radically and completely altered in a single generation of infants. We need to keep this in mind to clarify our thinking upon the muddled problem of minority groups.

We need to remember, too, that the Yakima are just one of a large number of minority groups in our country, and if we can profit by our knowledge of them, it is quite possible that we shall have tools to work with the others. The concrete data incorporated in this report are specifically Yakima, but the problem they present is not confined to the reservation in the Yakima Valley. Neither are the conclusions in this chapter. They will apply, except for illustrations, to most Indians on reservations in our northwest, and even to other minorities. [136]

CHAPTER V
Suggestions

It is well in the beginning to come to an understanding of aims in suggesting measures to be adopted in Indian policy. The conviction upon which the following proposals rest is that the Yakima must be absorbed in the dominant white population and lose his identity as an Indian if the problems that he presents and is confronted by as a member of a minority group are to be solved. It is also maintained that this process should be completed as speedily as possible without doing violence to the welfare of either the whites or the Indians.

It is not asserted that the goal of assimilation envisages a state that is inherently and unconditionally perfect. It posits an ideal condition and proclaims a social good only on the explicit assumption that the minority status of the Yakima is undesirable and that any course which contributes to either their social dependence or the prejudice which they now experience is to be rejected. In short, social good is defined primarily if not solely in terms of a reduction of social tensions. This definition of what is desirable like any other that can be imagined, arises from the applications of one particular scale of values that has been selected out of many possible ones. Furthermore, the choice of this measure of what is good for the Yakimas and their neighbors derives from a philosophy which can only be compared, not tested against, other social philosophies or value reckonings. In other words, it has not been arrived at by scientific methodology, nor could it be. Science deals with the values of means, not ends: It says what is or can be, not what should be. It cannot demonstrate that the goal of assimilation is better than any other; but starting with the assumption that it is, both the means of achieving it and the reasons for rejecting other approaches to it are amenable to scientific treatment. [137]

It would be possible to segregate the Yakima and to reconstitute them into a homogeneous tribe with a socially effective group spirit. Individuals in such a unit could be allowed to live their own lives in a secluded universe of thought and custom. Under those circumstances their individual self-respect, pride, ambition, and responsibility could be revived and group ideals to satisfy their needs as a vigorous society could be developed. All this could be done rather easily but the result would be the consolidation of a society within — but not correlative with — a larger society; and, given the fact that existing majority attitudes are what they are, we have little justification for supposing that this would be a happy situation for anyone concerned. Furthermore, we have little warrant for assuming that majority group practices — as opposed to theory — will in the foreseeable future operate to alter the minority status of the Indian. If the experience of the past is indicative, the emergence of such a subordinate cultural enclave would intensify rather than ease the strains in the local setting. Whether the future will or can bring a change in this reaction is problematical; now at least it is certain that the dominant population is not disposed to be sympathetic toward what it regards as the privileges, the conceits, and the infra-human behaviors of the minority element in its midst; and the sharper the definition of the minority group the sharper the imputation of these attributes and the more pronounced the intolerance of them.

Moreover, the more intimate the contacts between the two population elements the more marked the mutual antipathy is likely to be. The fact that many Americans say that they hold no prejudice against Indians, that they even think them an asset and a colorful addition to the American scene, is misleading. The attitude is commendable either, but it seldom bears up under the real test of tolerance. It is characteristic either of those who have had few intimate contacts with Indians as groups or those who regard tolerance as essential to their intellectual [138] Integrity. It is far from typical of the whites who live in the vicinity of reservations. They are confronted with the issues of inter-group contact and they find little that is appealing about them. It is a significant fact that the degree of tolerance which the average American manifests is in inverse proportion to the degree of his familiarity with Indian life. Those who live around reservations are prone to accept the common dictum that Indians are not worth bothering with, even though they might make a few individual exception.

It is easy for the rest of us to berate them. It is also easy to hope that the situation will change "'with time and with education." Something has already been said of this viewpoint with respect to Yakima education. The conclusions arrived at there also apply at this point. In spite of the inadequacy of our approach we cannot afford to relax our efforts against bigotry and ignorance. Tolerance should be championed in the home, the school, and from the public platform; and those who can should lend support with a battery of facts to bolster the cause. But, again, it is incumbent upon the social scientist to admit that there are disconcerting evidences of attitudes which are not amenable to this attack. While it remains to be proved, there is as much evidence for as against the conclusion that the tensions and conflicts which characterize inter-group attitudes are spontaneously generated at the point of contact regardless of the ideological background of the two groups. That they may be ameliorated by training can be freely acknowledged, that they cease to be potential areas of conflict has not been shown. The hope, therefore; that Americans whose lives impinge upon those of the Yakima can be educated out of their discriminatory attitude toward him while he remains an Indian is, as far as can be demonstrated, still a hope. If this is true, nothing is gained by blinking it. If it is disillusioning, that is no warrant for obscuring it. [139]

It is also unwise, became it is misleading, to posit the conflict of economic interests as the basic cause of Yakima-white difficulties, and to propose a mutually satisfactory adjustment of them as a means of realizing inter-group harmony. It is true that the Indians control a considerable quantity of valuable land and other productive resources that are coveted by the white man. It is also true, that there are a few jobs for which both the Indian and the white man regard themselves as eligible and for which they are therefore in competition. But in neither of these cases does the existence or non-existence of the competitive relationship define or coincide with the limits of the two racial elements. That is, not all Indian-prejudiced whites are in competition with Indians and prejudiced whites are not similarly prejudiced toward other whites with whom they compete; and no accumulation of particular instances would ever yield a dichotomy conformable with the interracial border. Since the areas of economic contention do not conform to this line of cleavage it is difficult to see how they can be regarded as either necessary or basic to its formation.

The truth is that the connotations of "Indian" and "white" take shape upon other grounds than the economic and can exist apart from this consideration. The polarization of group differences is structured on the basis of a varied assortment of real or alleged attributes which are at their inception pregnant with dissocative forces. Adverse reactions are either generated spontaneously or they are indoctrinated as a part of the group mores. They may emerge independent of any aggravation, in which case they are in themselves sufficient to creates patterns of avoidance and tension. Or they may be provoked by a challenge situation, in which instance the stimuli might be as varied as those that engender personal antipathies. In other yards, economic contention is only one [140] kind of provocation to inter-group aversions, just as it is in inter-personal relations, and in many instances it plays no part at all. Many whites living in the vicinity of the Yakima and other reservations may resent the restraint put upon their enterprise by governmental restrictions and therefore indirectly manifest an animus toward the Indian which may be said to have an economic foundation. On the other hand, most of them would scoff at the idea that the Indian is a competitor. He does not have the ability, and would not have, they believe, even if given the chance. The majority have no other reason for rejecting him than because he is different from themselves; and almost any business man would admit that he derives economic gain from the presence of the Indian. In short; a contest of economic interests can bring group patterns into sharper focus, and can even stimulate a search for common characteristics upon which to erect an sympathetic dichotomy, but the fact of competition is neither a necessary nor a sufficient explanation of the complex of mutual withdrawals, tensions, suspicions, and antagonism which extend beyond the range of competition and which define the problem of majority-minority relations. An adjustment in this sphere, then, does not offer a reliable prospect of its solution.

A more creative appraisal of the situation reveals that any kind of difference between the white man and the Indian is a potential source of discord. It is, therefore, a misnomer to call the problem a racial one. The fact of biological difference is just one element making for social distance between the two races. There are many other incongruities ranging over the entire cultures of the two peoples, and each one is important. As in the case of economic friction, it would only complicate the problem to be misled into a piecemeal attack upon selected segments. Long hair braids on men can be as irritating [141] to the intolerant white as the PomPom religion perhaps even more so, since he does not have to witness the "superstitious" rites of the cult, and may be ignorant of their existence. In any event, it does not seem feasible to grade later-group differences in point of seriousness; all are important, and the last vestige of irritation will not disappear before the last of them.

In some parts of our country the issue of assimilation is not now pressing. In sections at Arizona and Nevada Indians occupy marginal lands which have so far been comparatively unattractive to the white man. Often tribes have been set off in remote corners or are surrounded by unproductive wastelands. Under such circumstances inter-group frictions are at a minimal. But in places like the Yakima Valley Indian land is attractive, the white man has moved in, and presumably he is there to stay. At lease he will not be ejected without vigorous opposition. A policy of Indian segregation must envisage this clash; not only in the Yakima Valley but elsewhere. For with a homogeneous, healthy, and protected Indian community we must face the prospect of an expanding population and the need for more land to support it. Unless some form of population control or dispersal is contemplated, the demand for more living room must become an ever-widening one. This not too distant complication of the problem does not appear to have been squarely faced.

In view of these circumstances, it would seem that a consistent policy of isolation and reconstitution of the Yakima community would create more problems than it would solve. There is even less to be said in favor of a policy, if it be that, of letting the problem work itself out or of countenancing a continuation of the practice of the past whereby Indian policy fluctuated with the changing tempers and ideologies of the times. Either of these courses is expensive, self-perpetuating, and frustrating to Indian and white man alike. [142]

The alternative is a controlled dissolution and absorption of the Yakima community into the dominant American society. Such a program would at least have the virtues of clarity, consistency, and finality. It would not result in the immediate and enthusiastic welcoming of the Yakima into the American community; but it would promote their self-reliance and their self-respect, and it would diffuse them, as individuals, in the "melting pot" with more assurance of being accepted as individuals than present policy can promise.

If this is to be the program, then it becomes necessary to understand the Yakima and his psychology better than in the past. The ideal would be for every American to assume this responsibility, but it is above all incumbent upon those persons whose duty it is to administer policy, those officials in all departments who work directly with the Indian upon the reservation. Most of these people will protest that they do know the Indian and will draw upon a record of long and capable service to illustrate their contention. Without any desire to disparage these claims it must be said that there is an important difference between merely living near and working with Indians and actually making a systematic study of their customs and world view. The latter approach yields an understanding that the fragments gleaned from the former can never give. Indeed, it is a fact that can often easily be demonstrated that the hit-and-miss contacts that occur in the course of official duty give a badly distorted picture of Indian psychology. This applies even to the more intimate contacts made in the home by investigators of health and other personal conditions. The importance of their responsibility makes it imperative that such field workers be given training in social psychology and anthropology. It should be stressed that orthodox training in social welfare is not enough to meet the demands of the situation. Social workers, without spreading out into [143] fields ordinarily covered only by the anthropologist, tend to approach the Indian with the preconceptions and biases of our own culture, and for all their energy and good will they are liable to defeat their purpose from the start.

In line with this suggestion is the related one that we forego our impulse to attack the superficial aspects of the Indian's failure to adjust to our patterns and concentrate upon the more critical causes. We may deplore the medicine man's activity, for example, but, it does no good to rail against or intimidate him. He is but the symptom of a whole system of thought about disease. So, too, with the disregard of sanitation in the home, the murderous neglect of the sick, early mortality, etc. The root cause is the manner of viewing sickness, and many consequences that Americans deplore flow from this one set of premises. In the same way, a shabby house cannot be renovated by preaching the ideal of beauty to the owner, or even by giving him the paint and tools to repair it, for the reasons why he does not do so in the first place lie deeper and have other manifestations at odds with American ideals. Neither can we make permanent progress in providing for destitute and delinquent children by paying for their support or by hiring more social workers, policemen, or judges. The cause, as in the other instances, remains untouched by our patchwork, and the "cure" is but an expensive stopgap.

In the past, three principal causes have been employed to achieve the goal of assimilation. One of them, prominent in the early years, relied upon the power of the reservation authorities and took the form of threats, intimidations, and acts of physical force. It had an effect; as it probably always would; but such methods are hard to justify to others if not to one's own conscience. The results, moreover, were not entirely satisfactory. In the end only negative values were established. That is, coercion and suppression did [144] eliminate certain practices, but the same means were ineffectual in establishing other intended modes in their place. The prohibition of shamanism did not insure the adoption of scientific medical advice. Add to this the fact that very often suppression only succeeded in driving the banned custom underground, and the case for forcible persuasion, in the cultural sphere is not a very strong one. Officials today do not support it; reservation policy permits the practice of any peaceful custom.

The two other means were conciliatory; namely, education and a system of rewards. Neither of them, however, met with the degree of success that was anticipated, mainly because each of them produced a major dilemma. The case of education has already been discussed. It will be remembered that, while instruction of Indian children by white teachers has been productive of results, little headway has made with adults. This resulted in an ever-present drag on the efforts of teachers who could not offset the effects of home influences on their pupils. This is obviously a self-perpetuating involution which only time and immeasurable patience can gradually deflect out of its course. In the meantime, the success that was achieved was not consoling; it became apparent that the cultural meaning away of children from their parents disorganized their thinking and destroyed parental authority. The dilemma was whether to continue to feed these cultural orphans on the impersonal pap of the boarding school and contribute to the fragmentation of the society or to return them to the guidance of their fathers. Present policy has elected to reestablish the family bonds but to intensify education in the day school among white associates. Intermingling at the school age level will probably accelerate acculturation; the home influences will continue to operate against it.

It was a well-recognized policy of Agent Wilbur to dispense favors to those Indians who conformed to the standards which he set up. He made the most [145] of the regulation which restricted annuities to those who worked for them, using it as an instrument to press men into the civilised habits of wage earning, faming, and cattle tending. He even went beyond this and cautiously discriminated against those who would not attend his church services and persisted in polygyny, shamanistic activity, and gambling. A few individuals flourished under this regime; many others cynically accepted his gifts and paid lip service to his demands; and there remained an adamant block of conservatives who were embittered and drew even further away from the imposed ideals. The outlines of these three levels of adjustment are still quite apparent.

Upon first thought it might be supposed that a system of awards would be the most effective and painless of any means to induce the acceptance of a desired role. It is perhaps a truism to say that any person will do anything if the reward is great enough.

This is as true of the Indian as it is of anyone else; but in his case the only reward that is great enough is a jealously guarded privilege that has not been tendered to him. For it is nothing short of our full acceptance of him on a par with ourselves. We have rejected his scheme of life as unsuitable, even for him, and yet we will not permit him to enter ours as one of us. We resent his being an Indian; but withhold the one thing that would induce him to become a white man. That is our dilemma, as it is his tragedy. It is not possible to compromise with it and offer him substitutes and half measures and expect him to be satisfied. When we ask him to work, he asks why. Wealth brings him no returns in the real values of esteem and emulation on the reservation, and off the reservation he is still an Indian. To put it succinctly, we expect him to conform to our restrictive measures, but have denied him the rewards of this sacrifice of his selfishness and willfulness. As long as he cannot look forward to acceptance in our society, the only one that is left, he can see no point in paying the price of self-discipline. [146]

If all these things are true, and if we are willing to face the facts fearlessly, then we are led to the conclusion that our past failures to remodel the Indian have resulted from our failure to cope with all the ramifications of the problem, from our near-sighted effort to prune branches when it was the root that needed attention. If we are to save ourselves this unending labor, and, more importantly, if we are to meet the task with foresight rather than with a series of expedients, the problem as a totality must be considered. That in the conviction upon which the following suggestions rest.

Granting the goal of complete and rapid assimilation, four propositions are offered upon which to build a program. The first is that the Indian community must be treated as a whole in any measures that are to be applied to it. That is, the effective techniques must be those which will organize the mass opinion of the community, in all its parts at the same time and in the same ways, thus giving it unity and consistency. The molding of adult opinion is therefore an essential aim, and it should not be divorced from that of the children. Young and oil should proceed together, and the special attention given to children in school must be in the nature of a reinforcement of total group opinion.

The second proposition is that the obvious imposition of external controls defeats its own purpose. It alienates support and engenders resistance simply because it is external and therefore lacks internal sanctions. Even if passively accepted, conformance to the stipulated ideals is without the spirit and conviction that is essential to a self-propelling society. Briefly then, the Indian must <u>want</u> to become a white man.

The third proposition is that this end cannot be gained by any of the transparent methods that have been tried on Indian reservations, and therefore [147] that subterfuges are necessary. This is a proposal that is pregnant with alarms, and it could be obscured to avoid them. But, once more, it is necessary to appraise the facts with candor. If we are agreed that it is to the best interests of both the Indian and the white man that there be a fusion of the two and that the process should take place with a minimum of injury and exhaustion; we cannot well afford to shrink from a tool that is available for that purpose. Furthermore, providing tools for social control is the aim of social science, and unless we are prepared to accept the consequences it is better that we call a halt to our search before more are developed. In America we have ample reason to disavow the unscrupulous use of deceit and obscurantism in the manipulation of populations, but as long as we maintain the ideals upon which our democracy was founded we need have no fears and should, indeed, welcome knowledge of social control as weapons for our defense.

The fourth proposition is implied in the last two. It is that the problem of cnverting the Indian is one in motivations; hence the attack msst be on this level and not on the academic one which stultifies the efforts of the school-teacher. Indians, like other people, can learn whatever we wish to teach them. They can learn – that is, appreciate intellectually — that cleanliness is healthful, that adultery is an evil, that milk is nutritious, that intensive agriculture or stock raising is profitable, and all the rest that we have endeavored to teach them. Many, if not most, of them will agree to our conclusions — rationally. They do not even need a blackboard demonstration to be impressed with the truth of some of the things that we insist upon. They are observant, and they have object lessons all around them. Most of them accept us as their intellectual superiors and will grant that we have found irrefutable answers to many problems which confound them. [148]

But to acknowledge the truth of our contentions does not imply a conviction in their supreme importance. To admit that a careful tilling of the soil brings a more certain return than does hunting over it, or a greater income than does the leasing of it, does not commit a man to the life of a farmer. This holds for Indians as it does for us. Schoolteachers themselves will admit that their being a utilities executive would be more lucrative for them; but there are nevertheless many who remain schoolteachers, and cheerfully so. In other words, something more is involved than a knowledge of addition or long division, something more than an appreciation of the technical superiority of electric lights over kerosene lamps. Basically, men pursue different ends because they value them differently, and they come by their convictions on the worth of ends to be striven for as a result of social processes toward which we are only beginning to manifest a scientific attitude.

It is true that the reservation schoolteacher labors diligently to inculcate our ideals in the minds of his young Indian charges. He spends much of his time trying to establish our standards of health, wealth, and happiness. But the only devices at his command are pedagogical; by precept, by argument, and by rational demonstration he tries to convince his students. Yet the mainsprings of their action are emotional, and these are conditioned by subtle, persistent stimuli, often, unconsciously applied through intimate association, and beginning in early infancy. Their effects are enduring, and they are not likely to be altered through schoolroom associations and by logical demonstrations.

People "like" things even though they "know" that they are wrong, pernicious, or unprofitable, and they will often go on liking them, fighting for them, and even dying for them without caring or being able to care whether they [149] can be justified by reason or not. If necessary, reasons will be manufactured to vindicate habitual, unreasoned acts and prejudices, and counter-argument is a puny instrument for an attack, upon them. All this is, of course, quite apart from the fact that the Indian frequently begins his reasoning with a different set of premises than we do, and that these are likewise unassailable by logic.

It is not the purpose here to assert a well-defined dichotomy in human thinking, and to insist that reason and emotion are mutually antagonistic forces or complexes. We need not; and should not, call some acts reasonable and others emotional.

Element of both are present in every act. But there are the two components, and the one is educable by our schoolroom techniques while the other, the motivational component, remains beyond their control. At most they can impair and confuse this element; they do not clarify and constructively redirect it.

Some of the techniques that are appropriate to this component are well known and are in daily use in our society. They are so subtle and painless that most people are not aware that they are being employed, and they are so potent that their manipulators spend millions of dollars each year for the privilege of utilizing facilities for their operations – and think themselves well repaid. We have come to call these techniques of persuasion "salesmanship" or "advertising" or, more ominously, "propaganda" and have learned to some extent, to be on our guard against them. This, however, has not destroyed their effectiveness as an instrument for molding mass opinion. Their power, and their appropriateness in the present discussion; lies in the fact that they are capable of implanting a new idea so deftly in the mind of a subject that it seems to him that he has evolved it himself. Under such circumstances there is no [150] question of his conviction of its value. By these means a group of people can painlessly be induced to want those things that others have decided that they should want.

Books of many descriptions have been written upon this subject, and it is not to the point to enter upon it here. However, since the multiple devices of commercial advertizing, high-pressure salesmanship, and political campaigning have never been exploited for the conscious purpose of culture change, it is pertinent to relate them to the problem that we are discussing. An Indian reservation, with its inhabitants in the status of wards, and with definite and restricted boundaries, affords ideal conditions for a program of this kind. Utilizing well tested principles of applied psychology, simple, direct ideas might be presented, then stressed by repetition and indirection; shibboleths and slogans could be developed, constructive sympathies mobilized, and contrary views excluded or neutralized. The powerful forces of vanity and emulation could be stimulated and oriented toward the desired end just as they are in our advertising. With the resources and experiences at our disposal, it would be premature to assert that a well organised campaign would fail to induce Indian women to buy <u>and use</u> vacuum cleaners, soap, and hats; or that men would reject a new type of leadership under its compulsion. Emotional fillips such as bands, parades, and community singing should not be despised as aids in gaining the desired end. It might even be possible, with more experience and knowledge of their control, to make use of manufactured events and rumor.

It need not be emphasized that in such a program caution is imperative. The idea should not be to stir up an emotional orgy, but on the contrary to organize motivations in support of a well conceived system for substituting our ideas for those of the Indian. Some of the most potent motivations spring from [151] the negativistic emotions such as fear, suspicion, and doubt. At the same time, to attempt to capitalize upon them without more experience than we now have might result in disaster. They should not be excluded from consideration, but in the meantime it might be wiser to concentrate upon activating the forces on the emotional level which are more likely to produce constructive results. The urges that manifest themselves in expressions of devotion, dependence, and self-expression are suitable areas for exploitation, to mention only a few.

Closely allied to these verbal mechanisms of motivational control are the visual stimulants. The tremendous possibilities offered by visual instruction in the educational field has only recently been fully realized, mainly as a result of the need to teach millions of men in the armed services. A wide variety of visual aids have been developed for this purpose; and it is probable that teaching methods will be widely effected everywhere with expanding research on them. Indian pupils should certainly be given the opportunity to gain by this improvement, but for the purposes of our argument another possibility is of greater moment. Indians have for years been subjected to a kind of visual instruction in the form of actual demonstrations. The functions of field matrons, extension agents and government farmers have been just this; namely, to show the Indian what to do, using actual situations and materials. We have concluded that the results have not been wholly satisfactory. The reason has been, of course, that although the Indian might know what to do, he was not interested in doing it, and often time could not even be induced to learn. The implication is that visual materials can and should be used not so much as an instrument for imparting knowledge as one for instilling motivation; not as a device for teaching how to do a thing, but as a means for activating the will to do it. [152]

The potency of each mechanisms as the moving picture for doing just this has long been appreciated in our national life. As a molder of mass opinion, as a purveyor of ideas and ideals, as an arbiter of fashion and fancy, it is an instrument second to none. And no one will deny that major operations under its anesthesia are painless. Indians like movies, too. They see ours when they can — some of ours. Most of them are not intended for their consumption and so they cannot emotionally identify themselves with the situations portrayed. With specially prepared and adroitly oriented productions this obstacle to their conversion to our norms could be removed. This stipulation obviously holds for any program that might be organized. It must meet local conditions; and that means the needs and ideologies of individual tribes. We do not get much out of a Chinese movie; neither should we expect a Yakima to participate fully in a broadcast for the Navajos or a motion picture for the Cheyenne. If the expense of such an intensive program be urged as an insuperable obstacle, we might, as an alternate consideration, recall the sum of expenditures for Indian welfare since 1865, and add an indefinite annual plus for the coming years. Some groups like the Navajos already have radios and broadcasts in their language, but it does not appear that they are used for the purposes here discussed.

So far only the techniques for mass indoctrination have been considered. There are other possibilities for applied psychology on the individual level. The laboratory and clinical studies that have been made on suggestion, reconditioning, and personality reorganization have never been put to use as aids in cultural change just because they have individual reference. The possibility exists, nonetheless, of utilizing these techniques indirectly to achieve desired social ends under the circumstances that occur on a reservation. The devices themselves, such as those for instilling suggestion, might be employed to [153] inaugurate patterns of habit substitution through a selection and remotivation of key individuals. It would be possible, for example, to establish avoidances and compulsions in an individual under hypnosis which would not be too repugnant to his nature and therefore would not create emotional conflicts prejudicial to his personality structure. In this way suggestions designed to alter personal habits, such as those connected with eating, dressing, and sleeping arrangements, might be made, and later reinforced if necessary, with the expectation that a group of influential subjects would be strongly motivated to lead the others along the desired course of behavior. If the changes that could be effected by this means seem trivial, it should be remembered that they are nevertheless important points of friction in themselves and, furthermore, that small bits of behavior go to make up larger significant patterns that must necessarily change with the deflection of their component parts. It must be borne in mind, too, that many individuals would be happy to alter their habits if conviction could be brought to bear and uncertainty dispelled by doing so.

Closely connected with this aspect of the proposal is a second possibility: namely, that the majority of Indians in the confusion of their minds offer a ripe field for the purposeful services of a capable confidant and advisor. No one with Indian friends can doubt their need for unburdening themselves. Even reservation officials, who have no time to establish confidences, must listen to innumerable petty complaints and confessions. With the proper approach and design, a psychologist-confessor could not only do much individual good, but could lay the foundations for the trust and conviction that is necessary for a new program of action. Both of these possibilities relate in the first instance to the individual, but the emphasis should be upon using the appropriate techniques to alter the conditions of the group. [154]

A more distant possibility for accomplishing this purpose falls in a different category from the suggestions already made. It cannot be discussed in concrete terms because so far only a beginning has been made toward developing the concepts necessary for the realization. It calls for a new start upon the study of the subject of cultural change with some forthright statements of aim and procedure. It is believed that our attacks upon the problem of inducing changes in custom must be only partially satisfactory until such time as we have a more enlightened knowledge of the processes of change in the cultural sphere. At present we know very little about the nature of group habit modifications, in spite of all our random attention to the subject. Our descriptions of change have been in the nature of historical generalizations rather than in terms of mechanisms for the operation of which the time-place factor is irrelevant. As a consequence, we have not developed any incisive and productive concepts to define the process of modification, and hence can see no significant relations between one instance of it and another.

The basic problem in this approach is therefore an analysis of what change in custom is. Its basic assumption is that we can know something in advance of the ways in which a people will react to new ideas, since that which has been discovered to be true in one case can be expected to occur in another when the same factors are operative. Stated in another way, it assumes that there are repetitious occurrences in human group responses to similar stimuli, and that there are similar stimuli and equivalent factors in diverse and historically unrelated instances. This approach takes the view that our lack of progress in this study is the result of our inability to perceive similarity in diversity, a result which springs from our customary and unimaginative ways of defining sameness and difference in cultural data. It is reasoned that our [155] traditional ideas of like and unlike are unenlightening when applied to the material with which we work; and that when they have been recast, the way will be open for a redefinition of the interrelations of man-made things, and with that will come the possibility of a fresh understanding of developmental processes in the social sphere.

To establish the validity of this approach to our social problems; that of the Indian included, it is necessary that considerable research be done. The materials are at hand, but they must be investigated carefully. We must, for example, devote ourselves to a minute analysis of what takes place when customs undergo change in the normal course of events in our own and other well-understood cultures. We must make repeated studies of customs selected for the knowledge that we have of all the factors bearing upon their alteration, with attention to the degree and kind of change which they experience. Our inventions, our fads, our acceptance of new ideas, foods, and mechanical contrivances from abroad, or as a result of deliberate campaigns here at home, offer a fertile field for the study of recurring patterns and the limiting conditions for their developments. The question of limits is especially important, since it has been one of the stumbling blocks to success in this endeavor. We have realized that no generalization, even in the physical sciences, has absolute universal validity but must be hedged and qualified by conditions for its applicability, we will have come a long way toward understanding regularities in social phenomena.

That there are recurrences and well-defined processes in some aspects of cultural development — the new things do follow patterns — has been clearly demonstrated in the case of language. Word alterations and groupings reveal some striking consistencies operating over long periods of time, and the persistent [156] affects of grammatical structure in molding the thoughts of its users is a significant phenomenon for students of cultural change. As yet we know little of the controls; and limiting conditions for these developments, but that some regularities are apparent in linguistic forms should cause us to hesitate before declaring them to be unlikely in other aspects of culture. Some hopeful investigations have been made in these other areas of custom, and some tentative conclusions seem warranted, They are involved, as indeed they must be, and have no place in this general discussion. Much work lies ahead, moreover, and caution must be exercised. It is the necessity for the encouragement of these attempts, and the recognition of their importance; that must be stressed at this time if we are to gain any control knowledge of our social problems.

Presuming that these suggestions can be organized into a practical program for the cultural adaptation of the Indian in a way that would reduce the antagonism toward him, there would still remain the racial barrier to complete assimilation. Physical differences generate repellent forces fully as potent as cultural ones, and these cannot be changed in a day. But physical absorption must go along with the cultural if there is to be an end to the Indian problem. A public appreciation of the implications of race will help to bring this about, but we cannot expect too much of mere factual indoctrination. It is important, for instance, that everyone be convinced of the established fact that the Indian is not one whit inferior, mentally or physically, to the white man before we can hope for popular tolerance of intermarriage; but the emotional block is still there for most people regardless, and it will ever remain for the unusual individual to actually take the step of marrying an Indian.

This ultimate deterrent we must acknowledge, but there is hope in the fact that today there are many mixed bloods whose intermediate physical status [157] increases their eligibility as mates for the white man. With them both whites and full bloods unite with less hesitation than with each other. In some places there is a decided tendency for the hybrid element to marry with full bloods, thus producing a more marked concentration of Indian blood in the succeeding generations. This is not an unexpected development; the same cultural and emotional factors are at work in it as in the aversions to full white-full Indian unions, and they can be reduced in the same ways. The hope of complete assimilation rests with the salvaging of those of intermediate status. Through them the Indian as a physical type may eventually disappear, and except for a romantic twinge we must, as realists, look forward to this day.

Plate III
a. Modern dwelling
b. Modern dwelling: a councillor's home
c. Modern dwelling: a councillor's home
d. Aboriginal pole-and-earth construction for taking a steam bath; used at the present time

Plate IV
a. Brush shelter for summer; on camp ground near White Swan
b. Same; for cooking and eating accommodations
c. Similar brush shelter adjoining house shown in Plate IIIb
d. Cooking and eating arrangements under shelter on camp grounds

Plate V
a. Fish drying racks find living quarters at Celilo
b. Summer "home" at Celilo
c. View of Medicine Valley looking north; showing contrast between partially irrigated land along stream and arid land in foreground
d. View of unwatered upland of wild grasses; from same point as c, but facing south toward White Swan

Place VI
a. Creek bottom agriculture in the White Swan district; small plot of corn, squash, and melons
b. A family of Indian hop pickers, including the baby in a buggy in the background
c. Interior of an Indian house
d. Same, showing the kitchen

Plate VII
a. Scene at the Treaty Day Celebration on camp grounds near White Swan, June 9, 1942; hot dog stand in background
b. Women in a native costume at the Treaty Day Celebration
c. An elaborately beaded buckskin dress much as is still worn by women upon festive occasions
d. The man's four piece beaded garment of buckskin

Plate X
a. Indian graves with numerous objects deposited on them
b. Indian grave deposits
c. Child's grave with toys

Plate III

a. Modern dwelling
b. Modern dwelling: a councillor's home
c. Modern dwelling: a councillor's home
d. Aboriginal pole-and-earth construction for taking a steam bath; used at the present time

Plate IV
a. Brush shelter for summer; on camp ground near White Swan
b. Same; for cooking and eating accommodations
c. Similar brush shelter adjoining house shown in Plate IIIb
d. Cooking and eating arrangements under shelter on camp grounds

Plate V

a. Fish drying racks find living quarters at Celilo
b. Summer "home" at Celilo
c. View of Medicine Valley looking north; showing contrast between partially irrigated land along stream and arid land in foreground
d. View of unwatered upland of wild grasses; from same point as c, but facing south toward White Swan

Place VI
a. Creek bottom agriculture in the White Swan district; small plot of corn, squash, and melons
b. A family of Indian hop pickers, including the baby in a buggy in the background
c. Interior of an Indian house
d. Same, showing the kitchen

Plate VII
a. Scene at the Treaty Day Celebration on camp grounds near White Swan, June 9, 1942; hot dog stand in background
b. Women in a native costume at the Treaty Day Celebration
c. An elaborately beaded buckskin dress much as is still worn by women upon festive occasions
d. The man's four piece beaded garment of buckskin

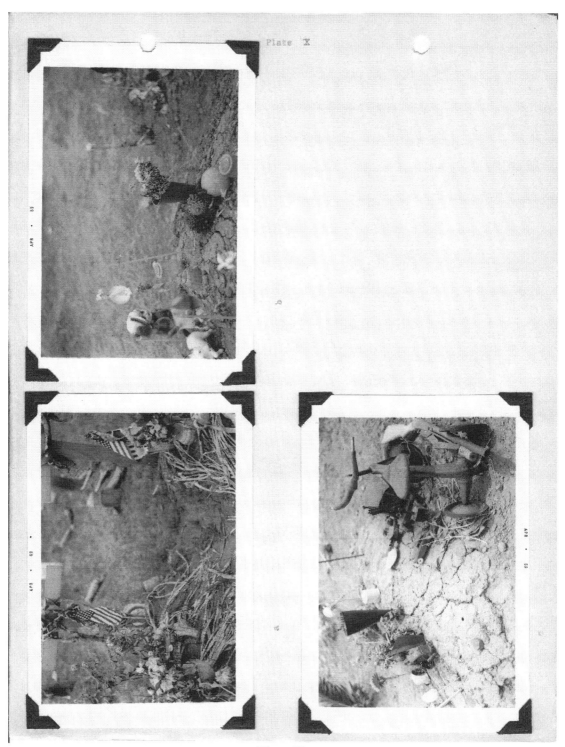

Plate X
a. Indian graves with numerous objects deposited on them
b. Indian grave deposits
c. Child's grave with toys

THE CATHOLIC UNIVERSITY OF AMERICA ANTHROPOLOGICAL SERIES

No. 14

Gambling Among the Yakima

BY

GERALD R. DESMOND. O.S.B.

A DISSERTATION

SUBMITTED TO THE FACULTY OF THE GRADUATE SCHOOL OF ARTS AND SCIENCES OF THE CATHOLIC UNIVERSITY OF AMERICA IN PARTIAL FULFILLMENT OF THE REQUIREMENTS FOR THE DEGREE OF DOCTOR OF PHILOSOPHY

THE CATHOLIC UNIVERSITY OF AMERICA PRESS

WASHINGTON, D. C. 1952

Copyright 1952

THE CATHOLIC UNIVERSITY OF AMERICA PRESS, INC.

Authors who may desire to reproduce passages from the present work in the form of quotations are hereby granted permission to do so by the publishers.

This dissertation was conducted under the direction of the late John M. Cooper and Regina Flannery Herzfeld as major professors, and was approved by Cornelius J. Connolly as reader.

MURRAY & HEISTER
WASHINGTON. D. C.

PRINTED BY
TIMES AND NEWS PUBLISHING CO.
GETTYSBURG. PA.. U.S.A.

CONTENTS

Section
I	Introduction	1 ~ 4
II	The Yakima	5 ~ 10
III	The Game and Equipment	11 ~ 16
IV	The Wagers	17 ~ 27
V	The Circumstances of Gambling	28 ~ 48
VI	The Functions	49 ~ 57
	Bibliography	~58 ~
	Biography	~ 59~

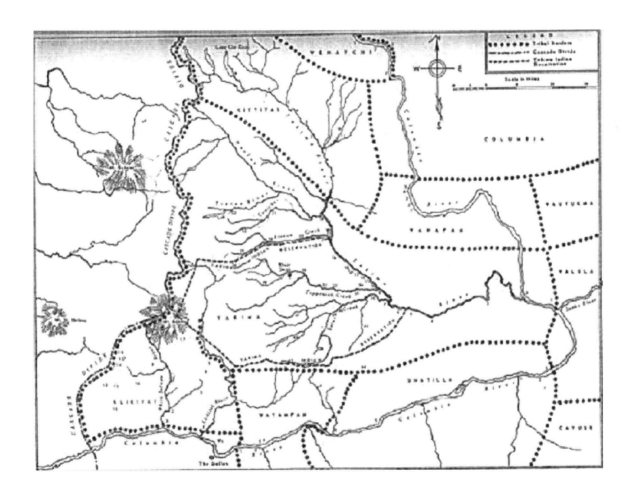

Introduction

SECTION I

INTRODUCTION

The purpose of the present study is to describe the gambling complex as it existed among the Yakima, in the period from 1860-1880, to see its integration into Yakima culture and to discover, so far as possible, its functions in that culture.

The data were obtained by the author during a residence of three months in 1944 at White Swan on the Yakima Reservation in south central Washington. Since no ethnography of this people is available it was necessary to obtain some insight into the culture as a whole.[1] Informants were therefore told that the purpose was to obtain an account of the old ways before they would be forgotten, and that some interesting phase would be selected later for publication. Thus, data could be gathered on aspects of the culture toward which less resistance could be expected while building rapport to the point where gambling could be discussed with less danger of having the informants accommodate their accounts to the past or present views of the whites. Furthermore, it seemed that a declared interest in a single phase of culture would unduly hamper the spontaneity of the informants.

The search for informants was started by enlisting the help of a storekeeper and gas station operator, both of whom had lived in White Swan for many years and were acquainted with everyone in the vicinity. After the project had been explained to them, they offered the names and qualifications of prospective informants and contacted them and other persons as they came to town. Thirty possible informants were considered and their qualifications discussed with fifteen well-informed residents. The field rapidly narrowed down to three principals, two raised in villages on Atanum [p2] Creek and the third in Kittitas Valley. The dozen subsidiary informants were all raised on the Reservation. All spoke their native Sahaptin language,[2] but their command of English

---

[1] The only accounts of Yakima culture as a whole are a brief one by Curtis (7:3-37, 159-161), and the material in Ray (1942, 99-258), which latter has the limitations as well as the virtues of the method used. Gambling is mentioned by both Curtis (7:159-160) and Ray (1942, 185) and by Ross (1:21). Gibbs (404, 406) and Culin (158, 307), but the information is indeed meager.

[2] Jacobs (1931, 93-98) classifies the widespread Sahaptin stock language into southern, west central, and northern languages. In the last language, he distinguishes northern dialects subdivided into two mutually unintelligible divisions, viz., the Nez Perce groups and Northern Sahaptin. In Northern Sahaptin, he further distinguishes the mutually intelligible Warmsprings, Walu'la-palu•'s, Umatilla, and northwestern Sahaptin, which latter was spoken with only slight differences by the Yakima, pcwa'nwapam, Klikitat, Wanapam, ski'n, and a few groups living in or west of the Cascade Mountains. Chinook jargon was also spoken in the area covered by the Northern Sahaptin language.

On our map, Jacobs' pcwa'nwapam and ski'n are respectively designated Kittitas and Wayampam together with those Umatilla groups living north of the Columbia River.

Introduction

was so good that interpreters were not necessary. A small fee was offered to the informant but without exception it was refused. Gifts, though not promised, were given to the principal informants at the end of the work.

Most interviews were held in the homes of those giving information, and records of the interviews were written on the spot. A free hand was given to the informants in presentation, and they frequently interpolated their own and others' experiences. Some information was given in confidence. At subsequent interviews the account was read to the informant, and he was asked to give fuller Information on some points and to check the whole. The material from one informant was also cross-checked with that from others. Some informants inquired among their friends for information they could not recall. Regular interviews usually lasted for four hours. At the close of an interview, an appointment was made for the next, and, in order to give the informant a better opportunity to recollect the past, he was asked what topic he would like to talk about next time. If none was volunteered, the author offered one for approval. Approximately three hundred hours were devoted to interviewing the three chief informants, and each of the others were interviewed from four to twenty hours.

Mr. George Olney, Mr. Simon Goudy and Mrs. Mary Mann gave accounts of all the important aspects of Yakima culture. Mr. [p3] George Olney (born 1862) not only gave a very full description of the culture, but also sponsored the author's participation in the gatherings held during the time he was on the Reservation. Mr. Simon Goudy (born 1869), a member of the Indian Police for many years, was especially well acquainted with conditions in Kittitas Valley. Mrs. Mary Mann (born 1871) was very helpful in affording the author an opportunity of learning the culture from the women's point of view. Some features of the language were explained by Mrs. Mann's daughters and son as they translated a little book of instructions for Yakima children written in the native language by Father L.N. St. Onge. The subsidiary informants who described various aspects of the culture were: Mr. Philip Olney, Mr. and Mrs. Al Goudy, Mr. James Olney, Mr. and Mrs. David Eneas, Mr. and Mrs. Oscar Olney, Mr. Chester Spencer, Mr. Enoch Abraham and Mr. Joe Dan.

Before attending gatherings, a description of the chief features was obtained. Observation and participation were directed accordingly. Afterwards the author wrote his own account, compared it with the preliminary description, and went over the material with the informants. Some information was gathered informally from individuals at gatherings, and some from casual acquaintances such as hitchhikers.

The territory north of the Reservation was known to the author as he was raised in the Kittitas area. Sites in the eastern part of the Reservation were visited, and a trip was made to the old hunting and berrying grounds on the upper drainage of the Klikitat River near Mt. Adams in the western part of the Reservation. Another trip was made via Goldendale to the old fishing and trading centers on the Columbia River near The Dalles, and to others on the lower Yakima River. Thus, the important features of the geographic setting became known well enough to facilitate interviewing.

Only a small part of the material, which the informants so graciously and patiently gave, can be used in this study of gambling. Even though it will not find expression here, the fuller knowledge of the culture proved important in understanding the gambling complex.

The author is deeply grateful to Professor John M Cooper and his colleagues, Dr.

Cornelius J. Connolly and Dr. Regina Flannery, [p4] for their inspiring works as teachers, for their unfailing encouragement, and for reading the completed manuscript. He is also indebted to Professor Cooper for guidance from the inception of the study, and to Dr. Flannery for most helpful criticism and advice. The author also wishes to express his appreciation to the informants for the kindness, indispensable accounts of the culture, and many happy hours afforded by them, and to the Benedictine Community at St. Martin's College, Olympia, Washington, for leave of absence to undertake the study.

SECTION II

THE YAKIMA

For the purposes of this study, the name Yakima will be used for all of the groups that, in the period from 1860 to 1880, had winter villages in the Yakima drainage from the southern boundary of the Reservation north to include the area marked Kittitas on the map, with the exception of a few groups moved to the Reservation.[1]

Prior to 1860, there had been political grounds for dividing this area in two. Gibbs,[2] the ethnologist with the railroad surveyors, observed the Yakima in 1853. He considered them as divided into two very closely connected bands, each made up of a number of villages. The northern band, with two principal chiefs, held the drainage of the Yakima River from its head-waters to Wenas Creek inclusive; the southern band, with three principal chiefs, held the drainage from the mouth of the Yakima River to the

---

[1] Although a few place names have been added and the Yakima groups living below the southern boundary of the Reservation have been excluded from the study, the map published here is essentially the one published by Ray (1936, 119), which reflects the relatively stable conditions prevailing toward the middle of the nineteenth century. Ray (1936) alone indicates the villages, but the boundaries differ in only minor ways from those of Jacobs (1931, 94) and of Spier (1936, 42-43) who reviews most of the literature on this thorny problem. Cf. Spier (1936, 5, 6, 12-15, and especially, 16-17).

The informant from the Kittitas area was chosen to check the reliability and completeness of his account by comparing it with the material of Ray (1942), and to test for variations between the Atanum and Kittitas areas in general culture and in specific cases like in-group vs. out-group sentiment in reference to gambling. Actually, the conformity between the material of Ray (1942) and the account of the Kittitas informant is remarkably close, and both of these sources vary very little from the accounts of the Atanum informants. The informants themselves claimed that there were no important differences in the culture of the two areas since the people spoke the same language with only minor differences, intermarried extensively, thought of themselves as one people, and for other reasons that will become apparent.

[2] Gibbs. The date is inferred.

[6] Naches River inclusive. One of the three latter chiefs dominated both bands.

Informants corroborated this division,[33] although the political basis for it was eliminated shortly after Gibbs had been in the territory. In 1855 a treaty was proposed for all of the Indians east of the Cascade Mountains providing for the establishment of Reservations, purchase of the remaining land, and other customary services. The treaty, however, proved unacceptable to the Yakima, and war, which spread through the Columbia Basin, broke out on the site of the present Reservation. The outstanding political leader of the northern division was killed.

Conditions remained seriously disturbed until 1859. During this time, some Yakima migrated east of the Columbia River. One of these was the principal political figure of the southern Yakima, who never returned to the area. When the present Reservation was established in 1859, the boundaries were so drawn as to include practically all of the villages and camping sites of the southern division.

Besides the migration from the area, some non-Yakima groups were gradually moved to the Reservation, and some Yakima villages were consolidated, but the Yakima villages, both inside and outside the Reservation, remained substantially as they were for two more decades since white settlers were not numerous enough to interfere greatly with Indian activities in the region until the railroad began operation in 1883. Nevertheless, the two divisions had lost their leaders, and since no other individuals gained sufficient influence to replace them, the effective political control fell to the headmen of the villages,[44] which, even under the old regime, tended to be autonomous.

These more or less outstanding men ruled in the villages with the aid of a council made up of the men of the village. On request, a headman invited a few leading men to help him adjudicate disputes, and he assessed fines or prescribed flogging as the case seemed to require. The village crier .was an important functionary who acted as master of ceremonies, repeated aloud the headman's speeches to the council, and went through the village each evening announcing the news of the day and activities planned for the next day.

---

3 Subdivisions of the area, of which Atanum is one, were known to the informants, especially subdivisions of the southern area. But the terms they applied thereto were used vaguely by them. For the most part, they were names of important villages on streams of the same name, but now and then the same names were used to include a number of villages. When an informant was asked, for example, the difference between the *atanum* and *t'xopanic*, he gave the familiar explanation that they were the same people, but that long ago the *t'xopanic* moved to Toppenish Creek because of a quarrel. The name Yakima was said to have been derived from a scurrilous story and to have been properly applied to a single village near the confluence of the Yakima River and Atanum Creek.

Spier (1936, 16) pays some attention to the smaller units.

4 How loose the political organization was can be seen from the fact that if a dispute occurred when the parties were away from their winter villages, the headman nearest at hand might be called upon to adjudicate, whether he was the headman of their own village or not.

Conflicting views about the chieftainship and the conduct of the war were factors, along with others, in keeping alive the rivalry between the two divisions of the Yakima which was reflected in the gambling situation to which we will refer. Moreover, the contacts of the Yakima with other people, although somewhat restricted after abandoning buffalo hunts and war, were much the same as they were in pre-Reservation days. For example, Gibbs,[5] points out the close relations of the Yakima with a number of groups. Their intercourse with Klikitat was constant — with them they shared root grounds and raced horses. Both Yakima groups visited and traded west of the Cascades in summer, members of the northern group going there more frequently, Inter-marriage with the Wenatchi was common, and with the Snoqualmi fairly frequent. Furthermore, the Yakima joined the Flatheads in their buffalo hunts which brought them in conflict with the Blackfoot in Montana.

The informants stated that actually these contacts were more widespread, frequent and intimate than Gibbs indicated. For example, the leading men in the Yakima villages were themselves nearly all blood or affinal relatives, and, as a whole, were related by marriage to all of the notable Northern Sahaptin-speaking groups, to the Wenatchi and other Interior Salish-speaking groups living between their territory and that of the Flatheads, and to the [8] Snoqualmi and some other Coastal Salish-speaking groups living east of the Cascade Divide. They also hunted buffalo with the Nez Perce with whom they fought the Shoshoni. Friendly relations with most of these groups were maintained up to and beyond 1880, their only enemies being the Blackfoot and the Shoshoni.[6] Consequently, the gradual movement sponsored by the Indian Agency of some neighboring Sahaptin-speaking groups, some Chinook-speaking Wishram, and some Interior Salish-speaking Wenatchi onto the Reservation did not notably affect Yakima culture.

It should be noted that the Yakima were little disturbed by the white settlers who began overland migrations to the Pacific Northwest after 1835 since the main overland route passed along the Snake and Columbia Rivers to the south of the Yakima. Nevertheless, besides the native goods of divers origins, including wares from the Plains to the Pacific Ocean and from Northern California to British Columbia, some white goods were also available as early as 1804.[7] The Yakima also had horses for sale as early as 1811.[8]

Through the efforts of the Indian Agency, stock raising and agriculture, begun by the Yakima before any white men lived in their territory, was expanded on the Reservation. Still, the old hunting-fishing-gathering economy was far more important for the people as a whole and broke down only gradually. The effects of Christian religious instruction, begun in 1847, of schooling and individual family housing, introduced during the period beginning in 1860, and of currency which had a much longer history, became

---

[5] Gibbs, 403, 408, 411.
[6] See the maps in Ray (1936, 103) and Spier (1936, 42-43).
[7] See the very interesting description in Lewis and Clark (4: 289). See also Spier and Sapir (224-228). Teit (121-122) mentions that the Columbia and Wenatchi made annual trips through Yakima territory to the trading center near The Dalles.
[8] Ross, 1:19.

important elements in the breakdown of Yakima native culture only after about 1880 when the occupation of the land outside the Reservation by white settlers began to seriously curtail the activities of the Yakima.

At about this time, the Indian Agency began to allot eighty acre tracts to individual Indians and continued to promote agriculture, stock raising, irrigation, and separate family homes. These and [9] other changes eventually broke down the village system of the Yakima and progressively lessened the value of the older individual and social ways.

Today there is relatively little external evidence of the old culture. Some of the older women have not kept pace with current white fashions in clothes, and some prefer moccasins to shoes, just as some of the elderly men prefer older styles of clothing and retain the long braids, but most of the middle aged and younger people dress like their white neighbors of the same income level.

Horses have largely given way to cars and trucks for transportation. Although horses are still highly prized for sentimental reasons, and much riding stock grazes on the Reservation, only a few are broken to the saddle, and hundreds run wild. A few are used by the cattlemen and old people for riding, and draft horses are employed in farming in about the same proportion as among the whites. The younger people ride for recreation.

Most incomes are low. Renting land, farming and cattle-raising are the principal sources of income. Much of the irrigated land on the Reservation is rented to white farmers. Working for farmers: on a wage basis, exercising fishing rights at the old sites on the Columbia River, and gathering a few huckleberries and roots supplement the resources of some. A "tribal" council, which was provided by the treaty, sponsors two cattle associations and some other concerted activities.

Elements of the old culture are more in evidence at festivals. The Fourth of July has been a traditional day of celebration for many decades. A parade is held in one of the two larger towns on the Reservation, the feature being the Yakima and other Indians on horses, floats, and a-foot, dressed in Indian costumes mostly of Plains inspiration. The celebration lasts at least three days. An "Indian" village, consisting of about twenty canvas tipi and a large tent, is erected. A series of bone (hand) games and separate card games for men and for women are played at the village in the evenings. A rodeo, which is widely attended by Indians and whites, is held on the three afternoons of the celebration.

About the first of June and the middle of August, three-day-festivals are held at the same time in several places on the Reservation. The most prominent feature and ostensible reason for the [10] festivals is a first-fruits' rite, which is conducted according to the present conception of old religious rites. The first-fruits' ceremony is held in the daytime. In the old days, the people left at once for digging roots or gathering berries. Now, however, gambling games are organized after the ceremonial feast and are continued late into the night. During the evening and night, several exhibitions of "Yakima" dances are given in the "Longhouse," which are attended by all who are interested. Gambling continues during the dances, and both dancing and gambling go on for two afternoons and nights after the feast day.

Card games[9] are used almost exclusively in the more or less private gambling sessions held throughout the year. Besides the bone game sessions held at the festivals, others are held in the fall when many of the Yakima and Indians from elsewhere are employed in picking hops. Card games, however, predominate at all times.

The author attended the Fourth of July celebration and the first-fruits' rites in August 1944, under the guidance of one of the principal informants. [11]

SECTION III

THE GAMES AND EQUIPMENT

Among the many contests on which the Yakima gambled, a hand game, which the informants called *palyowi't* {*palyuut*} in their language and the bone game in English, was the most popular. The game was played by two lines of players kneeling in front of two parallel lines of poles about eight feet apart. When the game was played indoors the floor plan of the typical plateau dwellings provided such an arrangement. The essential part of the game was guessing the position of four bones hidden in the hands of two opponents. The equipment consisted of a set of bones, a set of tally sticks, and a club for each player.

The four bones, called *s'kuma*, were two-and-a-half inch sections of the leg bones (femur or humerus) of a deer, each of which was rounded off on the ends or gradually tapered from the middle to the ends. Two of the bones were marked with a band of buckskin or sinew sunk in a groove around the middle, and the other two were unmarked. The four bones were played as two pairs, each consisting of a marked and an unmarked bone. The twenty tally sticks, which were about ten inches long and three-fourths of an inch in diameter, resembled short thin arrow shafts. Usually the clubs, which were about eighteen inches long and two inches in diameter, were of any convenient shape, and each player furnished his own club. But sets of clubs with

---

[9] Although cards were known to the Yakima even before the period under consideration, they were not used very much by the Yakima when playing among themselves or with other Indian groups.

shaped handles were sometimes provided.

The game was started by a challenge between two persons who became the principals of the opposing sides and decided the number of tallies, whether officials were to be used, and which side would be first to hide the bones. A full set of officials was a "bone game leader," who stationed himself at the end of the lines of poles to supervise the play, and two custodians for the wagers, who usually stationed themselves opposite the leader. When the betting was finished, each principal took a position at the center of a line of poles with a variable number of team mates on either side of him. A pair of bones and half of the tallies were given to each principal, [11] and the principals decided which side would be first to hide the bones by alternately hiding a pair of bones and guessing for the position of the unmarked bone until one succeeded while the other failed. Whenever a side was hiding the bones, the principal sang his power song, and his team mates then repeated it over and over while beating their clubs on the poles in front of them about one hundred times a minute.

The principal who won the right to start the game took possession of both pairs of bones, and he might elect to play one of the pairs of bones himself and choose a team mate to play the other pair, or he might select a team mate at his left and right to play them. The opposing principal either elected to guess the position of the bones or chose a team mate to do it.

The use of the bones and tally sticks was quite simple. Whenever the guesser located an unmarked bone, he won possession of the pair of bones; whenever he failed to locate an unmarked bone, he lost a tally stick. The game came to an end when one side had all of the tally sticks.

Because a marked and an unmarked bone was played as a pair, the two unmarked bones could assume only four positions; hence, four gestures sufficed to indicate their positions. Three of the gestures were made by quickly clasping the biceps of the right arm with the left hand and pointing the right arm with the forefinger extended toward the right, the left, or between the two bone hiders. The fourth gesture was made in the same way except that the forefinger and thumb were opposed somewhat like a Y.

In the following chart X stands for the marked bones, 0 for the unmarked ones when the four bones were in play. The numbers in parentheses indicate a particular arrangement of the bones and a particular gesture so that they may be referred to as position (1), gesture (1), and so on.

Position of Bones	No.	Gesture Which Won Both Pairs of Bones
XO XO	(1)	Arm extended to the right pointing the forefinger
XO OX	(2)	" " between the pairs pointing the forefinger
OX OX	(3)	" " to the left pointing the forefinger
OX XO	(4)	" " between the pairs with the thumb and forefinger opposed

[13] The chart shows the positions of the bones and the gestures that won possession of both pairs of bones at once. If gesture (1) was used when the bones were in position (2) or (4), the guesser won one pair of bones but forfeited one tally stick. If gesture (1) was used when the bones were in position (3), he failed to locate either unmarked bone and lost two tally sticks. The other gestures produced the same

results, but, of course, against different positions which can be readily worked out on the chart. For any gesture the guesser might use when both pairs of bones were in play, he had one chance to win both pairs of bones, two chances to win one pair of bones and lose one tally stick, and one chance to lose two tally sticks without winning either pair of bones. When only one pair of bones was in play, he had an equal chance of .winning the bones or losing a tally stick.

Bone game sessions were usually started in the evening, and game followed game until morning. A game could be won in half an hour, but it usually required from an hour and a half to two hours. Generally, about six games were played at an all-night session. Toward the end of a session, a game sometimes became so prolonged that it was broken off and continued the next day. On some occasions, sessions were held on three successive nights.

From the point of view of interest and high stakes wagered, perhaps horse racing ranked first, but it was not as frequently played as the bone game. Although several races might be run on the same afternoon, each race was restricted to two horses. The owners of the race horses challenged one another to race and agreed on the officials, the distance to be run, and the kind of race course to be used. Two kinds of race courses were recognized, straight away and double courses. Straight away courses started at a distant point and ended at a line near the spectators. The double courses were run from a starting line near the spectators, round a distant pile of rocks, and back to the starting line. Although longer and shorter distances were run on each kind of course, the straight away courses were usually from three to five miles long, and the double courses about two miles.

For the double course, an official was sent to the pile of rocks to see that each racer passed the pile of rocks before returning to the finish line, and a judge started the race and declared the [14] winner. For the straight away course, a starter accompanied the racers to the distant starting line, and a judge remained at the finish line with the spectators to declare the winner. Custodians were also appointed to guard the wagers.

Shinny was an exciting game in itself, and betting might, under certain circumstances, become quite heated. As played by the Yakima, each team consisted of from ten to twelve players. Each player provided himself with a shinny stick about four feet long by one and a half inches in diameter which was curved toward the end somewhat like a golf club or a hockey stick. The ball was usually a rounded oak burl, about four inches in diameter, hardened by fire. The playing field was from two hundred to two hundred and fifty feet long with a pair of stakes at each end for goals. The stakes were usually set about twenty feet apart, and sometimes a hole about a foot in diameter was dug between the stakes for goals. In the center of the playing field, midway between the goals, a shallow hole about ten inches in diameter was dug for a starting point.

A supervisor and custodians for the wagers were the only officials. At the beginning of the game, the two teams formed lines about twenty feet apart near the goal posts. The leader of each team stood near the hole in the center of the field in which the ball was placed. At a signal from the supervisor, each leader tried to hit the ball to those members of his team nearest his goal. As soon as the ball was out of the hole, all players broke ranks and tried to hit the ball along the ground until they drove it between their goal posts or into their goal hole. After each goal the ball was returned to the starting hole, and the supervisor signaled for the play to begin again. Each goal counted one point, and each game was played for a pre-arranged score, usually from five to ten points. A single game lasted two hours or more.

The rules did not permit taking up the ball in the hands. It might be kicked, but this was seldom done because of the danger of being struck by a shinny stick. Pushing and tripping opponents with a stick or foot were allowed, but striking them deliberately with a stick or fist was forbidden. Shinny games were intensely contested, and fights and injuries were frequent. Injured players were removed from the game and replaced by others. [15]

Wrestling and foot racing were two sports which ranked among the major gambling situations. A supervisor and custodians for the wagers were the officials. The wrestlers stripped to their moccasins and breechclouts, faced each other, and usually encircled one another's torso with their arms, clasping their left wrists with their right hands. This back hold, however, might be barred by the supervisor. If he barred it, the hands were placed on the opponent's sides, just above the hips, or on the shoulders. Each wrestler then tried to throw his opponent to the ground by tripping him, or oftener by thrusting one leg between the opponent's legs and pushing him over on his back or side. Three out of four falls won the match. Short rest periods were taken between falls.

The courses for the foot races were straight away and double, as for the horse races. The officials for important matches were the same as for the horse races, and the course and distance to be run, a matter for agreement. Adults and champions usually ran two or three miles, but longer and shorter races were also run.

Of less importance for our purpose, either because they were infrequently played or betting on them was mild, were broad and high jumping, swimming contests over straight away and double courses for two or three hundred yards, tug-of-war between teams of about six members, and canoe races on the lakes at the headwaters of the Yakima River. All of these contests followed the usual pattern of two opponents or teams at a time. In this category of events on which betting was mild were two games played by women — beaver-tooth dice and double-ball shinny. Double-ball shinny was played under the same rules as shinny, but straight sticks were used instead of curved sticks, and a pair of three or four inch cylindrical pieces of wood were used instead of the ball. The number of players on a team varied from a minimum of four to the usual number of ten or twelve.

Beaver-tooth dice was played by two women, facing each other across an elk or deer skin. The dice were four first incisor teeth from the upper jaw of a beaver or "whistling jenny" (marmot). Two of the four teeth were marked on one side with a line of dots; the other two, with transverse lines. The dotted teeth were called .men, and the lined ones, women. After placing bets, the women alternately tossed a pair of dice to determine who got both pairs [16] of dice to start the game. The winner then tossed all of the dice for tallies. Certain combinations won tallies and others lost the dice to the opponent. Unfortunately, the single description of the scoring obtained by the author is obviously incorrect. Spectators also bet on this game.

Finally a few contests may be mentioned upon which wagers, if made at all, were small. These were arrow-shooting contests in which, as usual, two players at a time competed to see which could shoot the farthest or hit a four by six inch ball of grass at about thirty feet. Boys sometimes forfeited the arrows they used like boys in our society play marbles for keeps. Another method of testing skill in aiming was to see which of a pair of players could stop a rolling hoop by shooting his arrow so that the hoop would come to rest around the arrow. Similar to this was the well-known hoop and pole game which, among the Yakima of the period under consideration, was played very simply, and, as far as I know, without magico-religious associations. [17]

SECTION IV

THE WAGERS

The informants had described the artifactual and other possessions before they were asked about the wagers, and they seemed to find it difficult to give particular wagers much beyond horses, blankets, clothing, and some money. But they made such general statements as, "You could bet anything of your own manufacture, but not grub (food)." "Anything you had. Hardly anyone ever bet food though."

The following lists will give some impression of the wagers and a rough indication of their value. The lists, however, are not complete. The values will be considered in more detail below.

The items in each category were not exactly comparable in value, but since the bettors had a strong tendency to bet the same kind of wagers — such as a horse against a horse, and so on — it was easier for them to arrive at comparable values. Wagers of the same kind also varied in value. For example, when speaking of horses the informants regularly distinguished between good and ordinary horses. Although much work remains to be done, the following notes will give some further indication of values.

The Yakima were sentimentally attached to horses, and they placed a high value on them. Every man wanted to own not only enough of them for himself and his family, but to own as many as possible of the finest horses. Although horses were never used for food, they were useful for riding and packing, their natural increase was a source of wealth, and they functioned well as a means of saving and a medium of exchange. They were also used as wagers, as presents in the exchange of gifts between relatives of the bride and groom at marriages, and they were not difficult to raise since the area was well suited to horse raising.

At the beginning of the period under discussion, the Yakima were poorer in horses than they were before the war in which horses were killed, confiscated, and taken from the area permanently. Considering the period as a whole and the family as the owning [18]

Wagers

	Very little value	Little value	Valuable	Very valuable
Horses and cattle				horses cattle
Skins:	chipmunk squirrel cottontail rabbit	mink weasel muskrat	deer beaver coyote wolf fox badger	elk buffalo bear mountain goat or sheep
Blankets: (robe, cape)		woven strips of cottontail fur	sewed skins	Hudson's bay mt goat
Ornaments and raw materials	deer hooves few small trade beads porcupine quills undyed feathers	a dyed eagle feather	quantity of trade beads abalone shell dentalium shells clam & other shells large bone beads	necklaces, bracelets & ear pendants of bone, shell & trade beads finger rings
Clothing:	plain moccasins buckskin headbands	*M—fur caps M & W—mittens W—plain leggings, 1/2 or knee-length	M—decorated shirt W—decorated gown M—" thigh length leggings M—decorated moccasins W—basketry hat ornate tobacco pouch calico shirt overalls handkerchief or scarf	M—outfit of ornate buckskin or cloth W—buckskin outfit or calico gown

[19]

	Very little value	Little value	Valuable	Very valuable
Equipment for hunting and fishing:	ordinary arrows hawk feathers for arrows arrow head small wood or bone fish hooks wooden club mesh gauge Indian hemp fish line, temporary "baskets" of tule, etc. cedar roots, dyed grass, etc., for better baskets small hemp bag	few well-made arrows bow quiver of fawn hide 1, 2, 3-prong spears dip net net shuttle horn-handled whip hair-rope		guns
Containers, utensils, etc.:		basketry cup bone awl 18" wooden needle	ornate water-tight cedar-root basket ornate rawhide parfleche	
Money:				money
Miscellaneous:		snowshoes tobacco	knives strike-a-light	

*M—man's
W—woman's

[20] unit, the mode was probably about ten horses to a family. When getting lists of the important men in the villages, the informants consistently indicated those who were wealthy by giving the number of horses they owned. Owners of three hundred to eight hundred horses were considered very wealthy, but relatively few people were wealthy in this sense. At the other end of the scale, there were a considerable number of people who owned but one or a few horses. Young men found it rather difficult to start a herd. Even though the fairly common number of ten horses might be exchanged between the

relatives of the bride and groom at the marriage, few, if any, went to the young men. Moreover, there seems to have been a general reluctance to part with horses, and also services were seldom paid for.

The sentimental attachment to horses, much of which remains today, was indicated by the delight the informants showed in telling about the horses they owned in their youth, the care they took to mention the speed riders made on trips, and the following incident. When calling on an informant for the first time, I saw her holding the reins of a well groomed and saddled horse. Although I shuffled my feet as I walked toward her across the graveled barnyard, said good morning, and coughed several times, she remained perfectly still, gazing into the horse's face for fully four minutes before the horse attracted her attention to my presence. She greeted me rather embarrassedly and soon gave the horse to her son who had come up. As we watched him ride away, she said, "You know, that horse is part Arabian."

Besides distinguishing good and ordinary horses, the informants also distinguished race horses. They were the most valuable of all horses and were very rarely wagered. All of the Indian groups east of the Cascade Mountains readily accepted Yakima horses in barter, but the Indians west of the Cascades did not use horses, and the whites generally preferred their own breeds. For the last reason, it was not easy for the Yakima to convert their horses into money, and for the same reason, it is doubtful if a money value can be placed on them. Yet, in his report for 1874, the Indian Agent, who included Indians other than those called Yakima in this study, reported 13,000 horses of all ages and 1,200 cattle, estimating the average value of the horses at $15.00 a head, and the cattle [21] at $12.00 a head.[11] The informants said that cattle were scarce, and that ownership was concentrated in a few hands. But they could be easily sold to, the whites for money. Cattle, however, were seldom used as wagers, but one of the informants mentioned an instance in which a cow was wagered against a horse.

The value of the various skins depended on a number of factors. Among the very valuable ones, buffalo hides were the most valuable. These hides were never plentiful since the Yakima had to travel to the plains to hunt buffalo. They were quite scarce during the period under discussion because the Yakima no longer hunted buffalo. But they could still get hides from the Nez Perce, who continued to hunt them, and through the Wishram and other traders. Elk were scarce, and the elk hides were very valuable because the people wanted them especially for burial wrappings. Mountain goats or sheep and bear were quite scarce in the area. Bear hides were the least valuable in this category, Deer hides, which are listed as valuable, had the greatest utility for the Yakima themselves. Although the Yakima considered deer plentiful enough for food, they sought deer hides especially from the Salish-speaking groups to the north who wanted horses. Apparently about four tanned hides were exchanged for an ordinary horse. The other skins listed as valuable and of little value could be disposed of to white traders. All of these were in good supply in the territory except beaver which had been nearly trapped out.

There was little difference between a blanket used for bedding and a cape or

---

[1] Report of the Commissioner of Indian Affairs, 1874, 339.

robe. The value of the blankets made by the Yakima depended on the value of the skins used in them. The Yakima did not make blankets from the wool of the mountain goat or sheep, but got them from the Wenatchi. One of the informants said that his mother gave a good horse for one. "Hudson's Bay" blankets were the most valuable of all. They were very highly prized as robes, were not used for bedding, and were not easily obtained because of the scarcity of Yakima goods acceptable to white traders and the limited work opportunities with them.

All of the listed ornaments and raw materials for them were obtained through native or white traders, except porcupine quills, [22] deer hooves, some bone beads, and some kinds of feathers. Abalone shells were from the California coast. The other shells and shell beads were obtained by direct or indirect trade with Indians from Puget Sound and the Oregon and Washington coasts. In gambling, one advantage of the ornaments and raw materials was divisibility.

During the period under consideration, each man and woman maintained a full outfit of buckskin clothing as highly decorated as he or she could afford. By the middle of the period, most women also had a muslin or calico gown. In summer men spent most of the time in breechclouts and moccasins, except at gatherings. Besides their fine buckskin outfits, they usually had a set of ordinary buckskin clothes, and quite a few of them had an outfit of some articles of European clothing. European clothing was expensive. The buckskin outfits, which required more than two deer skins, varied in value according to the amount of decoration. Clothing, however, was wagered as complete outfits or as individual pieces.

As a rule, each man made his own hunting and fishing equipment, except guns; hence, the exchange value was rather low. Guns were rather scarce at the beginning of the period, and they remained expensive throughout the period, their use being restricted largely to hunting large animals.

The value of the baskets can be estimated, to some extent, from the statement of an informant that an expert basket maker who devoted her full time to it could make an undecorated watertight basket of medium size (about one gallon) in about seven days. These baskets were usually of about two gallon capacity, and most of them were completely decorated with varicolored dyed grass. The exchange value was rather high in native trade, and they were desired by all of the native groups. Dozens of baskets and containers were used for gathering foods, storage, transportation, cooking, dishes, etc. Some European utensils were also in use.

Although perhaps a majority of the Yakima had some money, at least at times, it was relatively scarce, and the wealthier men, including certain headmen who received some money from the government, had notably more than others. As mentioned above, the Yakima had little goods acceptable to the whites except furs and the scarce cattle. Although there were a few work opportunities at the Agency and with white cattlemen and settlers, wages were [23] so small that little money was put into circulation from these sources.

Among the articles listed as miscellaneous, the snowshoes were made by the men for deer hunting, and the knives and strike-alights were obtained from the whites. The smoking material used by the Yakima was a half and half mixture of kinnikinik leaves and an unidentified plant found in the mountains. Although some tobacco was obtained from the whites, smoking was not general. The informants said that the *twa'ti* {twáti} (shamans) and headmen were the only ones who smoked in the old days, and that when others began to smoke, people would say to them, "I see you are smoking. Are you a *twa'ti*?" The shamans smoked in the curing rites, and the headmen smoked at important councils. The two other uses of tobacco were to cure insomnia and to produce unconsciousness and dreams. The fact that tobacco had a limited use, and that it was not highly desirable, lessened its utility as a wager. Even today the Yakima do not smoke much.

Among the things not used for wagers were: objects associated with the magico-religious beliefs such as bells, drums, and magical objects; such personal effects as breechclouts and fighting clubs (either a rock-filled buckskin or a stone with a wooden handle); such tools as mauls, chisels, mortars, pestles, and digging sticks; large fishing equipment such as seines and traps; canoes; shelters; and, as mentioned above, food.

The drums and bells were used only in connection with the so-called PomPom religion which included the first-fruits' ceremonies, but PomPom was entirely dissociated from gambling. Although magical objects were used in gambling, they were used secretively. This probably had something to do with excluding them as wagers. The fighting clubs were used somewhat like side-arms. These clubs, however, were forbidden by the Indian agent, and his injunction seems to have been carried out rather well. The tools and fishing equipment mentioned were generally unwieldy. The shelters were not only unwieldy, but the typical ones were the joint product of several families and were not exchanged in any way. Neither land nor fishing sites were exchanged. Although some of the fishing sites were owned by families, and they were passed on by inheritance, the land itself was not divided into family plots [24] or family hunting territories. In reference to saddles, the informants said that, although most men rode bareback in the old days, some made them of buckskin at first and later made them of the skins of horses that died. Wooden stirrups were added to these saddles. They also made pack saddles, and some men got "Dragoon" and "Bacheer" saddles from the whites. They claimed, however, that saddles were not wagered because they were too valuable.

The staple foods were several kinds of small roots, huckleberries, venison, and salmon. Besides the staple roots and berries, other roots, plants, berries, fruits, and seeds, making some twenty varieties in all, were gathered by the women. In addition to the venison and salmon, men hunted wild fowl and other kinds of animals and caught other kinds of fish. The women preserved for winter use not only most of the kinds of food they gathered, but also the venison and salmon taken by the men. Wives owned all of the foods they gathered and also the foods taken by the husbands, and they were free to barter them.

A considerable amount of wealth was the product of the combined efforts of husband and wife. The skins which the husbands obtained by hunting and trapping were tanned and made into clothing, blankets, and other articles, and also decorated by the wives. It seems that the wives also owned a considerable portion of these articles.

Wives did all the bartering in food, which was carried on not only with members of the same and neighboring villages, but also with traders and members of other groups. Wives usually accompanied their husbands to the villages of the Wishram and other groups on the Columbia River where they traded roots for the highly prized sixty pound baskets of dried and pounded salmon. They also traded articles of their own manufacture such as baskets, as well as some food and some skins, mostly for ornaments. In this way some food was converted into wagerable wealth, but the informants could not recall a single instance in which food was bartered specifically to convert it into wagerable wealth. The men did all of the herding and, roughly speaking, owned all of the horses. They also bartered horses, skins, and the less acceptable hunting and fishing equipment. Men carried on the barter with the whites and also bartered horses and some skins in native trade. [25] Even when a husband discovered a bargain in native trade, it was customary for him to call his wife, and, if she approved, she did the bartering.

As in barter, men often consulted their wives about articles to be gambled, although they also gambled without consulting them. The informants said a wife would say in almost every instance, "Go ahead. Maybe you will get two." They also said that husbands and wives rarely quarreled over the gambling losses of either party or over reluctance to use wealth for gambling. Although they recalled a few instances of wife beating on account of gambling, they said wife beating was done by only the "meanest" men, and that infidelity or suspicion of it was the usual reason rather than anything connected with gambling. It appears that the women encouraged their husbands to gamble, and that the men were limited in wagerable wealth more by their ability in hunting, trapping, horse raising, and manufacturing rather than by the reluctance of their wives to process or part with goods.

When it was pointed out to the men informants that since most men did not have many horses, women seemed to own much more property than men, they seemed surprised and, after some thought, said they guessed it was so all right. The women were well aware of the situation. When the women informants were asked what women thought of men, some of them said that they were like big boys in many ways. The older women still have a quiet confidence in their competence which gives them considerable dignity. When working, they go about their tasks with a certain flair which shows an awareness of their ability and a willingness to display it.

Besides those already mentioned, there were a few other ways of obtaining wealth. Although the services of chiefs, headmen, leaders of hunting parties, and other services were not paid for, shamans were promised liberal rewards when asked to cure, but they also gave away a great amount of wealth at winter dances. As one informant put it, "It kept stuff in circulation." Gifts were quite often made to the old man who assisted in power quests and to the go-betweens in marriages. Gifts were also made at little parties and at funerals. And gambling was a means of obtaining goods. [26]

The method of betting was quite simple, and, with some exceptions, men or women were free to bet with whomever they might wish. Those who wanted to bet horses led them into view, and those who bet smaller articles or money held them in their hands. Each bettor then sought a desirable wager (usually of the same kind of goods he was offering) among the bettors who were supporting the opposing contestant or team. When an agreement, which could be reached entirely by gestures, was made, the wagers were tied together and called to the attention of the custodians of the wagers who directed the small articles to be piled near their station and horses to be tied to a nearby sagebrush or tree. Although the dyad pattern of one person reaching an agreement with another person was always observed, each bettor could bet several wagers with the same individual or with as many others as he wished. From the point of view of the wagers, betting was on a strictly double or nothing basis, i.e., there were no pools or other arrangements by which a person could bet a small wager and win a large amount of wealth. Even the contestants had to bet on themselves if they wished to gain wealth on the contest since no prizes or other wealth were given to them for their part. Although the informants were unable to estimate the average wager, they maintained that people were seldom excluded from gambling because they could find someone who was willing to bet as little or as much as they desired, and relatively few games were played at a single session. Out-betting, however, was rather common, gamblers fairly often bet all of the wealth they had with them, and on rare occasions a fairly rich man would spectacularly bet nearly all of his wealth on a single event, reserving but a few horses and some clothes.

There was practically no loaning among the Yakima, hence, all wagers had to be on hand for the contest, promises were not offered or accepted, and there were no debts at the end of a gambling session. The only example of a loan made specifically for gambling which the informants could remember illustrates the elaborate means the borrower took to break down the resistance against loaning and also the only instance in which a song with words was used in connection with gambling. Before a bone game, a member of another band who was visiting the Yakima in the fall [27] sang a song with tears running down his face, which told how he was a wild boy in his youth who refused to obey his father and lost everything playing the bone game, and that he wanted just a few gifts. The informant said the song was an easy one and those present picked it up and sang along with him. He then asked for just a few gilts so he could play the bone game. Again, an informant mentioned a case in which two famous gamblers met and soon proposed to race their horses. Both of them wanted to bet more than they had with them, so they called off the race and set a later date so that each could bet more wagers. The informant said that this was not unusual. In this case promises were not sufficient.

Although the informants said the winners always collected their innings, one informant remembered an exception, an instance which also illustrates the fact that Yakima would wager things which they would not part with under other circumstances. "My father was a great gambler. He had to go to work when he was a boy because his mother was a cripple. He worked for the Hudson's Bay Company. He was coming home one time with a Hudson's Bay blanket. They were dear in those days. He met a man who wanted to buy it from him, but the man did not have enough to pay for it. He offered to play my father for it. They played all night and my father won everything the man had. My father took a few things he wanted and gave the rest to the man." [28]

Functions

SECTION V

THE CIRCUMSTANCES OF GAMBLING

Seasonal changes and the corresponding changes in the activities of the people brought marked differences in the number of gambling sessions, the number of contests used for gambling, and the number and social relationship of the participants.

The Yakima lived in winter villages from about mid-November to mid-March. Although these villages were so situated as to exploit nearby pasture and avoid the heavy snows of the mountains, some snow could be expected at any time after the first of December. The mean temperature in the vicinity of the villages was roughly 25° F. in January. Outdoor activities were further hampered not only by short colder periods when the temperature dropped as low as −5° or −10° F. but also by varying amounts of snow as affected by the Chinook winds.

The usual trails, connecting the areas marked on the map "Yakima," "Kittitas" and "Wayampam," crossed elevations of more than two thousand feet. Since in winter these were seldom passable on account of deep snow, the areas were relatively isolated from one another. Intercommunication between the villages within the respective areas was, although markedly decreased and difficult at times, actually maintained throughout the winter. No village within a given area was much more than ten miles from its nearest neighbor.

All the residents of a village were usually related by blood or marriage, the few non-relatives being slaves or outsiders who had obtained permission to reside there. Ordinarily there were from five to twelve lodges, each accommodating about four closely related families, and a few tipis accommodating single families. In addition there were a dance house (longhouse) and a few sweat lodges. The average population seems to have been about two hundred for the larger villages, and about fifty for the smaller ones.[11] [29]

The food quest was reduced to subsistence fishing for sucker and whitefish and an occasional hunt for deer. Much time was spent by the adults in the manufacture and repair of equipment to be used at this and other seasons and the older children were

---

[1] The incomplete data from the informants indicate that the more important villages or occupied centers in the Kittitas area during the period considered here were those numbered 2, 3, 4, and 9 on the map; the smaller ones were 5, 6, 7, and the remaining numbers indicate summer camp sites or abandoned sites. In the Yakima area, 7, 13, 17, 18, and 25 indicate the more important villages; 5 and 20, the smaller ones. But a few villages of groups brought to the Reservation and a few minor shifts in the sites are ignored. As in the Kittitas area, the remaining numbers indicate mostly summer camp sites or abandoned sites. Ray (1936, 143-147) gives the names of the villages and camps.

The Yakima population in the period 1860-1880 cannot be accurately determined from the published materials, and the informants' reports are not satisfactory. Rather than omit a figure, 2,500 is offered as a rough guess. See Reports of the Commissioner of Indian Affairs, 1852-1881 and Kroeber, 138.

taught these crafts. This was considered by the Yakima a very dull and monotonous time of year although the daily routine would be broken by an occasional village council, or, less frequently, by the rites accompanying birth, illness and death. Furthermore any who so desired were free to attend the winter dances sponsored by the most important shaman in each of the larger villages- These dances were so arranged that there would be no conflict in dates. The ceremonies lasted five nights and it was on these occasions that youths began to validate their powers. While the winter dances were of special interest to those who possessed power — particularly to those who hoped to become shamans or curers — actually nearly all the fellow-villagers of the sponsoring shaman attended that ceremony and many outsiders came, though in no one case were all the members of the other villages of the area present. Again, although PomPom[23] was vigorously opposed by the Indian Agent during the span we are considering, and interest in the cult varied from village to village, at least one village had ceremonies almost weekly to which members in other villages might come.

There was absolutely no gambling connected with either the [30] winter dances or the PomPom ceremonies. On account of weather conditions all sports were abandoned, and active recreative life, so much fuller at other times, was more or less at a standstill.[38] In individual villages, however, a party of women occasionally played, beaver-tooth dice for an hour or two at a time. Occasionally, small parties of men, or of men and women together, also organized bone game sessions. Since these were intravillage games, the opponents of necessity would ordinarily be related to each other, the immediate family of one brother, say, playing against the family of another brother or against the family of some more distant relative. It should be noted, however, that a husband and wife never bet against each other or played on opposing sides in the bone game or any other contest, and that parents did not bet against their children. In such intravillage games, neither the competition nor the betting was very intense. Only goods of very little value were wagered, and usually there was no supervisor present nor were custodians of the wagers or other officials appointed.

On rare occasions when a fellow-villager challenged a professional gambler, there would be wider interest and excitement. The so-called "professional" gamblers were those who were markedly successful in the bone game and horse racing, and who were usually wealthy enough to afford losses and willing to accept all challenges. There seems to have been one or two such men in each of the larger villages. Professionals in the bone game usually claimed specific supernatural power for gambling which was sought in the same way as the quest for other powers, namely, by going alone to an isolated place with the expectation of hearing a voice which would give a wordless song with a promise to succeed in certain endeavors. Any class of natural things — rocks, animals, birds, fish — could give power, but some powers were stronger than others,

---

[2] By 1860 Pom Pom (a Chinook Jargon word) was already a syncretism of prophecy, first fruits' rites, and other elements. Cf. Spier (1935) and also Du Bois.

[3] Winter was pre-eminently the season for story-telling. Sessions for children were commonplace in the individual lodges, and quite often a special session by an outstanding story-teller was announced by the crier. In addition, adventure stories were told to youths as they learned the arts and crafts under special leaders.

and some individuals had as many as three powers. Not all boys and girls, however, sought power nor did all those who sought it obtain it, but those who did and wished to use their [31] power were obliged to dance at the winter dances to "treat their powers right" and thereby retain them.

The data obtained do not indicate that anyone received specific power to win in the field sports, but such power was nearly always associated with the bone game. Along with power to cure specific diseases or injuries or to succeed in salmon fishing, hunting or one of the crafts, the specific gambling power was considered to be in a lower class than the power of the shamans (*twa'ti*) who could both cause illness or death by their power and cure illness caused by their own power or the power of another shaman who had a weaker power than theirs. Nevertheless, it was believed that the players in the bone game by singing the power song of the principal and beating the rhythm on the poles were helping that principal to use his power — a concept identical with that underlying the same practices at the curing ceremony of a shaman. Although no exact data were obtainable on the precise operation of the power to influence the gambling or on the ideation in making it work, the principal who had the stronger power or who received better support from his singers and beaters was thought to have a better chance of winning, and one informant stated that in the bone game whoever hid the bones was also using the power of the leader on whose side he played.

Although the informants knew that magical objects were prepared and bartered at high prices by certain people who were not shamans, only one of the two they were able to describe was used in gambling. One of the informants said that his brother brought a dried humming bird to bone games and secretively touched it to his hands and the bones when hiding them. The heart of a humming bird was also one of the ingredients of the other magical object described — a mixture which was said to make anyone touched with it fall in love with the owner.

The bone game was always started with a challenge, which varied according to the circumstances. A simple suggestion from one person to another sufficed for a small game between village members or other intimate groups, but when a fellow-villager challenged a professional gambler the challenge was a little more formal, and the game was played in the professional's lodge. The challenge for intervillage games in which professional and [32] non-professional players and bettors participated was usually made through a messenger who arranged the date and place — ordinarily in a professional's lodge. Intervillage games occurred in each area on an average of once in a fortnight, but no one village would witness a game very often at this time of year. Attendance was not very great and the sessions rarely lasted more than one night. Nevertheless, the intensity of play and the betting were stronger than in the intravillage games. As a rule, women did not take part in such intervillage games, not that they were excluded, but men were usually more interested.

By March the snow had disappeared from the vicinity of the villages and the pastures had begun to improve, but fishing and travel were impeded for some time thereafter by swollen streams fed by the melting snows on the hills and mountains. Since the food supply of a considerable number of families was apt to run low about this time, efforts to hunt, fish and gather roots, as well as to make trips to barter for fish with groups on the Columbia River, were made as soon as possible.

Some roots in the vicinity of the villages were ready for gathering toward the end of March. In preparation for the salmon run, the first of which usually occurred about April 1st, families who owned fishing sites prepared dams and obstructions along the Yakima River and its tributaries. When the first run appeared most of the villages held a one-day first-fruits' salmon rite in their respective dance houses, after which the people left at once for the fishing sites. Groups of men in relays caught fish night and day, while the women prepared, dried and packed the fish. This intensive activity lasted a week or two. Then the population of the villages dwindled as the families began to leave singly or in pairs for their favorite root grounds. There the women dug and peeled the roots, sun-dried some and cooked others according to the variety. All that were not needed for immediate consumption were then cached. Although some men always remained with the women, hunting parties of five to twelve members, organized under a leader, went out-from time to time.

With the disappearance of the snow, active outdoor recreative life was gradually resumed, especially by the children and youths. Although a relatively large amount of time was spent by the [33] children in the 4-7 age group in imitative play, especially of hunting and of root-digging, foot racing and arrow-shooting contests were common. Children from 8-14 played hoop-and-pole and hide-and-seek in addition to the arrow-shooting and foot racing, and all rode horses as often as they could get hold of them.

From the age of fourteen onward the boys and girls were segregated in their recreative activities, and imitative play was replaced by work following the lines of division of labor between the sexes. In sports the youths preferred shinny, wrestling, foot racing, hoop-and-pole, arrow-shooting contests and tug-of-war in about that order. Girls indulged only in double-ball shinny and foot racing among themselves.

Men enjoyed watching the sports of the older boys and occasionally even joined in these sports in a spirit of fun. When opportunity afforded they helped to train promising wrestlers and runners and shinny players, some of whom would undoubtedly attain championship status. In order to try out these coming athletes, their proud fathers would arrange both intravillage and intervillage matches within the area. A few intervillage contests between recognized individual champions and teams would likewise be arranged during the spring.

As the pasturage improved, much spare time was spent by the men and older boys in breaking and training horses. The Yakima territory was well suited to horse raising, and the hardy little horses, very important in the lives of the people, had a powerful hold on the imagination of the Yakima. Accustomed to horses from childhood, every Yakima man and woman was a skilled rider.

The ambition of every man was not only to own enough horses for himself and his family, but also to own as many as possible of the finest horses available. Everyone was interested in the racing qualities of the horses, and no horses were so valuable or so much admired as the champion racers. Some of the so-called professional gamblers were interested primarily in horse racing, and their number included some of the most prominent men. These professionals and others spent much time and wealth developing promising race horses and buying champions. Among the prominent Yakima men mentioned as professionals primarily interested in horse racing were cucu'skin, a headman of an important village [34] in the Kittitas area, and *sulu'skin* who, although not politically important, was prominent as a descendant of a former

Yakima chief. "Chief" Moses of the Sinkaquai'ius band of the Columbia was considered not only a great athlete but also a "great race horse man" who was willing to pay almost any price for a race horse he wanted. Smoxa'la of Ghost Dance fame,[44] the most prominent man among the Wanapam, was also considered a professional gambler on horse racing who, in a race between his champion and a white man's horse, bet ten horses, and he and his followers added a hundred dollars to the wagers on this single race.

Each man knew his fastest horse and tested its chance of winning from other horses owned by others in his own group. In the spring, intervillage races were arranged in the search for champions, and sooner or later the best horse owned in one group was tested against the best horses owned by those in other groups.

During this season of busy economic activity, the women gambled very little, if at all. Bone game sessions were still held indoors, just as in winter, until the salmon run started. Intervillage matches were more frequent than in winter, but the salmon run and subsequent dispersal of the families for root digging brought a marked decline in all games and sports.

Determined gamblers, however, could still find a bone game about every two weeks in the intervals between hunting trips, but the sessions were held away from the camps in order to avoid disturbing the women who were tired from their work of digging and preparing roots for storage.

At the intervillage sports contests and horse racing, attendance was not very great at this time of year, and a single contest — shinny game, wrestling match, foot race or horse race — was often the only event. Spectators would bet on such an occasion whether the event were a contest between "amateurs" or "champions," each one backing the representative of his own village, and one has the impression that all this was merely anticipatory of the large scale gambling that went on at the big gatherings of people in summer. [35]

As the first of June drew near, the Yakima began looking forward to the high light of the year — the "big time." Certain roots of high quality in the vicinity of the former villages, marked 10 and 11 on the map, in the Kittitas area were particularly abundant at this time of year. Practically all of the Yakima from the Kittitas area and most of those from the Yakima area foregathered there since they used the roots from this site for barter. In addition many of the Sahaptin-speaking Wanapam and a goodly number from the Salish-speaking Wenatchi and Sinkaquai'ius {Snk^{y}use} band of the Columbia came regularly each year, and some few visitors as well from nearly any of the groups living between the Cascades and the Rockies in this region could be expected. Those living west of the Cascades were, however, prevented from coming by the snow remaining in the passes.

Although the approximate time of the feast, which was the first important feature of the "big time," was well known, the headman or headmen of the villages nearest the site decided the date at which it should be held. They then sent messengers to invite all of the surrounding groups and appointed local leading men and women to organize groups of fellow-villagers to gather food and firewood, to supervise the cooking, serving,

---

[4] Mooney (part 2 708 ff.) gives an account of *smoxa'la* but not of this incident.

and so on.

The Yakima families did not travel to the site in village groups, but came pouring in from those places to which they had scattered after the April salmon run. The women drove the pack horses loaded with tipi and equipment, and, since the pasture was now at its height, the men were free to bring along as many other horses as they wished. Most of the visitors reached the site the day before the feast. They were greeted by the headman and settled in camp sites where the women erected the tipi, village groups usually camping as such. In the evening the criers went through the camps giving the news and announcing the feast.

On the feast day, the people took sweat baths as was their wont before any important undertaking. The morning meal was prepared and eaten separately by families, and the rest of the morning was spent on grooming their hair, applying a cosmetic of deer tallow and red tree-fungus to their faces, and adorning themselves with their best clothes and ornaments. The feast, which began about noon, was served outdoors to the lines of men and women [36] sitting with their feet under them before long tule mats. No public religious rites were connected with this feast, however, nor with any of the events of the "big time."

The work entailed in the feast was done by the hosts without any help from the visitors. The feast usually lasted until three o'clock or later, and the remainder of the day was devoted mostly to renewing friendships, telling stories and jokes, exchanging news, and visiting with relatives who had married into other groups. It was not customary to have a bone game the night of the feast, but formal challenges to bone games, horse races, and other field sports were made and reported to the crier, who announced a program of sports for the following afternoon. Nearly all of the contests were arranged between champions from different groups — Wenatchi, Sinkaquai'ius, Wanapam, Yakima from the Kittitas or Yakima areas, and so on. The program at the "big time" always included several horse races and a bone game, but the other contests varied. Wrestling, foot racing, shinny, jumping — both broad and high — and tug-of-war were preferred in about that order, but the quality of the champions in the different groups attending, the rise of new champions as tested in the spring, and other factors influenced the selection of the particular contests. For the Yakima, the situation involving the greatest rivalry, and consequently the keenest interest, occurred when one opponent was from a village in the Yakima area, and the other was from the Kittitas area.

People discussed the coming program with great interest. The owners of horses that were to run the following day took them off pasture. Next morning, the athletes who were to be on the program took sweat baths, the owners decorated the gaunted ? race horses, and the people again dressed in their gala clothes and rounded up the horses and selected the other wagers they expected to bet. All repaired to the race course or playing field about noon. The crier called each event in turn and helped to choose officials and custodians for the wagers. The last event of the program was always a bone game, which usually began after the evening meal and lasted all night.

At a large meet of this kind, horse racing was the most important of the daytime events. Most owners decorated their horses with colored feathers in mane, tail and forelock; some even painted [37] them with stripes. The riding equipment usually consisted of a hair rope tied to the horse's lower jaw as a bridle, and a whip with an elk horn handle. However, bridles and several kinds of saddles obtainable from white traders as well as the native stuffed skin saddles were sometimes used. Many of the champion horses were owned by older men who customarily obtained Jockeys among the young men of light weight who stripped to their breechclouts for the race.

Although well-established courses, whether straight away or double, were likely to be accepted without change, the distance to be run was a matter to be decided between the owners. As stated above, challenges had been brought to the attention of the crier the previous evening. At times the distance for the race was also set at that time because some of the owners wished to choose among their horses for speed and endurance according to the distance they would run. At the meet, if the course and distance were not already decided, the crier helped the opponents to make the decision and to choose the officials. The criers themselves were often asked to act as judges, and as such they were leaders who, as in the case of all leaders, were given absolute obedience when performing their functions. Some of the criers were among the best remembered, liked, respected and trusted Yakima. To no small degree the success of a meet depended on the crier's knowledge of spectator values and crowd psychology. One of the requisites of a crier was a "good strong voice." When the arrangements with the owners were finished, he announced the event to the assembled crowd and the betting started.

Gambling was taken seriously and was not considered a time for joking or laughter. Neither was it hurried. Wagers of all values were made according to the wealth of the individual man and woman, but, in general, betting was heavy, and horses were more frequently offered as wagers on horse races than on any of the other events. Those from the home village of the owner of a competing champion bet on that champion, but others who were not represented by contestants, so to speak, were free to bet on either side. There were some cases where area loyalty or even "tribal" loyalty was quite strong, but, in general, it was much less binding than village loyalty. There was a general desire, [38] appreciated by all but seldom expressed, to offer bets until an opponent refused to go further. The owners, who were often fairly wealthy professionals, not only often made the heaviest bets on the race, but also quite often indulged in out-betting. Although of rare occurrence, cases were known in which a fairly wealthy professional bet on a single race all of his wagerable wealth except his racer, a few horses and his clothes against one or several bettors. At the "big time," many youths as young as fifteen years placed their first bets, except for the arrows they forfeited in the arrow games from about seven years of age. It should be noted that the rules of all the games were so simple and well known that language was no barrier to participation, and the method of betting permitted the transaction to be carried out in simple gestures. In fact, the whole gambling complex was well adapted to intergroup use. As the betting neared an end, one side might still be offering wagers which the other side refused to cover, but the crier often let the situation stand for awhile until the crowd was becoming uneasy before suddenly calling for the racers.

The starter lined up the two racers if the double course had been chosen, while the spectators cheered encouragement; or should the course be straight away, they cheered the starter and the racers as they set out for the more distant starting line. A signal from the starter got the race under way. As the two horses approached the finish line, the jockeys used their whips to get the most from their mounts, while the crowd yelled and cheered. When the race was over the losers fell silent and the winners continued to cheer for awhile before collecting their wagers from the custodians. Good sportsmanship was the rule, and expressions of admiration for a good race were common even among the losers.

The crier showed no haste in starting the next event, whether it was another horse race or some other sport such as wrestling or shinny. If it were the latter, he consulted the leaders of the two teams and helped them to choose a supervisor and custodians, and to decide the number of goals that would constitute the game. When the crowd settled down and was becoming a little impatient, he announced the event, and the betting began. Excitement ran high during the game as fights broke out, injured players were removed from the field and substitutes replaced them. The [39] spectators supporting each side cheered their team when they made a goal, and as the score mounted on one side the spectators offered additional wagers in the short intervals between goals. As in horse racing and all other events, village members always supported their own team and bet on them.

Just as keen interest was displayed in wrestling matches. Wrestling, as described on page 15, was "a real Indian game," and when champions were involved, betting was intense. The intervals between falls also offered opportunity for additional betting which not only boosted the morale of the contestants but also made possible further contest between rich bettors. On one occasion, for instance, two well-known wrestlers from different villages were competing. One threw the other, and then the roles were reversed. The crowd was obviously favoring the second opponent when a wealthy uncle of the first went over to him and asked, "Nephew, can you throw him?" To which the nephew confidently replied, "Yes, I am on to him now. I can do it." Whereupon the uncle went a-round taking all bets. The nephew was as good as his word and threw his adversary for the next two falls and thus won the match.

Open gloating over success in gambling was not the rule. At the end of a match, there might be a shout followed by excited talking and laughing as the victors collected the winnings, but, in general, there was no attempt to humiliate the losers, who usually remained quite subdued and silent until betting began on the next event.

Thus event followed event, according to program, until the evening meal after which the bone game session was announced. This was played outdoors, and the poles on each side of the line of fires were of maximum length to accommodate the many players. Foreknowledge of the games gave the players an opportunity to prepare by taking sweat baths for five days previous to improve their chances of winning, by practicing with the bones, by preparing magic to be applied in the game, by selecting wagers to be offered, and by talking about the impending matches.

When the challenge was between individuals, they acted as the principals of the opposing sides. When it was between two groups, as was customary in the scheduled events of the "big [40] time," the most successful professional of each group was principal by assent. Each side had a strong conviction that it would win, and the stage was set for a real contest between two powerful opponents. A crier acted as master-of-ceremony at such a series of bone games as the night would witness, often acting as "bone game leader." In any case, after announcing the bone game, the crier and the two principals came together to agree on a "bone game leader," custodians for the wagers, and the number of tally sticks to be used. The custodians stationed themselves at some convenient place near the playing area, more often at the end of the line of poles, and then the betting was in order. Although horses were seldom bet in a night bone game, the principals bet very heavily against each other and might place bets with others if they wished. Betting was brisk in any case, and nearly every individual spectator risked something on the outcome, those bound by village or other loyalty supporting their respective professionals, and the "unrepresented" placing their bets according to their judgment of which side had the more power. Wagers were greater in value and quantity at the bone games of the "big time" than at any other season, and the custodians sometimes directed the wagers of the heaviest bettors to be placed in the playing area between the lines of poles, directing others to be placed near their station as usual.

When the betting was over, the two principals took positions opposite each other at the center of the lines of poles and called out, "All who want to be on my side come in." As many as thirty players, including those who had bet the heaviest, lined up on the left and right of each principal. Others found places near their principals from which they could watch the play. Such a game was dominated by older men. Women rarely played, and pregnant women stayed away lest their children be born with a "pride" for gambling. Children under two years were also kept away lest the power injure them, and mourners did not attend to avoid bringing "bad luck" to their companions.

Before the game got under way the "bone game leader" stationed himself at one end of the line of poles and sometimes made a proclamation that sleight-of-hand, by which the position of the bones was changed after the guess, and certain ways of swinging [41] or holding the arms, which facilitated the change, would not be allowed. A player who was caught violating the injunctions of the "bone game leader" was removed from the game, and another player was substituted. However, certain practices like the false motions made by the guesser to trick the hider into revealing the position of the bones by eye movements or changes of facial expression were within the law, and in any case a little skullduggery was appreciated, especially by the members of the group whose players worked the tricks successfully. The bone game sessions at the "big time" was the supreme occasion for skillful manipulators to show off their prowess to the best advantage.

When the players were in place, squatting back on their heels along the poles, the professional, whose special set of equipment was to be used, removed it from the buckskin wrapping in which it was kept when not in use. He then distributed clubs to each player, and gave a pair of bones and half the tally sticks (usually ten) to the other principal, retaining a pair of bones and half the tallies for himself. The principals stuck the tallies in the ground in front of them and prepared to determine which side would first take possession of both pairs of bones, at which time the tallies would also come into play. The teammates of the challenged principal, who was usually given the privilege of starting this play, took their clubs in their right hands and listened while he sang his power song with moderate volume.[55] As he began to repeat it, they joined in

---

[5] Curtis (7: 162, 11, 13) gives songs entitled a Klikitat hand game song, a song typical of the kind used by Yakima shamans, and a Yakima power song. Although I learned one of the songs used in one of the bone (hand) games I attended, I am not

and commenced to beat with the clubs on the poles, bobbing up and down to the rhythm of the song with a motion not unlike that produced by riding a horse at a trot. The challenged principal accompanied by his teammates sang the song [42] again and again until he thought his power was ready, when, as his teammates continued and his opponent watched every move, he "treated" the bones by rubbing them between the palms of his hands, tossing them on the ground, rolling them about, and so on, before hiding them in his hands. There were some who could do this while holding their hands in plain view — a skill highly appreciated by the onlookers — but most found it necessary to put their hands back of them or to conceal them with a skin or mat. It was during this procedure that those who used magical objects, such as the humming bird, applied them to their hands and to the bones. With a bone hidden to his satisfaction in each fist, the challenged principal joined in the singing again and, with arms akimbo, exposed his fists and swung them back and forth before his chest. After some time, he stopped singing, while his companions continued, and brought his arms to rest either crossed with the left fist on the right shoulder and the right fist on the left shoulder, or the upper arms against the body with the forearms parallel to the ground, or kneeling upright with the arms extended and a fist on the breast of the player to his left and right.

The challenging principal in the role of guesser then spent some time stretching his arms and rubbing them with downward strokes while showing signs of stress and gazing intently at his opponent from time to time before trying false gestures to induce telltale eye motions or changes of facial expression in his opponent. When he finally gestured his choice, the hider put his fists to his shoulders and opened them to expose the bones. The roles were then reversed and the procedure continued until one side got possession of both pairs of bones as described on page 11.

With the tallies now in play, the bone hiders and guesser were selected as described on page 12, and the game was under way with the treatment of the bones and accompanying power song. As the bones changed from side to side, one team abruptly stopped its song and almost without a break the other started its song, and the game proceeded in deadly earnest. Excitement rose and fell as did the volume and quality of the power songs while the tallies changed hands and the heated players stripped off their shirts, some of which along with even moccasions [sic] became wagers [43] as the night wore on. When one side won all of the tallies, that game ended and the same or another principal challenged for the next game. Sometimes betting was carried on during the game.

The author witnessed a tense moment in one big bone game when a woman, whose side had lost all but two tally sticks to the opponents, removed at this critical moment a ten-dollar bill from her purse and held it out toward the opponents with an air

---

competent to record it properly or compare it with Curtis' examples.

Informants who did not want to talk about power gave a standard explanation that the songs and beating on the poles were to confuse the opposition. As far as the form of the game is concerned, the bone hiders whose teammates were singing and beating on the poles were trying to resist the efforts of the guesser to locate the unmarked bones by tricking them into facial expressions or eye motions and by other means.

of studied confidence. One of the opponents met the bet and the two bills were placed side by side between the contestants. Whereupon she quietly produced another ten-dollar bill to raise the ante, but this bet went unmatched. The significance of her action can be better appreciated in view of the fact that the average bet in this particular game was about two dollars. Informants stated that this kind of additional betting on the side, as it were, was very common at the all-night bone game sessions of the "big time" during the period considered here.

Although not all attended the bone game, there was little sleep in the encampment on the night of the "big time." As dawn came, the bone game broke up, the morning meal was taken, and most people sought some rest.

The groups remained camped at the site for a week or more. The women spent most of their time digging and preparing roots for storage after the announced program was brought to a close by the all-night bone game. With the exception of one or more councils, at which among other things the unsettled problem concerning the relation with the white man was discussed, the men were free to spend their time as they chose. Since most professional gamblers attended the "big time," and since many others who were not on the program wanted to compete, special matches in sports, which drew crowds of spectators and bettors according to the reputation of the participants and the groups to which they belonged, were arranged. If the circumstances warranted, another afternoon of sports was set aside at which attendance was general, and bone games sometimes ran for three successive nights. Meanwhile, a rather brisk trading business was carried on in horses, food, skins, ornaments and other objects. The "big time," moreover, offered ideal conditions for making marriage arrangements.

Yakima families dispersed again at the end of the "big time." [44] Some went to their own fishing sites, and some went to the Wenatchi sites to intercept the second salmon run; others established camps at different root grounds from which the men went hunting; still others, especially headmen and wealthier men, went on visiting trips, often accompanied by their families; while some of the professional gamblers toured the fishing sites on the Columbia River.

In July, when the average temperature at the lower elevations reached about 70° F., and short warmer periods reached temperatures of 95° F., many families moved their horses to better pasture at higher elevations. Some of these locations were used regularly by headmen and wealthy men, and their camps became centers where hunting parties formed, and visitors as well as the families of fellow-villagers came and went. Thus, most men alternately hunted and fished, and most women dug roots and preserved fish, but small groups of men arranged bone games about every two weeks, and visitors provided sporadic opportunities for horse races and the accompanying betting.

About August 1, a second "big time" was held near villages 6 and 7 in the area marked Klikitat on the map. This "big time" was not so well organized in the period from 1860 to 1880 as it formerly had been, but the camas grounds still attracted many families from the Yakima area and a considerable number from the Kittitas area. Traders and professional gamblers from various groups attended, but relatively few families other than the Klikitat and Yakima families came to this "big time." Wishram traders, though few in number, attended regularly. This "big time" was carried out in much the same way as the one in June, and lasted for a week or more, but the feast was not always given. Inter-area and inter "tribal" rivalry in sports and gambling was just as keen, although the crowds of spectators were not so large. By the middle of August most of the Yakima families, whether they had attended the "big time" or not, had left for the huckleberry-patches in the high mountains.

As the berry season tapered off toward September, hunting deer and elk for the winter supply of venison increased. While in the mountains, the Yakima met families from west of the Cascades with whom they traded regularly. But during the berry and [45] hunting season, practically no games or sports were played. Some families continued to hunt well into November; others intercepted the final salmon run in September at sites in the mountains or at the usual sites on the Yakima River and its tributaries.

From October on, however, the people in increasing numbers returned from the mountains, gathered cached supplies, assembled into village groups, established winter quarters, and made final trading trips to the Wishram and other groups on the Columbia River. Although the establishment of winter quarters required some work, and fishing occupied some of the families, the period from the close of the hunting season to the onset of winter afforded more leisure time for both men and women than any comparable period since spring. Good weather conditions and the social situation were conducive to sports, games, traveling, visiting, and so on.

The people coming from the mountains stopped at the villages along the way for visiting and gambling. Those who went to trade with the Wishram and other groups on the Columbia River gambled there and also stopped at the villages along the way. Others, especially groups of young men, went to different villages merely for social visiting and gambling.

Many visitors were entertained at the villages in the Yakima .area at this time of year, and bone games, beaver-tooth dice, and sports matches were held more often than at any other time. At some places sports programs were held as often as once a week. Most of these programs were arranged as inter-village matches.

Formal challenges were usually delivered by a third party rather than by a contestant, except in the bone game. After the challenge was accepted the announcers in the respective villages proclaimed the events and the date, which was usually set from five days to a week from the day the challenge was made. The prospective contestants entered a training period and took a sweat bath daily to gain strength. Sweat house rites were used generally by the Yakima to rid the bathers of sin and of contamination from contact with the dead, as well as to give strength and success in their projects such as hunting and gambling. The procedure included songs by the sweat house leader, talking to the sweat [46] house as if to "a wise old man, a shaman," and asking for success. Dieting and sweat baths fulfilled the dictate "to keep light and clean" in order to attain success in many projects, including gambling, and sex abstinence was likewise advised and often followed. The participants in the forthcoming match practiced their respective specialties and included the trying out of a considerable number of tricks, among them, for instance, how to get advantage at the start of horse or foot races, various holds and deceptions in wrestling, making false motions in the bone game play, and so on.

Meanwhile village members talked about the impending match, were interested in their champions and in what wagers they intended to risk. The contestants had to bet on themselves, if they bet at all — and often young contestants performed without betting. Village loyalty was displayed by the wagers as at the "big times," fellow-villagers standing solidly behind their own champion or professional.

The women were less busy in the fall of the year than at any other time and so the women's games were played more frequently then. All of these games and contests tended to be intravillage and did not, as a rule, attract all of the women within the village either as players, spectators or bettors. The younger women tended to play double-ball shinny and to compete among themselves in foot racing, usually without betting; the older women played the dice and bone games which always involved wagers. The same pattern was followed as in the men's games and sports, so there were women champions in foot racing, women leaders, supervisors, custodians for wagers, etc., as officials at the games and contests.

Men sometimes bet on the women's games but usually only when a group of men challenged a group of women to a dice or bone game once or twice at this time of year. Such games between the sexes were looked upon as being carried out more in a spirit of fun and as not so fully competitive. The stakes were not very high. Informants stated that there was really no reason why women should not challenge men to a game, but they could not recall a single instance where such had been the case. Women, nevertheless, were free to bet on any and all games inaugurated [47] by either men or women, and to participate, as they sometimes did, as players who sang and used clubs in bone games where the principals were men.

Thus, while the weather still permitted easy traveling, inter-village challenge matches, contests between local hosts and casual visitors, and intra-village play, all accompanied by gambling, were the order of the day. As winter set in, sports were abandoned and inter-area visiting was brought to a stop, intra-area visiting much less frequent, and each village settled down to the comparatively dull and monotonous routine of daily life.

In summary, the hand game was the most popular all year round gambling activity, and the only one for which specific magico-religious power was believed to be available. The bone game and the dice game were never played without the inclusion of wagers. The sports, however, were often indulged in merely. for fun although all of them offered opportunities for gambling. Wagers were always of the dyad type, regardless of value. The intensity of interest and the amount wagered, however, depended primarily on the social distance of the opponents. Little was wagered on intra-familial or intra-village games and sports. Competition was much keener and the stakes higher on inter-village contests especially when the villages were in different areas or represented different linguistic groups. Rivalry was most marked between the inhabitants of the Yakima area on the one hand and the Kittitas area on the other, although there was little to distinguish the two culturally or linguistically. Village members invariably backed up their champion or professional and the other villages of the area tended to fall in line when it was a question of, say, a champion wrestler from one of the villages in the Yakima area meeting a champion from a village of the Kittitas, Wenatchi or other area.

The opportunities for entering into the keenly competitive situation depended primarily on the seasonal round of economic activities. In winter there were no sports and the areas were isolated one from the other. Aside from the occasional inter-village bone game, gambling was limited to the small-wager intravillage games where those competing were related by blood or marriage.

In spring the weather conditions were better but the food [48] supply needed replenishing and much time was necessarily spent in fishing, hunting, root digging and trading expeditions. Some minor inter-village sports contests were carried out, but these were more in the nature of try-outs for coming champions and neither attendance nor betting was great.

In summer at the two "big times" when especially valuable roots were available at particular places, and circumstances permitted the gathering of people from over a very wide region, the opportunity for the meeting of out-groups was favorable. Competition and interest were more intense and wagers higher than at any other times.

Between the June and August "big times" and up to the beginning of the homeward trek in October, people were scattered in family groups. Yet there was intermittent gambling among visiting groups, especially on the bone game and on horse racing. In October, after the height of the hunting season had passed, the villages in the Yakima area were hosts to many visitors from other areas. The weather was favorable and there was more leisure. Consequently intervillage sports programs were organized with great frequency and gambling was more concentrated than during other seasons.

SECTION VI

THE FUNCTIONS

One of the main functions of gambling among the Yakima seems to have been that it augmented recreative life for those who otherwise would have been mere spectators — offering interest and excitement and at the same time opening another path to prestige for the individual without causing disastrous results.

Much of Yakima recreative life centered on sports, horse racing, and the bone game. Participation as principals in these activities was limited — in the case of sports, to the young, the strong, and the skillful; in horse racing, to the older wealthier men, as these were usually the only ones who could afford to own the highly valuable champion racers; in the bone game, mostly to those who had successfully sought specific supernatural power. No such restrictions of age or ability, of power or wealth curtailed participation in gambling. Men and women, young and old, strong and weak, rich and poor, all could gamble provided they had anything to wager and could find a taker. Status, either acquired or achieved, was no bar to gambling, the only exceptions being mourners and pregnant women, for whom gambling was temporarily taboo.

Lack of wagerable wealth did, however, practically exclude children from serious betting until about the age of fifteen when they began to acquire their own property and gradually to become economically independent. While gambling was not actively encouraged among children, as was the development of proficiency in sports, it was certainly not disapproved. As pointed out above, mere boys forfeited arrows in childhood contests. The general attitude was formulated by one informant as follows: "Anyone who had anything to bet could bet. No one advised against it."

Participation in gambling was actually high, and it is estimated that after an individual was about fifteen years of age, even relative poverty rarely prevented him from gambling at least on a modest scale, and in the course of a year the economic position [50] of practically every Yakima was altered to a greater or lesser extent through winning or losing bets.[61]

Informants all held that gambling provided a good time regardless of whether a person won or lost. Whereas a contest between expert and evenly matched opponents was enjoyable and exciting to the Yakima, the fact that the individual had a stake in the outcome lent even greater interest and excitement, part of which was the possibility of getting "something for nothing." The Yakima were convinced not only that "people had a good time" by gambling, but also that "some people got rich that way."

Nevertheless accumulation of wealth as such was not an admitted goal in Yakima society. Miserliness was openly censured, and it was denied that wealth in itself was the basis for any other status. Those who accumulated property were supposed to dispense it liberally, and a reputation for generosity gave prestige. Just as those who had more than others were expected, for example, to pay more for services rendered by the shaman, shamans in turn were expected to, and actually did, give away property lavishly at their winter dances. Again, just as it was a sign of generosity for one with means to offer a more valuable article for a less valuable one in barter, so in gambling there was further opportunity to gain a reputation for liberality and good sportsmanship.

A person who was in a position to meet wagers offered by an opponent and who consistently refused to do so, or one who bet only on a "sure thing," was considered niggardly and lost status, regardless of his other attainments. The regular bets were publicly displayed and everyone would know who bet what and could estimate how big the wagers were in proportion to the property owned by the individual. Thus, even a person in relatively modest circumstances could maintain prestige by betting according to his means. Still greater prestige accrued to the individual if he acted beyond expectation. Offering considerable wagers at critical points in a contest, especially if one's own side seemed to be losing, as well as betting a wager notably more valuable against one of less [51] value offered by an opponent were additional methods of display. The most spectacular type of betting occurred on those rare occasions when some well-to-do person would venture to risk nearly everything wagerable he had on a single contest. This, was looked upon as especially courageous, and his reputation as a sportsman was made. The situation was similar to the rare occasions on which a particularly adventurous and fairly wealthy man who, when he arranged for, say, a second wife, would give nearly all of his wealth, reserving only a few horses and some clothing. Such conduct was greatly admired, and whether he had given too much for his bride would become a repeated topic of conversation in which the groom freely entered. Incidentally, informants were careful to casually mention cases in which they paid "big money," usually by merely stating what was paid and leaving the inference of the relative magnitude of the transaction to the auditor.

---

[6] Report of the Commissioner of Indian Affairs, 1865, 253. In this report, the Agent speaking of gambling says, "I have imprisoned at times for this."

In addition to being an avenue of prestige to the many, the gambling situation afforded special prestige to a certain few. Those who were known as "professional gamblers" occupied an admired status comparable to those occupied by the rich and by outstanding athletes, although none of these were called leaders. The supervisors of the contests, especially of the bone game, and the crier who acted as master-of-ceremonies, however, were so designated and were accorded the same recognition as was given to outstanding men in certain other activities such as headman in political life, shamans and sweat bath directors in religious life, and those who directed hunting parties and salmon fishing groups in economic life, and the like.

That such wide participation in gambling, motivated as it was by the excitement inherent in the situation as well as the desire for gain and prestige which could be satisfied by this means, was not disastrous for the Yakima was due principally to the nature of the wagers and to the pattern of betting.

First, the wagers consisted of surplus property. Although food was an important article of barter, it was never wagered. It was exchanged mainly for other types of food and was never converted directly into wagerable goods at the immediate time of gambling. On the one hand, food was generally not available beyond that needed for immediate consumption for a considerable [52] part of the year, the rest being scattered in caches. On the other hand, there was an abundance economy in the sense that the level of Yakima culture in relation to the natural resources permitted the people to make an adequate living without drudgery, and, in the course of exploitation, some surplus property beyond food came into the hands of every normal adult. Shelter was never offered as a wager, and as for clothing, while it was an acceptable wager, especially if it was decorated, the minimum required for decency was not gambled, and the amount needed for protection from the weather was easily replaceable since the Yakima dressed rather lightly with a simple type of clothing. Therefore, gambling losses could be sustained without affecting the basic physical requirements of life.

Whatever was to be gambled had to be available on the spot at which the contest was to take place. Borrowing was discountenanced under any circumstances among the Yakima, and in the gambling situation it was extremely rare. Nor was it customary to extend credit, so to speak, either in barter or in wagers. Promises to pay were not acceptable, so that debts, gambling or other, were not accumulated.

The individual bet exclusively his own property, with the exception that after consulting his wife a husband might risk what appears to have belonged to them jointly. As a rule, the wife not only agreed to this but apparently urged her husband to gamble by suggesting that he might win. If goods wagered by either husband or wife were lost, there were no recriminations. Thus the use of goods for gambling was not inimical to family harmony, and while gambling losses might leave the family short in some articles, the members were never left in absolute want. Even the heroic gambler, who risked all of his wagerable property but a horse or two on the outcome of a single event and lost, actually suffered no physical hardship. While such losses in material wealth were not only inconvenient but deeply felt, they would be compensated in large measure by gain in prestige. Furthermore, in this culture, where industry was admired and laziness scorned, it was possible to recoup by dint of hard work and astute trading.

Secondly, the pattern of betting placed some limitations on the amount of property which could be won or lost. Since there were [53] no pools, no odds, no prizes, or other means by which a great amount of wealth could be gained for a small wager, the most a bettor could win on a given contest was double the amount of his wager, often of the same kind of goods. At an important gambling match, enough horses to constitute a modest fortune and impressive piles of other goods changed hands, but these were distributed among many individual bettors. At least half of the individual bettors at most gambling sessions were away from their villages or camps which usually precluded their returning for more wagers during the session. They could estimate ahead of time how much property they could afford to risk, always keeping in mind their reputation for liberality, and would bring only so much. For this reason, both they and their opponents, even if the opponents were in their own village, were limited by the amount of property they brought.

Moreover, an all-night bone game session involved only about six separate games, and an afternoon of sports, only about four or five events. One was considered a moderate gambler among the Yakima if he bet a single item at each opportunity during a session.

Informants were unable to estimate what portion of an individual's wealth was won or lost in gambling, but they maintained that none, not even professional gamblers, could live by gambling alone, and that few, if any, became really rich by it. It was added, however, that among the young men, for whom it was always difficult to start a herd of horses, a few might get a start if they were lucky in winning some property which might then be gradually built up by further gambling and other means, such as barter, until they ultimately obtained a racer which helped them to acquire wealth, including other horses. In any case, the pattern of betting was such that gambling was neither an opportunity for the poor to "get rich quick" nor an occasion for really ruinous losses.

A second important function of gambling among the Yakima was that it helped to cement in-group solidarity without causing out-group rivalry of such dimensions as to threaten harmonious relations. Strong in-group solidarity resulted, of course, in out-group competition, but the gambling situation was such that it had no serious consequences.

The winter village constituted the basic in-group in reference [54] to gambling. For all practical purposes, the village was an autonomous political unit, the members of which were bound by many ties, kinship through blood and marriage being the strongest.[72] Fellow-villagers carried out such economic activities as hunting, and such public religious ceremonies as the first fruits' rites were performed essentially by and for the members of each separate village. This same feeling of unity pervaded the gambling situation.

Although gambling is of its very nature competitive, intra-village contests were not taken very seriously; interest was mild and betting was light. Furthermore, members of the simple biological family never bet against each other under any circumstances. Consequently, only mild rivalry in gambling developed within the village. The real competitive spirit became evident, however, as soon as the contestants were from any two different villages and was most marked if one opponent represented a village in the

---

[7] Jacobs (1932) gives kinship terms for the neighboring Klikitat. The two lists obtained by me from the informants were practically identical with Jacobs' list of Klikitat terms.

Yakima area and the other a village in the Kittitas area.

In some cases, particularly in the fall of the year when the village groups had formed, challenges were sent from one village to another as a whole rather than to individuals or small groups for a particular kind of contest. In these cases, as in others, the village reputation was considered to be at stake, and the village responded as a unit. For five or more days, the people and champions prepared for the encounter. All of the members of the village attended to loyally support their champions and defend the "honor" of the village by betting at least according to their means. The rich were expected to make a good showing for the group by offering and accepting as extravagant wagers as possible, and should any of their number succeed in putting up something so valuable that no one from the opposing village could match it, this was considered in the nature of a victory, regardless of how the actual contest turned out. The village group then, as a group, all won or all lost together.

Generally speaking, whether village "honor" was at stake or not, when a village member was an active contestant against a [55] member of another village of the same area, another area, or another group, fellow-villagers who attended either played on his side, or bet on him, or both. When village members were unrepresented by a champion, so to speak, they were free to bet on either champion, but they seldom bet with fellow-villagers who elected to bet on the opposite side.

In spite of the fact that inter-village gambling was competitive to the point of reaching a high emotional pitch among the Yakima, informants were unanimous in maintaining that there were no untoward results, except the fights which sometimes occurred in shinny. In general, the culture provided adequate controls.

First, the role of supervisor was important. Since he was a leader, he was considered to have authority, and, as in all other cases where leaders were recognized, the rule was to give him absolute obedience when he was exercising this role. He actually exerted considerable influence by enforcing fair play and by anticipating incipient disagreements. He was empowered to make his own rules to thwart cheating, and, if rules were broken, he could remove players from the game.

Again, the function of the crier, or master-of-ceremonies at large sports meets, helped to smooth the way, as it involved his assisting the contestants in coming to agreements and selecting other officials, and his was the task of so ordering the program and timing the betting that things would not get out of hand, as it were.

And finally, the method of handling the wagers appears to have helped in controlling the situation. The fact that the wagers agreed on by two bettors were tied together left no doubt as to what kinds of goods and what specific amounts had been risked and made it impossible for a loser to shirk his responsibility. And since the contests were always of the same pattern, one contestant or team opposed to another, and the opposing bettors were also about equally divided there could be no doubt about the identity of the winners. Depositing the wagers with custodians not only guarded them during the play but also made it unnecessary for the winners and losers to come, into face-to-face relations at the critical time when, at the end of an event, the winners were elated and the losers depressed and annoyed. In any case, quarreling was [56] vigorously disapproved under all circumstances, and good sportsmanship admired. No gloating over the losers occurred, and all informants insisted that "there was a good feeling in it" even when they played "for blood" as in the contest between the Yakima of

Functions

the two areas.

Thus, although out-group rivalry was keen, and expressed itself characteristically in gambling, it was so controlled that the harmonious relations among all the people of the region — based as it was on intermarriage, frequent contacts for trading, common exploitation of some resources, and the like — were not unduly disturbed.
[57]

BIBLIOGRAPHY

Culin, S. Games of the North American Indians. Twenty-fourth Annual Report of the Bureau of American Ethnology. Washington: Government Printing Office, 1907.

Curtis, Edward S. The North American Indian, Vol. 7. Cambridge, Mass.: The University Press, 1911.

Du Bois, Cora. The Feather Cult of the Middle Columbia. General Series in Anthropology, Number 7. Menasha: The George Banta Publishing Company, 1938.

Gibbs, George. (In Stevens, I.I., Reports of Explorations and Surveys to Ascertain the Most Practical and Economical Route for a Railroad from the Mississippi to the Pacific Ocean. Vol. 1. Washington: The Government Printing Office, 1855.)

Jacobs, Melville. A Sketch of Northern Sahaptin Grammar. University of Washington Publications in Anthropology 4:85-292. Seattle; University of Washington Press, 1931.

―――――. "Sahaptin Kinship Terms." American Anthropologist 34:688-693, 1932.

Kroeber, A.L. Cultural and Natural Areas of Native North America. University of California Publications in American Archeology and Ethnology Vol. 38. Berkeley: University of California Press, 1939.

Lewis, Meriwether, and Clark, William. Original Journals of the Lewis and Clark Expedition, 1804-1806. Edited by Reuben Gold Thwaites. Vol. 4. New York; Dodd, Mead and Company, 1904-1906.

Mooney, James. The Ghost Dance Religion and the Sioux Outbreak of 1890. Fourteenth Annual Report of the Bureau of American Ethnology, Part 2. Washington: The Government Printing Office, 1896.

Ray, Verne F. "Native Villages and Groupings of the Columbia Basin." The Pacific Northwest Quarterly 24:99-152, 1936.

―――――. Culture Element Distribution: XXII Plateau. Anthropological Records 8:99-258. Berkeley: University of California Press, 1942.

Reports of the Commissioner of Indian Affairs. Washington: The Government Printing Office, 1852-1881.

Ross, Alexander. The Fur Hunters of the Far West. Vol. I. London: Smith, Elder and Company, 1855.

Spier, Leslie. The Prophet Dance of the Northwest and its Derivatives: the Source of the Ghost Dance. General Series in Anthropology, Number 1. Menasha: The George Banta Publishing Company, 1935.

―――――. Tribal Distribution in Washington. General Series in Anthropology, Number 3. Menasha: The George Banta Publishing Company, 1936.

Rev Gerald Raymond Desmond, OSB, PhD
(1904 - 1990)

Born 9 June 1904, Gerald Raymond Desmond was the son of Patrick and Rose Hand Desmond, herself born in Ireland. After attending Ellensburg schools, he went on to St Martin's high school and college, joined these Cassinese Benedictines on 11 July 1923, and was ordained 14 June 1930 in St James Cathedral by Bishop Edward O'Dea. Graduate work at Catholic University in DC led to an MA in 1931 (Relation of Delinquency to Recreation in 35 Cases) and a 1946 PhD, published in 1952 as *Gambling among the Yakima*, after he was president of the Seattle Anthropological Society in 1951. He served as Dean of St Martin's College (1935-42, 46-48), and was elected Abbot on 30 Dec 1964 to assume increasing duties from and succeed his elderly abbots, Raphael Heider (1903 - 12 Feb 1971) and Dunstan Curtis (1921 - 28 July 1981). He retired 1 May 1972 (at 68), died 4 April 1990 (at 86), and is buried at his abbey in Lacey. A lecture series is named in his honor.

Index

4
4~H club, 123

A
adultery, 31, 42, 99, 101f, 148
American State Bank, 87
anthropologists, 68f, 145
arrows, 33f, 56, 174f, 184, 194
Atanum, 164f, 167 #3

B
Badger Creek, 36
Bannocks, 39, 92
Barnhard, Albert, 47
Barnhart, Albert, 16
bear hides, 176
beaver-tooth dice, 173, 183, 193
bells, 9f, 18f, 30f, 40f, 49f, 55f, 61, 178
"big time", 185f
Bill, Tom, 29, 32
bison, 65
Blackfeet, 65
Blackfoot, 20, 168
Blanchet, FN, 11, 55
blindness, 24, 47, 86f, 114, 119
blood, 34, 42f, 68, 89, 139, 181
blue, 18, 22f, 42f, 55f, 61f
bones, 92, 169f, 175, 180f, 189f
Bruno, Jerry, 14
buckskin, 16f, 23f, 32f, 50f, 61, 66, 81f, 141, 170, 177, 189
bum-bum, 6, 10 #2 cf *pom pom*

C
Catholic Ladder, 11
Catholics, 11, 17f, 37, 54f, 65
Cayuse, 14f, 21, 37, 42
CCC, 82, 109
Celilo, 35, 70, 80, 106, 118
Charlie, Williams, 36
Chehalis, 9, 109, 113
Chemawa, 108f, 113, 120
chicken pox, 120
Chief Joseph, 20, 66
Chief Moses, 186
Chief Newshirts, 37
Child Welfare, 86
Christmas, 10
Clackamas, 10f
complaints, 72f, 98f, 106f, 129, 137, 151
confession, 11ff, 17, 30f, 40f, 50f, 61
Connolly, Cornelius J, clxxi, 166
consumption, 37, 46f
Coon, Jack, 28
Coon, Minnie, 26, 30f
Cooper, Fr John M, clxii, 165
Cooper, James Fenimore, 67
Court of Indian Offenses, 98f
Crook, Clifton A, 126, 127 #4
cult phases, 13, 56
Cushman Hospital, 113, 120

D
Dalles, 6f, 12, 18, 21, 67, 165
Dawes Severalty Act, 72f
deer hides, 176
Demonstration Agent, 122f
dependents, 85f, 99, 115f
diphtheria, 120
divisibility, 177
Dreamers, 6, 9f, 14f, 20*, 38, 91f
drums, 9f, 18, 22*, 40f, 55f, 91f, 178

E
eagle, 31f, 53, 57, 61, 63, 64, 67, 70, 185
eagle down, 41, 53
eagle feathers, 16, 23, 35f, 46f, 53*, 175
earth ~ *titcam*, 22, 28, 31f, 40, 54
Earth Thunderer, 32f, 57
east, 13, 18, 22, 39, 44f, 50f, 61f, 64
eel, 46
Edwards,O.C., 27, 37
egg, 23
Ellensburg, WA, 132, 202

F
Father Woods, 10f
Ferguson > Yakima County, 67
fighting clubs, 178
flags, 10f, 20f, 29*, 56*
Flannery, Regina, clxxi, 166
foot racing, 173, 184f, 193

202

Index

formulae ~ dicta, 49
Four Lakes, 66
four roads, 18
Ft Simcoe, 66, 73, 124
Ft. Klamath, 39
Ft. Vancouver, 11f, 23

G

Goldendale, WA, 67, 165
Goudy, Simon, 165
Grand Ronde, 11, 66
Granger, WA, 129
grizzly bear, 33

H

hand game, 170f, 189 #5, 194
Harrah, WA, 73, 80, 129
hiders, 171, 190f
Hood River, 6, 19, 26f, 51
hot lunches, 126f
huckleberries, 24, 25*, 79, 169, 176f, 193
Hultucks, Charlie, 36
Hunt Spidish, Susie, 22f, 30f, 46
Hunt, Jake, 21f, 25*
Hunt, Jo, 13, 18, 26f, 33, 47
Hunt, Laushlai, 22f, 46, 51
Hununwe ♀, 16*
Husum, 20f, 30f, 45f, 56f

I

Ike, Oscar, 9
Ike, Sally, 37
Indian Cattleman's Association, 122
Indian policemen, 98f, 110f, 165

J

Jack, Willie, 37
Jacobs, Ruth, 14f
Johnson-O'Malley Bill, 126
Josephine, 28f
Joyce, Sally Ann, 9, 23f, 28, 32
Junior Tribal Council, 98

K

Kaimet ~ Jake's sister, 33
Kamayakin, 65f
Kanine, Jim, 17, 42
Kashkash, Jim, 37
Katxot, 9
Kilasasomkin's wife, 42
Kishawa, Elisha, 37, 42
Kittitas Valley, 164f, 185f, 191f, 198
Klamaths, 39, 42 #19, 47, 57 #27, 101 #3
Klikitat, 6, 9f, 20, 25f, 34, 59, 165f, 192
knee dancing, 9f
Kumsuks, 12

L

La Center, 10
Lane, Mary, 8
Lawyer, 66
left side, 16, 22, 28, 39f, 44, 50, 171f, 190f
Lincoln, Sophie, 47
Lindsay, Elizabeth, 9, 14, 17
Lishwallait, 14
livestock, 70f, 116, 122
Luls, 15*, 20

M

Mackay Creek, 14f
Mackay, Billy, 38
Mann, Mary, 165
Marmot ~ "whistling jenny", 173
mass indoctrination, 150
mattresses, 117, 123
McClellan, Lt George B, 65
McKinley, Isaac, 36f, 47, 51
Merritt, Anthony, 48
Methodists, 11, 18, 66
Milroy, Gen RH, 72
miserliness, 196
Mt Adams, 13f, 165
Mut, 12

N

Nez Perce, 14, 164 #2
Nixon, NV, 39
Nukshai ♂, 16*

O

Olney, George, 165

orange, 41

P

Padawa, Allen, 14f
Palus, 20
palyowi'tu ~ bone game, 170
Parker, Samuel, 12
Parker, WA, 19, 36, 129
Paviotsos, 36, 38*, 48
penalties, 99
Pendleton, OR, 3741, 106
Pinapuyuset, 16, 23
poles, 10f, 18, 22f, 34, 47, 56*, 170f, 190
Polina, Pete, 39, 47f
PomPom, 6*, 15, 22, 91f, 141f, 178, 183; cf bum bum
Presbyterians, 16, 37f, 48
Priest Rapids, 21, 70, 91

Q

Queapama, 36
Quinn, Mac, 37

R

rainbows, 53f
red, 11f, 22f, 54f, 56*
Reed, John, 13
Riddle, Jo, 54
right side, 10, 15f, 22f, 39f, 50, 171f, 190f
Rock Creek, 20, 35f, 56
root feast, 15*f, 49

S

Sabbath, 15, 22, 24
sacraments, 11
saddles, 33, 79, 169, 178*, 188
Sahaptin, 2, 6f, 34 #15, 35 #16, 48, 164 #2
Sanat ♀, 36
Sarah, 48
séances, 28f, 35, 47
Selatkrine, Charlie, 9, 19, 41
seven, 9, 12f, 24, 31f, 40f, 49, 59
Shakers, 6f, 24f, 35f, 43f, 50f, 61, 141
shamans ~ twa'ti, 177f, 183

Sidwaller, Remi, 36f, 42, 50
Silas, 30f
Simnasho, 36
sins, 23, 40, 54, 60
Sioux, 64f
Skin, WA, 17f, 35f, 56f
s'kuma ~ game billets, 170
Slocum, John, 93
Sloutier, Annie, 26
Sloutier, Isabel, 26
Sloutier, John ~ Cascade chief, 26f
smallpox, 11, 120
Smohalla, 6f, 13*, 14*, 20, 91
soldiers, 65, 95
Spearfish, WA, 27, 35, 44, 57
Spencer, Chester, 165
Spidish, Lucy, 12, 51
Spidish, Martin, 11f, 27, 47
Spidish, Susie Hunt, 22f, 30f, 46
spinning, 31, 40f, 60f
spirit, 16, 21, 33, 41, 50, 55, 83, 119
Squimkin, Tommy, 17
staffs, 34
Stevens, Gov Isaac, 65f
Stuart, Robert, 13
suckers, 182

T

tally sheet, 119
tally sticks, 170f, 189f
tamanos ~ taaxmanawis, 33
tambourine, 6, 31, 45f, 55f
Tariutcus, 12
Tenino, 9, 14, 20, 57
Thompson, Tommy, 35
Thunderbird, 25, 32f, 57, 62; 5 brothers, 34
thunderbolt arrow point, 33f
Thunderer ~ Nashat, 32
titcam ~ earth, 22, 28, 31f, 40, 54
Titcam Nashat ~ Earth Thunderer ~ Jake Hunt, 32
Toppenish, 36, 67, 73f, 80f, 90f, 100f, 133
trachoma, 113, 119f
trails, 42, 182
tug-of-war, 173, 184f

Index

U

Umatilla, 6f, 14f, 20, 31, 36, 42, 47, 56, 106
Umtuch, Alice, 47
Umtuch, Thomas, 36
upper jaw, 173

V

vomiting, 40f, 61

W

Waiem ~ Celilo, 14f, 35*, 42
Waiet ~ Jake's sister, 37
wakes, 50f
Walula, 14, 20
Wanapam, 14, 20, 164 #2, 186f
Wapato, 73f, 87f, 92, 126f, 132 #9
waptashi ~ feather, 7
Warm Springs, 6f, 12f, 30f, 40f, 50f, 106
Wasco Jim, 27f, 51f
Washani, 6*
washat, 6*
Washington State College, 132f
Washington State Normal, 132
waskliki ~ spin, 7*
Watchino, John, 10
water, 8, 15, 21f, 31f, 40f, 59, 62, 70; holy water, 11
Watilthkai, 12
Weewa, Charlie, 38f

Wenatchi, 168, 177, 186f, 191f
wheat, 71
Wheeler-Howard Act, 96,
whiskey, 33, 41f, 102
White Salmon River, 7, 21f, 34
White Swan, 28, 36, 47, 73f, 80f, 112, 130f, 154f, 164f
Whittier College, 87
Wholite, Billy, 36
Wilbur, Rev James H, 66f, 71, 146
Williams, John, 18
wind, 33f, 182
wing dress, 44*, 61, 89
Winishut, Frank, 37f, 51
Wishram, 11f, 18f*, 27, 35, 168, 176, 192f
Wiyetrinawit, 14, 20
wolf, 33, 175
Work Relief, 86f
WPA, 82, 113
Wright, Col George, 66

X

Xiwili, 26

Y

yellow, 17f, 25, 36, 44, 50f, 55f*, 61

Please Help Banish Typo Gnomes

Sold @ Amazon.com

Made in the USA
San Bernardino, CA
14 January 2019